GLORIA MAXWELL

Touched by Evil

Touched by Evil

Michèle Knight

**HODDER &
STOUGHTON**

First published in Great Britain in 2008 by Hodder & Stoughton
An Hachette Livre UK company

A Hodder & Stoughton Book

2

A CIP catalogue record for this title is available from the British Library.

ISBN 978 0 340 95128 6

Typeset in Sabon by Hewer Text UK Ltd, Edinburgh

Printed and bound by Clays Ltd, St Ives plc

Hodder Headline's policy is to use papers that are natural, renewable
and recyclable products and made from wood grown in sustainable forests.
The logging and manufacturing processes are expected to conform
to the environmental regulations of the country of origin.

Hodder & Stoughton Ltd
338 Euston Road
London NW1 3BH

www.hodder.co.uk

To my two miracles. My beautiful son Julien and my eternal love, Margi Land, who showed me what it is to be truly loved.

Acknowledgements

Overwhelming thanks and love to the gifted, brilliant and stunning soul, Jane Alexander, who co-wrote this and was the Eeyore to my Tigger. Without you it would not have been possible.

Thanks also to Judith Chilcote, dream agent and all round angel; Julie Hill, my 'adopted' daughter who kept my life together, and Julie Pickford, the best friend and PR anyone could want; Jane M for the inspiration, wit and your unequalled mind; Dougie Brimson, for being a constant strength and my very own knight; the two Adams: Adam Stone (Rokk Media) gorgeous Web genius, and Adam Fronteras, whose idea it was for me to write this book; John Carroll, the guardian of Somerstown; Annie R for the astonishing kindness, you really are amazing; never leaving out Cazza, my best mate through thick and thin and Caroline Reynolds, my soul friend who only knows love.

Finally, of course, to Lucy: you should have made it, it was all worthwhile in the end!

Contents

x   *Contents*

Author's Note

My story is not a pretty one – at least not at the beginning. But I want to share it because I believe it is a message of hope. However desperate and bleak the start in life a child has, it can still turn into an adulthood filled with joy, happiness and fulfillment.

Yes, we can have it all – and more. How we do that is neither complicated nor particularly mystical. For me, it comes down to two simple truths, truths that I have been aware of since I was a small child: always believe in the power of love and always know that we can create our own reality and therefore transform it.

So, no matter where you come from – or where you are now – my wish is that this book will give you the courage and hope to know you can have a dazzling future. The magic of life means anything is possible.

One other very important thing: this is my life as I remember it. It is my truth, based on my memories, diaries and medical records. The early years are written from a combination of memory, memories recovered by hypnosis, tapes of interviews with my mother, and also include some channelled material.

Names and other identifying details have been changed throughout to protect the privacy of the individuals concerned.

Prologue: Wishing on the Scarab

My sister Lucy saved my life. Time and time again. It's just what she always did. We're twins — closer than close in the way that only twins can be. Although I was born first, it always felt as if Lucy were older and wiser — maybe that's why she felt she had to protect me. It's a good job she did, because if it weren't for her, I'd be dead by now.

The day I was born, Lucy died. But she didn't leave me; she stayed behind for me, keeping me safe. As I grew up, she was always around, helping me get through the bad times — really bad times in fact, some of the worst a child can have. I never thought of her as a ghost, or as anything weird. In fact, as the years went by, I even forgot that she was my twin, my sister. She was just Lucy and she helped me out. She looked out for me. She gave me advice. I didn't always take it, of course. Whoever listens to good advice all the time? Plenty of stuff happened to me that Lucy couldn't stop: sometimes all she could do was be there with me and comfort me. Because that's what twins and big sisters do, isn't it? Twins keep secrets too. Lucy was a big secret – until I was thirteen years old.

I was playing pinball in Italy when Lucy told me who she was, that she was my twin. I was so shocked I couldn't believe it. I felt as if I were making it up. I had been crazy about Elvis for years and he'd had a twin who died. Was I taking the idea from there? For a few mad moments I wondered if I were going crazy, if I had made Lucy up entirely. But the more I thought about it, the more sense it made. Of course she was my twin. How could I ever have forgotten? Then Lucy said I should tell Mum about her.

– No, Lucy. She'll think I'm mad.
– Tell her.

Lucy hissed in my ear. She was in one of *those* moods and I knew I'd get no peace until I did what she said.

'I know I had a twin sister who died when I was born.'

Mum's face went quite grey.

'What you say?' Her voice was shaking. Mum had grown up in Italy and she still spoke with a very strong Italian accent, punctuating her speech with Italian phrases.

'My twin sister. Lucy.'

'*Porco dio*. How did you know that? Nobody knew about her. Only two people knew and both of them are dead. How did you know that?'

So I told her. I told her that Lucy had always been there,

as long as I could remember. She was stunned. I remember her hands trembling as she lit another cigarette.

'So you really do have the gift, eh?' She shook her head. 'It's a blessing and a curse,' she said. Then she told me about how Lucy and I were conceived; about how she wished on a scarab – and how her wish came true.

It was a gloomy winter's day; dark and overcast. Rain lashed against the windows of the small west London flat. Mum had been sitting in the kitchen, a cup of tea turning cold on the formica table. Dad had brought her a painted plaster scarab beetle back from Egypt. He worked in the travel business and frequently went all over the world, bringing my mother back curious and unusual gifts. This one came from a man selling 'genuine antiquities' from a stall at the approach to the pyramids – it had caught his eye (though he said he had no idea why as it was really quite an unpleasant-looking piece). Most wives would have thought an old scarab an odd or even unwelcome gift, but my father knew it would intrigue Mum. She was no typical suburban housewife, but an incredibly unusual woman – a hugely gifted psychic and palm-reader, descended from a long line of Italian wise-women. She could cure and curse. She could uncover the past and peer into the future. She was wild and tempestuous and a law unto herself. She was scared of nothing – neither living people nor the spirits of the dead. Just one thing terrified her – the possibility of not having a child.

She was turning the scarab over and over like a talisman in her hands, brooding on how cruel fate was, how unfair. She had been desperate to conceive ever since she and Dad had married sixteen years before. They had tried everything but it seemed that their four-year-old adopted son (my brother Nicholas) was going to grow up an only child. Mum was desolate. She was thirty-eight and her body literally ached to carry a child. Time and time again she had perused her palm, reading the lines, unable to understand why they lied. Had she been doing a reading for someone else, there would have been no doubt at all. There they were, quite clearly, the lines that signified the two children she would bear – how could they possibly be so wrong? Yet, despite the lines, despite everything she knew and believed, she couldn't possibly see how she, barren for over sixteen years, could have a child now.

There was something strange about this beetle. Mum could sense an ancient power in it, and felt sure it was some kind of amulet. But her intuition also told her that it possessed a dark power and warned her that, if she dared to wish upon the scarab, it might not go according to plan. This was a wild, anarchic force – one that would not easily be tamed. Mum told me that, in her heart, she knew that were she to wish upon the scarab, there would be a price to pay.

She didn't care. Always tempestuous, always courting danger, she didn't believe in living safely or according to the rules. The need for a baby felt like a physical ache; if she couldn't carry a child, life was no longer worth living. A baby would be a blessing, not a curse. So she clutched the beetle between her rough, work-scarred hands, and threw out a fervent prayer in her stilted English:

'Give me a baby. Give me a child to carry in my womb. *Per favore, per favore,* please give me the power of birth.' Over and over she said the words, and outside the sky seemed to darken. The bare light bulb flickered overhead and Mum felt a tingle down her spine. An uneasy prickling sensation filled the air. Mitchy, the old tortoiseshell cat, who had been curled quietly on the tattered brown leather pouffe, howled and fled from the room.

Something was happening. She kept chanting, louder and louder, feeling the power tingle in the air like static electricity. The chants became sobs.

'Give me a baby. Give me a baby. Give me a baby. *Per favore. Per favore. Madre di dio.* Please. Please.'

Turning the beetle over and over in her hands, feeling its solid weight, heavy like a stone. Rising to her feet, closing her eyes, begging the universe to listen to her; calling on God; summoning all the powers and spirits that exist in this world and the next, to hear her plea, to give her her deepest desire. Suddenly, abruptly, the light went out. A huge silence hung in the air and Mum stood stock still, barely daring to breathe, aware of the rough carpet between her bare feet, aware of the dull heaviness of the beetle lying solidly in her hands.

One moment it was inert, dead; the next it no longer

lay still and heavy. There was a lightening, a quickening; something was moving between her hands, something alive, something that wanted to escape. Leathery wings were pulsing against her palms, trying to spread, trying to fly away. Mum opened her fingers a crack and gasped in horror and amazement– the dull plaster had transformed into a glistening black carapace. Real legs were scrabbling on her skin; real wings beating against the cage of her fingers; real beady black eyes were gazing with glittering intent at her. With a scream, she flung open her hands and the beetle fell to the floor, landing softly on the biscuit-coloured patterned carpet.

Shuddering, she stepped back, instinctively recoiling from the horrible creature. What had she done? How could this be happening? Mum was used to unusual, strange happenings but this was way beyond anything she'd come across. She thought she was going mad.

For what seemed like an eternity, she stared at the beetle – unable to move – and it seemed to wait and watch, gazing back at her, searching her soul. Then the light came back on, the spell snapped, and the beetle stopped moving. Cautiously kneeling down, Mum stretched out a hand, her fingers trembling, her heart thudding. She barely dared touch it, but forced herself to tap it, tentatively, with a fingernail. Once again it was inert, just an old, rather worn statuette. She picked it up and turned it over and over in her hands, scrutinising every inch. Then she wrapped it in an embroidered doyley and shoved it away at the back of the cocktail cabinet. She sank into an armchair, shaking her head, as if trying to dislodge the memory. Had she imagined it all? Her hand moved unconsciously to her belly. No. It hadn't been imagination. As only a born psychic can know, Mum knew with all certainty, with every bone in her body, that the impossible, the miracle, was going to happen. She was going to have a baby. What she didn't know then, what nobody knew (it was well before the time of scans and ultrasounds), was that she was going to have two babies. Twins.

My father couldn't believe it. He had long ago resigned himself to not having a natural child. However he was delighted and relieved – he knew how much it meant to Mum. Dad wasn't exactly the calmest of presences himself, but compared to Mum's wild passion and uncontrolled emotion, he was serenity incarnate. He somehow managed to restrain her wildest urges and kept her as calm as possible during the pregnancy, but it was difficult. She insisted on continuing with her work, cleaning houses for the local rich Italians and giving psychic readings. It was the 1960s and interest in the supernatural was running high. Madame Bruna, my mother, was in huge demand.

Her waters broke but nothing happened for two days. Then, after forty-eight hours of long, tough, painful labour, she finally had a caesarean. I was born first, and born blue. Then Lucy was born – and born dead. She had a hole in her spine; Mum thought it was possibly spina bifida. I nearly died too. Through a combination of regression (in which you hypnotise yourself to go back to the past) and what Lucy told me, I have been able to revisit my early years and even the time before I was born. It sounds incredible, but really it's a very simple technique that anyone can do. I realised that part of me had wanted to follow Lucy, to avoid a lifetime that I knew would be full of difficulty. But at some level I made the decision to stay around. In India avatars (incarnations of higher beings) are born blue – it's a sign of being spiritual. A way of marking you, from day one.

So I was branded from birth – as a psychic. I was going to follow in my mother's footsteps as someone who can look into different realities, who isn't held in by time or place. I can look at you and just 'know' what is going on in your life, what has happened in your past, and what may well happen in your future. It's a powerful gift and one I use with great care. Sometimes when I give readings, I sense enormous pain; I can tell that a person has been abused, has suffered enormously in his or her life. And I feel a huge rush of empathy because I too have suffered long-term abuse, terrible loss, and a violent, unstable past.

As I learned from my mother, prophecy and magic are in my blood. Sadly, I also inherited a pattern of abuse that stretches far down the generations. Back down through time the children in my family were abused by their protectors, by the adults around them. All families are complex, but mine was doubly so. First it was overshadowed by the sadness and loss of power that abuse brings. But, second, it was a family in which power came from other worlds – the dead walked with the living; uneasy spirits scratched on the walls, and tormented souls shrieked for attention and retribution. I grew up both powerless and full of power – it was a strange and perplexing combination.

I treasure my gift – it has let me help countless thousands of people, including some very famous ones. I know that the advice I have given has often turned people's lives around; sometimes it has even saved lives. However, as Mum feared, the scarab did contain a curse. First, Lucy died. Then my father was told he was dying – initially of bone cancer, then of leukaemia. Of course, as I lay in my cot, I knew none of this. Nor did I know that I was being born into a pattern of abuse that stretched back generations. Like Sleeping Beauty, I inherited a terrible curse, a legacy that was to blight my whole childhood – and threaten my entire life.

However, like Sleeping Beauty, I also had my 'good fairy' – Lucy. Even when life was the worst it could be, Lucy always pulled me back from the brink. When I found myself in impossibly dangerous situations, she was there to protect me. She helped me keep the powerful belief that people, inherently, are good. She helped me decide that the evil pattern of violence and abuse would stop, right here, with me and would go no further. Lucy saved my life – of that I have no doubt whatsoever. She helped me get to where I am now. Despite such a horrific start, I have managed to turn my life completely around. I have made peace with my past, and I think it's fair to say that nobody who meets me would ever guess that my childhood was a nightmare, and that I barely survived adolescence.

I still have that scarab, but I keep it locked away in the bottom drawer of my desk. I don't dare give it away (it wouldn't be fair to let someone else take it on), and destroying it would be equally dangerous. I don't look at it very often, but when I do I shudder. It reminds me of the monkey's paw. I can tell that it's got strange supernatural powers – that it can grant impossible wishes that can have unforeseen and terrible consequences. There is an old saying: be careful what you wish for as you just might get it. Mum wished on the scarab – and she got what she wanted. I was the consequence. I made the decision a long time ago never, ever to wish upon that scarab. I have taken what Fate decided to dish out to me, and I've taken it on the chin. I truly believe that we can determine our own lives. Yes, my past was awful, but without it I would not be the person I am today. I learned from each and every bad thing that happened to me.

Writing this book has been a remarkable process. Much of my early life was filled with pain. Reliving certain memories has at times brought up almost overwhelming emotions of anger, betrayal, terror and deep grief. For years I kept these painful memories at a distance. Much of what has been recorded here has come as a shock even to my closest friends, yet I felt compelled to tell the truth at last for many reasons, not least because I truly believe that we can overcome anything to be the person we want to be and have the life that we want. This book is part of my healing process. As anyone who has suffered abuse knows, it never ever goes away for good. You learn to live with it, but you do live with it all your life.

There are many ways to tell any story. I could recount my early years in terms that talk only about the very darkest of human experiences and emotions, yet always there was a shard of light that shone through for me. For every curse there was a blessing. A light in darkness. Sometimes it flickered only in the distance. At others, it drew me and supported me like a beacon. I never let go of that light. It's a light I still carry today. I always see the best in people and situations. I see the potential in everything. It is attaching myself to that potential that has enabled me to bring out the best in me, in others, and to transform myself and my life through every experience.

Today there are so many blessings in my life: I lose track trying to count them. Had my beginning been ordinary, safe and comfortable, I don't think I would be the person I am today. It's an old cliché, but it is true: steel is tempered by fire. I feel as though my early years were one long endurance course. In all good fairy tales the hero or heroine is tested to his or her limits. There are moments where, lost in the woods, beset by peril, alone in the darkness, they don't know which way to turn, what to do, or whom to trust. But always they must act. By acting they define themselves and danger itself becomes an opportunity.

Above all, however awful our past experiences, we owe it to ourselves to take control of our present and our future. By refusing to allow the past to dominate us, we become free to live our own lives in whatever way we want to live them. I believe I am truly blessed. We are put in this world to learn and to grow – and I am still learning, still growing. This is my story – and Lucy's.

I

Hush Little Baby

My parents were chalk and cheese, sugar and spice – so different it was hard to believe their marriage lasted a minute, let alone twenty years. My mother, Bruna, was Italian, so tiny that the word 'petite' hardly does her justice, but with the curvaceous figure of a Tinkerbell Venus. Her family had lost all their money, their business and their home in the war and by the time she met my father she was so poor that her everyday shoes were roughly hand carved from wood. Did it bother her? Not remotely. She was so proud and tempestuous, her temper so wild and violent, that she earned the nickname Vesuvius. When she got angry, anyone with half a brain knew they should slide out of sight and out of reach of her furious fists and sharp words. Curses tripped easily from her acid tongue. Her grandmother was said to be the village witch, a wise-woman who taught her all manner of seemingly impossible things, from clearing unwanted spectres to raising dead ancestors; from casting love spells to spinning dramatic (and horribly effective) curses. Hers was a world of faith and superstition. It blended magic with Roman Catholicism and she saw nothing remotely odd about believing in both holy water and tarot cards, in praying to Christ and summoning demons.

There was always magic around our house. Mum believed totally in magic and spells and charms and hanging weird talismans everywhere. On the one hand, she would be incredibly kind and gentle, so caring and healing. She was deeply loving and giving to strangers and took on other people's problems without a second thought, helping them wherever she could. She would carry out spiritual healing for hours, without charging a penny, and put up homeless people in her own home. But then, on the other hand, she was not adverse to the odd curse. Some of her clients would pay her to put curses on people and I found that really horrible. It felt so weird and alien to me. How can anybody with half a brain cell not realise that you shouldn't curse people? I always knew that magic existed, and I believed in it totally, but I also knew very clearly from the outset that it should only be used for good.

Yet my mother felt that she could make such judgements. She felt it was her prerogative to define if people were good or evil and, as far as she was concerned, there was never any middle ground. If a person were evil, she felt she had every right to punish them. I loved my mother deeply, but I was also terrified of her on a primal level. The combination of her aggression and her ability to do magic frightened me to my core. If she wanted, my mother really could wreak destruction and I wouldn't want to have been cursed by her.

She was eighteen when she met my father, in 1947. In some ways, spiritual ways, she was wise beyond her years. Her eyes were so intense that my father used to say you felt as if they would burn away your soul. Yet, in other ways, emotionally, socially, intellectually, she was still very much a child. She could barely write in her native Italian and she knew no English. Right up to her death, she would regularly spell my name the wrong way.

My father, Michael, on the other hand, was tall and suave, a stunningly handsome cross between Errol Flynn and David Niven – the archetypal English gentleman who had served his country during the war and had an insatiable hunger for knowledge. He spoke seven languages and was incredibly cultured and urbane. On paper, they had absolutely nothing in common. In real life, they had serious chemistry.

He caught sight of her across the crowded dance floor in the British Officers' Mess in Trieste and was lost in a second. He was only twenty, yet already a seasoned battle-scarred soldier. She was a simple village girl with an extraordinary gift. She was wearing her best dress (very old, yet carefully washed and pressed) and was inordinately proud of her fashionable ankle-strap sandals (not caring one iota that they were far too small and pinched her ankles and squashed her toes). She caught his eyes burning into her and, knowing exactly what she was doing, stared right back. As they gazed at each other, they both knew they had met their fate.

They fell head first into a starry-eyed love, an all-or-nothing love, an all-rationality-out-of-the-window, sink-or-swim kind of love. What did they have to lose? The war was just inches behind them. My father had seen sights no man should see. My mother too had come within a whisker of losing her life – she too had seen death at first hand.

In the last years of the war, my mother's family had had to leave their home town of Udine and were temporarily staying in the village of Filetto. They were living in wooden barracks and food was incredibly scarce. 'It was a battle for survival,' my mother recalled. 'There were some days when we had nothing to eat.' One day she never forgot. Black thunder clouds were gathering and planes were flying overhead. She could hear bombs being dropped, guns firing in the distance, machine guns that seemed to get closer and closer. She clutched the puppy she had found, and adopted, in one arm; and hung on to her mother with the other. They and the other refugees ran towards a small shelter and crammed in together. Inside it was dark, very dark. Years later I taped her telling the story – this is what she said:

'The children were crying. Some of the grown-ups were praying in the dark. We thought it was the end of the world, between the blackness of the shelter, the smoke, the rain, the sound of the guns. It was cold and wet; we were all starving hungry and scared, so scared.

'My little dog slipped from my hands and I ran out after him. When I turned around and looked towards the hill I was shocked out of my skin. We were surrounded by Germans. They all stood up with their machine guns pointing towards the barracks. I screamed and everyone came running out of the shelter. We were surrounded by soldiers, all heavily armed: they were laughing as if they were drunk.

'The soldiers put us in a line. I was wearing a very thin dress and cardigan and I could feel the cold steel of a bayonet touching my skin, sending shivers up my spine.

'When we were all lined up – men, women, children – the Germans stood looking, with their machine guns in position. The blood drained from our faces and I could feel cold sweat washing over my body. I clutched my mother's hand. Then suddenly I felt a feeling of calm and peace come over me. I was prepared and ready to die.

'But it did not happen. They seemed to be waiting for orders. Finally the Commandant arrived and split us up – the men were left outside the barracks. The rest of us were taken inside. We heard gunfire – all twenty-two of the men had been shot.

"*Raus! Raus!*" a voice barked. Get out! We walked in a daze towards the town, expecting to be shot at any moment. There were Germans everywhere, laughing, spitting, threatening us. But the town itself was empty, like a ghost town. We continued walking until we came to the priest's house and we begged for help. But he shut the door in our faces, leaving us to the mercy of the Germans.'

The tape ends there, but obviously they weren't shot, they didn't die. Eventually they went back to their home village and picked up the pieces, like everyone did after the war.

So my parents had been through hell and come back. They were alive and they were in love. They saw a chance for happiness and grabbed it with both hands. They were both gorgeous; both burned far too bright. They were flirtatious and avaricious with a desperate need for flattery. Underneath it all, of course, there was a yawning abyss inside them both – they needed to be noticed, to be understood, to be loved and cherished. Neither of them had any boundaries. Both incredibly child-like, they were one of the worst possible combinations any youngsters could have had for parents.

Neither family was terribly impressed by the romance. My Italian grandmother wanted Bruna to marry a nice local boy, to have lots of babies, to look after her parents. She wasn't remotely impressed by this suave debonair Englishman. On the other hand, my English grandparents, back in genteel Lyme Regis, were doubtless horrified at their beloved son falling for not just an Italian peasant (I suspect there were elements of racism and snobbishness there), but a bona fide witch to boot. I suspect both families were delighted when Michael's army unit was moved from Italy. They believed the romance would fizzle out and die when the lovers were parted. It didn't. I have a case crammed full of the most passionate love letters, showered with kisses.

Ti amo tanto, tanto, tanto. I love you so, so, so much.

They snatched time together in secret whenever my father had leave. They even managed to sneak away for a weekend in Venice (my mother pretending she was staying with an aunt), shyly booking into two separate rooms in a cheap *pensione* near St Mark's Square. The city worked its magic and my father proposed, with the twinkling lights from the boats dancing over the water.

On 15 April 1950, they married at Trieste. No relatives attended – only my father's army friends were there as witnesses. My father merely scribbled a postcard to his parents to say he'd got married.

They spent their honeymoon night in a cheap guest house whose only door was a bed sheet separating the lovers from their host. Not that they cared. They were launching on their new life together – anything was possible, everything was possible. They were young, they were beautiful, they were in love. What could possibly go wrong? My father's unit was moved to Germany and then, in the early 1950s, they came to London, to a small flat on Ladbroke Grove in Notting Hill. Dad left the army and decided to use his knowledge of languages by working for a travel agency. Mum worked for Boots and also started a business as Madame Bruna, psychic and medium, reading both the tarot and palms.

They were a golden couple and must have seemed very exotic for the 1950s. Dad was constantly travelling, bringing back wonderful tales and curios from far-flung corners of the world. Mum was an exciting foreigner, her kitchen smelling of garlic and olive oil, rather than chip fat and toast. Even more thrilling, she was a psychic, someone who spoke to spirits as easily as chatting to the neighbours. Notting Hill loved them and they soon built up a large coterie of friends and clients.

What my parents' circle didn't realise was that Mum's gift was no fairground sideshow. Magic and supernatural power ran deep and hard through her veins. She was a deeply spiritual person – the other realms were as real and meaningful to her as everyday life. Dad, on the other hand, had been brought up with the Church of England and had that staunchly English system of belief – in other words, taking it for granted, not really thinking about it except on high days and holidays. He humoured her on the whole. I think he found it all rather novel and appealingly bizarre to begin with, and their marriage progressed it just became part of everyday life.

She wasn't the only one with foibles. My father had repeated affairs and casual lovers which caused no end of rows. He had plenty of opportunities because his job took him all over the world. He was always a good-looking man, even as he grew older and became ill. Well-dressed, smart, intelligent, charming – women fell for him all too easily and he didn't put up a fight. My mother did, though, and the neighbours must have become used to the sound of Italian curses being screamed and the crashing of pans, the smashing of china. Their relationship was always wildly tempestuous – full of furious fallings-out and passionate making-up. He was the only person in the world who could handle her. She could be totally irrational, but he managed it somehow.

Interestingly, their sex life wasn't particularly fulfilling for her. She once told me that she found sex painful with him and that it was because she had 'an infantile womb'. But frankly, I think it was because he simply wasn't a great lover, despite all the affairs. Later on she told me she hadn't discovered the joy of sex until she was in her late forties.

He never thought of leaving her, I'm certain of that. He was very old-fashioned in many ways and he felt responsible for her. He had plucked her out of her life in Italy and brought her to England, so he had to live with his decision.

Mum desperately wanted a child to cement their love, to turn the two of them into a family. They tried everything. They saw doctor after doctor. My mother cast every spell she could think of, drumming up every incantation, every arcane ritual her grandmother had taught her back in the northern Italian hills. Their home reeked of incense as she burned it in endless clouds in front of a six-foot-high water-colour painting of Christ. To no avail. Her taped diaries from the time are enough to break your heart. She wanted a baby so very much.

Then, incredibly, she got one. Mum was cooking in the kitchen when she heard a commotion out in the street. She peered out of the window. A small crowd had gathered around her front door, staring at the step.

'Eh! What's happening?' she shouted out the window. 'Why are you all here at my door? Go away!'

'Hello, Mrs Saunders. Did you realise there's a baby on your doorstep?'

'A *what*?' My mother couldn't believe her ears. She dropped the saucepan with a crash and ran to the door.

They were right. Lying on the door-mat, swaddled in a blanket, was a tiny baby with the blackest hair and skin the colour of toffee. He opened his almond-shaped eyes and gazed at her. Mum was, once again, consumed by an intense love. She had prayed, begged, cast spells for a baby – and finally, after all those years, God had answered her.

'*Madre di dio*. It's a miracle.' Before anyone could say anything, she scooped up the baby and marched inside, kicking the door shut behind her.

'Shush, shush, it's OK, baby.'

There was a banging on the door, but my mother ignored it. This was her baby. He had been left on her doorstep, hadn't he? The banging continued but she walked away into the bedroom, and sat rocking the baby on her lap, softly crooning Italian lullabies.

Of course, someone called the police and they came to take the baby into care. Mum wasn't overly worried – she knew (the way she would just 'know' things) that he would come back. The police explained what had happened. The baby was the son of a Pakistani woman who had lived in the upstairs half of the house. She had had an affair and had left her husband to live with her lover – a huge scandal.

When she had given birth, she had brought the baby back to his father, her erstwhile husband, hoping he would care for the child. There was some horrible wrangling for a while, with the mother trying to extort money from my parents, but in the end – amazingly – my parents were allowed to keep the baby – Nicholas, my brother.

I'm stunned, when I think about it, but I suppose regulations weren't so strict then. He was to be raised by a C of E father and a Roman Catholic/pagan, spell-casting mother. Not the remotest thought for his Muslim heritage at all.

Nicholas was quiet and good as a baby – a serious child with huge brown eyes. For quite some time it seemed as though he had plugged the hole in her heart. But eventually, inevitably perhaps, the nagging urge returned. She wanted to be pregnant – *pretna* or *pregna* as she always called it – she wanted her own child, from her own womb. A symbol of the intense love she still felt for her husband.

Finally, of course, she wished on the scarab – and fell pregnant.

Mum told me the story so many times it became part of our family mythology, as natural to me as other children's tales of favourite puppies and seaside holidays. While we live most of our lives in this sane, rational world, there is – without any shadow of a doubt – another world out there beyond this. There is much more to life – and death – than we can ever know. What really strikes me is that, although many strange things did happen to my mother, this was the only time when she said that an inanimate object seemingly came to life. She was adamant that the scarab had been, for a few moments, alive and real and, when you think about it, why would she lie? Personally I do believe it happened and I do believe the scarab granted her wish. Just as I believe and fear that there is one wish left on that beetle. My mother was convinced that, in order to have her wish granted, she would have to suffer some terrible consequence. I know that we can manifest what we believe in (it's at the bottom of my sincere belief in cosmic ordering). I'm not saying she conjured up Lucy's death or my father's fatal illness – and heaven only knows she tried hard enough to have him healed – but I do think we often get what we ask for.

When Mum was eight months pregnant she was heading off on the Tube to do a psychic reading. In her home village in Italy fortune-telling was an everyday, matter-of-fact occurrence, but in London in the 1960s, it was an event. As the world opened up, with cheaper air travel, there was a surge of interest in other cultures and other realms. Travellers to India brought back yoga and a heightened interest in mysticism and the supernatural. Anything magical was wildly popular. My parents had always been ahead of their time: now my mother's gift was in great demand.

It was a gloomy March day and it was raining heavily. As she walked into the Underground station, her foot slipped on the wet steps and, before she knew it, she was tumbling helplessly down two entire flights of stone stairs.

The pain was terrible but the fear was even worse. It felt as if it lasted a lifetime, she said, as if she were going to keep falling for ever. Time seemed to slow down as she fell. Hands reached out to grab her. Voices, sharp with terror, chimed in her head. A horrible smell – of wet stone, sweat and stale urine – battered her nostrils. The red flash of adrenaline clouded over her sight. Finally, finally, she stopped tumbling. There was a horrible stillness, like a vast intake of breath. Then the voices started, a cacophony of sound; hands touching her, the hot press of a crowd. All she wanted to do was to curl up into a ball, to hide herself away from the world. But arms gently lifted her up. Someone laid a coat on the step and they made her sit. People wanted to call an ambulance, but she waved them away. She would be all right, she said – she just needed to get home. She forced herself to her feet and, brushing aside their protests, she limped off to the Tube train.

It was a miracle she wasn't killed. She was black and blue with bruises, her face swollen, her whole body aching and tender – but she hadn't even broken one bone. The journey home passed in a daze and my father was horrified when he came home from work to find her curled up on the sofa, still in her wet clothes, her hands clutching her belly.

'Bruna, what happened? Are you all right my darling?'

'I fell down the steps to the Tube. I'm OK. Just bruises.'

But that night she found she was bleeding. The doctor

came the next day and sent her to hospital for bed rest for the final month of her pregnancy. Neighbours rallied round to look after Nicholas. All was going to be well.

Mum said her abiding memory of her pregnancy was the smell of roast chicken. She craved it and would smell it everywhere – even over the intense antiseptic of the hospital. For a month she shared a ward with other mothers-to-be who, unlike my poor mother, would simply come in, have their babies and leave. Time dragged and Mum amused herself by telling the fortunes of the other women – reading their palms and laying out the tarot cards over the crisp hospital sheets. There was one woman who was Irish and stunningly beautiful. 'But so stuck up, you know,' my mother recalled with a smile and a shrug.

'I told her she would have a little boy, but that he would not be so beautiful like her. She didn't want to believe this but, hey, what happened? She had a boy, and he was the most ugly baby you ever see. She even knew it, the poor girl. She said to me, "Isn't my baby ugly?"'

The other women asked Mum to predict what they would have. Would it be a boy? Would it be a girl? Time and time again, Mum got it right. Boy, girl, girl, boy, boy, boy, girl . . . never faltering, never once getting it wrong. At first they found it exciting and fun, but after a while it became uncanny and unsettling – because my mother didn't just predict the gender of their babies; she also told them in some detail about the kind of lives these as yet unborn children would have as they grew up.

'Your baby will be a good son to you. You will have five grandchildren. He will look after you too.'

'Ah, your daughter, she will be so clever. She will go to college, make lots of money.'

The women went off smiling broadly, telling everyone on the ward about the good fortune coming their way. But, never exactly tactful, Mum dished out the bad news as well as the good. She told one poor woman that her son would have criminal tendencies and spend much of his life in prison; another that her daughter would run away from home by the time she was ten. As her predictions about their babies' gender came true time after time, the women fell quiet and thoughtful. Of course, if she was right about this one thing, what did that say about her other predictions? The ward became charged with a heightened, nervous atmosphere. The women whispered to one another if my mother left the room and an uneasy silence fell when she came back to the ward. They stopped asking, scared of what they might find out. Sometimes it's best not to know what Fate has in store. Funnily enough, while all her other predictions were so accurate, my mother could not foresee her own future. She thought her dream was coming true. She was waiting to have her baby, the natural child of her womb. Her family would be complete, her world perfect. Little did she know that what Fate gave with one hand, it would take away with the other.

But still, for all that, it was a peaceful time, the quiet before the storm. As Lucy and I came to term, our mother's waters finally broke. When I revisited the scene under self-hypnosis I found it incredibly tragic. What many people don't know is that right up to the time of birth, and even a little beyond, a soul still has knowledge of where it has come from and the tasks that lie ahead. You can regress back into the womb and realise why you chose the parents you chose, why you picked this incarnation. Yet, when we come to birth, there can be a period of panic, of yearning to return to the Source rather than face the life chosen.

Lucy and I were certainly in no hurry to come out into this world. My sister knew she wasn't staying and I wasn't entirely sure I wanted to head out on a solo mission. Floating in the womb, it seemed a simple decision, so much easier and nicer to bow out, not to take this particularly tough turn at the incarnation wheel.

– *You must. You have to. You know you have to do this.*

Lucy was insistent.

– *But I don't want to go alone.*
– *I'll stay with you.*
– *Promise?*
– *Promise. I'll be there for as long as I can. As long as you need me.*

Of course the doctors had no idea of the inner battle going on. They tried to induce us, but we weren't going for that either. Forty-eight hours passed in frantic negotiations, anguished debates – both outside and inside my mother's body. Lucy hid behind me, pushing me forwards, telling me I had to do it; I had to leave her behind and go into this life on my own. Finally the doctors gave up and Mum was wheeled into surgery. They were going to cut us out by caesarean. Nobody had any idea there were two of us. When they pulled me out I was so starved of oxygen that I was bright blue – like an Indian god. I was also angry, so very, *very* angry. How could I be facing this on my own, without my twin, my soul sister? I opened my lungs and screamed and screamed and screamed. But nobody cared. I was alive, that was all that mattered. I was carted off to an incubator while the doctors plucked out my sister, her tiny twisted form, and slung her into the waste sluice, discarded like so much rubbish. My father was horrified at this and when my mother heard she wept inconsolably.

In the incubator it was lonely. The lights were too bright, there was too much space: instead of the thumping of our mother's heart there was either silence or the far-off chatter of nurses, the beeping of instruments. Above all, there was no Lucy. After nine months of being together, arms entwined or nestling up back to back, squeezed together in the womb, I was all alone. When I look back on that time it is with huge sadness. That first feeling – of intense loneliness – was to be the predominant emotion of my life.

My sister was utterly forgotten. Nobody talked to my parents about her. Nobody offered counselling. She had no funeral. There are no pictures of her, no handprints or footprints, as would happen nowadays. She was a non-person and nobody mentioned her again – until that fateful day when I was thirteen. Even I forgot she was my sister, my twin, as the years passed. She just became 'Lucy' – a voice, a comforting presence. So, in some ways, I too betrayed her.

My mother suffered from anxiety and depression following our birth. While she was in the hospital she was fine, but the moment she came home she panicked. Although she had already brought up my adopted brother Nicholas from babyhood, this was something different. She felt totally overwhelmed. She told me that Dad popped out to the shop to buy a paper, and all of a sudden she found herself panicking at being left alone with the baby. He seemed to be away for ages, for hours, but when he came back it had only been about seven minutes. Probably it was hormonal, but she must also have been feeling intense grief for Lucy. Maybe there was some kind of anticlimax as well. After more than twenty years of wanting a natural child, here was the child. Was I a disappointment? Was I what she wanted? She said that her first impression was that I was hairy and black! She thought I might be a genetic throwback to earlier mixed ancestry. Maybe I wasn't the dainty little perfect princess she had imagined. I don't know.

Nicholas, however, was in no doubt whatsoever. I was an abomination. Until I came along, he was the undisputed prince of the household. Now this puking, puling brat had usurped his mother's attention. He wasn't having any of it, and as little children do, he took out his frustration on me. I was lying on the carpet in the lounge, kicking my heels as Mum went to get a fresh nappy. Dad was in bed. Quick as a flash, Nicholas saw his chance and took it. Grabbing a cushion from the settee, he knelt down and squashed it on to my face, pushing with as much strength as a four-year-old can muster. Lucy was looking out for me even then, because he paused for a moment (enough for me to haul in some air) and then put back the cushion and this time decided it would be more fun to trampoline on my stomach as well. In the nick of time Mum came back into the room.

'Hey. Don't do that, Nicholas, you naughty boy. You'll hurt the baby.' She tugged the cushion away from him and, as the air poured back into my lungs, I let out a piercing scream. Nicholas, in turn, burst into tears and my father came shuffling into the room in his maroon slippers and blue striped pyjamas, crumpled from bed.

'What the hell is going on in here?' he demanded.

'It was Nicholas. He tried to smother the baby,' my mother said.

Nicholas turned to his father, big brown eyes brimming with tears.

'I didn't, Daddy. Honest to God, I didn't. I swear I didn't.'

'Michael, he was hurting the baby. I don't think he really meant to, though. He is just a bit jealous.'

Dad looked at him and he looked at Mum.

Dropping on to his knees, my father scooped Nicholas into his arms and patted his back soothingly. 'There, there. It's OK.'

The family turned back into itself. My father and brother sat entwined on the floor, like a modern Pietà, with my mother leaning in, trying to bring herself back into the picture. I lay, feeling quite forgotten, on the rug, the cushion tossed to one side. My mother later told me what had happened – she was quite matter-of-fact about it. But when I revisited that memory in regression, it felt different. I felt an over-whelming sense of panic, of terror. It went a way towards explaining the panic attacks I suffered as I grew older. But on a deeper, psychological level, it felt like a rejection. It felt as if they were the family unit and I was the added extra. I was the intrusion that had upset the delicate balance. This conversation with Lucy went through my head.

- *I shouldn't be here, Lucy. They don't want me.*
- *Of course they do. Get over it!*
- *My brother tried to hurt me.*
- *But I stopped him, didn't I?*
- *They don't love me.*
- *They do. Maybe they think they love you too much. Maybe they think they should love Nicholas more.*

It was the start of a feud that would go on for half our lives. I loved my brother to bits but he couldn't help but know that I was the natural child, he the adopted one. It didn't matter to me and I know it didn't matter to my parents. But it mattered to him. It burned inside him. His fear made him angry, dangerously angry.

So, my childhood was already touched by fear, even when I was a newborn baby. The abuse started pretty soon after that.

2

Crazy Horses

In the late 1960s we were living in a maisonette in west London. My mother's diaries describe a strange time. Her dream of a family had come true – she had her heart's desire. Yet the dream turned dark. My father was becoming increasingly unwell with what I later discovered was bone cancer. Nicholas was clearly jealous of me. Looking back, Mum must have been grieving horribly for the death of Lucy. She told me later that she blamed herself for Lucy's death – that if she hadn't fallen down the stairs, Lucy might have lived. How strange that her death was kept such a close family secret.

But our family seemed to thrive on secrets. As I grew older and started looking into my past, I delved endlessly into my childhood. I have tapes and tapes of my mother talking about the past – both her own audio diary and also 'interviews' I did with her, to make a record of our lives, desperately trying to understand why my life turned out the way it did; why I felt the way I did. Lucy had told me a lot too – as I grew older, she would fill me in on what had happened in my past. She didn't tell me everything, though. There were gaps, pauses, silences.

I think that, when I was very young, Lucy used to take my place sometimes, so I could blank out the worst of times. She would gently push me aside and I would simply go into the blissful darkness while she faced the horrors instead of me. It's similar to what happens when a personality splits off (like *Sybil,* and the other famous multiple personality cases) in order to protect the fragile self. The gaps irritated me, though, and so I also did a lot of work on myself – using self-hypnosis to go back to the time before I had conscious memory. What I discovered, when I looked back, was that the abuse that plagued my life had started frighteningly early. When I finally was able to talk to my mother about it, she confirmed much of what I described and added her own recollections.

My nursery was a bright sunny room, facing south, with a big tree outside. When the wind came up, the tree's branches would tap against the window panes like bony fingers trying to get inside. The room had pale yellow wallpaper with a frieze of nursery rhyme characters wandering round the wall at waist height. My cot sat in the corner, by the window, with a row of brightly coloured beads stretched across and a mobile of Hey Diddle Diddle hanging overhead. The cat and the fiddle never moved for some reason, but the cow would spin lazily round and round.

Our next-door neighbours were a couple in their sixties, 'Aunty' Flo and 'Uncle' Duncan. Looking back, it was a strange friendship and I imagine it was born of necessity, rather than choice. As my father was ill so much, my mother was working pretty well non-stop. It must have been hugely stressful, having two young children and no spare cash for childcare. Duncan and Flo, on the other hand, had no children and time and money weren't an issue. They must have seemed like a gift from God. If only my parents had realised that they were quite the opposite.

One day – I must have been about eleven months old – I was lying in my cot, watching the cow spin mournfully round, when the door slowly creaked open. Uncle Duncan walked carefully, quietly, across the room and eased himself into the nursing chair by the side of my cot, pulling his thick tweed trousers up round the knees to stop them bagging.

He smiled, a crooked smile that curled his lips but didn't reach his eyes. His eyes were horrible, cold and hard.

'Hello, baby.' He didn't use the babbling baby talk everyone else did. He didn't coo or pull silly faces. He just stared. Intently. Fiddling with his trousers, moving his hand further up towards the fly. Then he was standing up, with his penis out, pumping at it with his hand, stroking my face with long bony fingers. I don't know what would have happened next, but my mother came into the room and found him, standing there, fly open, penis dangling out, half-erect.

He jumped backwards, knocking over the chair, scrabbling to get himself covered up.

'What you doing? What you doing with that thing out?' My mother was horrified, her face turning red with rage.

'I didn't mean anything, Bruna. I didn't. Honest to God. It won't happen again, I promise you. You *do* believe me?' He was babbling, endless words, backing away from the cot. Then he picked up the chair, set it back down and sank into it, his head flopped forwards into his hands. His bony back shuddered with sobs. My mother stood staring at him, shaking her head: anger turning to confusion and then to compassion. My mother always loved an underdog. She had an amazing capacity for tolerating human weaknesses and frailty.

'It was a mistake, eh?' she said. 'It won't happen again. You promise?'

'I promise, Bruna. I really do. I don't know what got into me.'

Mum became brisk and businesslike. 'Well, luckily there was no harm done, eh? She's only a baby. She won't know anything about it. She'll forget all about it. No harm done.' She kept repeating it as if trying to persuade herself.

What she couldn't see was that there wasn't a tear in his eyes, only that hard, cold, calculating look.

It's a curious thing, but people who have been abused often tend not to see it happening to others. It's as if they can't bear to think about it, can't believe the cycle will start up yet again.

My earliest childhood memory (of my own, rather than something Lucy told me about or one retrieved through hypnosis) was of crawling about our small square lawn in the back garden we shared with our neighbour upstairs. Her name was Mrs Clack, but we called her Mrs Click-Clack as we were convinced she wore wooden clogs purposely so she could tap dance over our heads and disturb us every night. Looking back, this was pretty unlikely as she was eighty-five and pretty well bedridden.

The garden seemed huge to me as a toddler. It was an entire world, a jungle, a savannah, a magical place that seemed wild and endless. A blackbird was singing that day and I remember very clearly being caught in a moment of pure magic – it was as if someone had suddenly switched the lights on and the world had shifted from being black and white to living breathing Technicolor.

I gazed up at the sky – duck-egg blue with a slow procession of cotton wool clouds. It was a moment of transcendence, maybe the birth of my consciousness. I felt a part of something bigger, the universe, the Whole. I became aware that I was more than just little Michèle – that I belonged 'out there', that some day I would 'go home'. It was magical, and I can still remember it with utter clarity. It was a moment of pure total bliss.

Then the real world crowded in. I realised with a horrible jolt that this world wasn't boundless. It had boundaries – a dark wooden fence that smelt of creosote. Through it I was aware of someone gazing in on my private world.

Someone staring. Someone watching my every move. It was
Uncle Duncan, our neighbour, and he seemed very old to
me, and very bent, and very horrible. He had white hair
and an extremely bulbous nose. He wore his shirtsleeves
rolled up and held a rake in his hand. He was tossing leaves
into a rusty bin and burning them. When I looked at his
garden it seemed curiously barren. He smiled at me, but
it was a dead smile.

'Hello, Michèle. How are you today?'

I didn't answer. There was something not right about
him, something I didn't like. At some level I knew he was
someone I couldn't trust, shouldn't trust.

- *I don't like him, Lucy.*
- *I know. Nor do I.*

'Michèle? Are you shy? Won't you talk to your Uncle
Duncan?' He raised an eyebrow.

I shook my head and plucked a blade of grass, keeping
my eyes firmly on the ground. If I didn't see him, maybe
he couldn't see me. I heard a door open and my mother's
voice rang out.

'Eh, Michèle! Why aren't you talking to Uncle Duncan?
Don't be rude. You say "hello" like a good girl. Uncle
Duncan has been good to you. He looked after you when
you were a baby.'

Uncle Duncan smiled, a sickly smile. I noticed a tiny globule
of spit at the corner of his mouth and watched fascinated

as it bobbed in and out as he spoke. He looked at me and, turning his head away from Mum, winked. I shivered.

'She's just shy, Bruna. I reckon she's forgotten her Uncle Duncan. I'll have to spend a bit more time with her, won't I?' He paused and stared intently at me. 'A *lot* more time.'

Mum came down the steps and I rushed over to her, hiding behind her legs, burying my head in her wide full skirt. It smelled of garlic, incense and perfume – a strange combination, now I think about it, but to me at the time it signalled safety. Mum had saved me from the nasty man over the fence. For the moment.

'Uncle' Duncan was married to 'Aunty' Flo. Aunty Flo was very short and had a limp, a legacy of childhood polio. She walked with a stick and had a face like a crow – squinty eyes, sharp pointed nose, and she would look at you with her head tilted to one side, as if you were always on the verge of committing some hideous offence. She was nice enough to my face, but I just knew that underneath the smiles she hated me. In fact, she hated all children. Did she know what her husband did, what he wanted to do? At some level, she must have done.

Their home was the tiny flat next door. As you walked through the door the sickly cloying smell of cheap perfume would hit you – it made me feel queasy. I can still see that flat so clearly. Every surface was filled with ornaments. They both came from Glasgow originally and every area was covered with hordes of knick-knacks in clashing tartans: miniature bagpipes and fake sporrans, a Monarch of the Glen, and dolls in Scottish costume. There were also loads of Toby dogs – and I think they must have had a real Jack Russell once as there was a dog's lead hanging on the back of the door – but no sign of any dog, which I found profoundly unnerving. Above all, they collected Toby jugs, those ugly fat men's faces leering horribly. It felt as if you were surrounded by a crowd of nasty dirty old men, all laughing at you, all making fun, all enjoying your unhappiness, all wishing they could share in what was happening to you.

By the time I was three my father's periods of illness were increasing. Sometimes he was all right and would go to work, but often he had to stay home. My mother was working incredibly hard, leaving me at home with Dad while Nicholas was at school. When Dad was in pain, which was often, I was left to my own devices or (more often) was sent round to Uncle Duncan's and Aunty Flo's. Of course I didn't want to go; I would have done anything not to have gone, but really I had no choice. I tried saying I didn't like Uncle Duncan but my mother would turn on me and yell, saying I was ungrateful, that if it weren't for Uncle Duncan and Aunty Flo I would have nowhere to go. Didn't I care about my father? Didn't I want him to get well? He needed peace and quiet, not a noisy kid bothering him. Guilt gnawed at me.

I remember one day in particular. It had been boring at home. The house was dark, the curtains closed, and none of my toys interested me.

I must have been annoying my father as he told me to go next door to Uncle Duncan.

Lucy didn't like it one little bit, and nor did I.

'Do I have to, Dad?' I whispered.

'I'm so tired, Michèle. I need to sleep. Go on now . . . off you go.'

'But I don't like it there . . .'

'Now Michèle, we've been through this before. Don't let me have to tell your mother you've started that nonsense again.'

I couldn't disobey my father and I dreaded my mother's fury, so I struggled out of our front door and up the stairs to next door. They seemed so steep, they were tiring. It was like climbing a mountain and I felt tired when I got to the top. I pressed the button and chimes rang out – a nasty tinkling sickly sound. Uncle Duncan's nose preceded him through the door.

'Your mum at work again, is she? Never mind. Uncle Duncan will look after you. Come on in, hurry up.'

I dawdled reluctantly in after him, every step torture. He went to the kitchen and I stood, shifting from one foot to the other, in the lounge.

'Here's a cup of milk.'

I was thirsty so I reached out and took it, gazing solemnly at him. I looked round for somewhere to sit.

'Come and sit on my lap and I'll read you a funny story.'

I really didn't want to, every part of me wanted to rebel, but I was an obedient child (at that time) and so I clambered up on to his lap. It felt bony with sharp bits and I wasn't really very comfortable. He cackled and started rocking me back and forwards, pretending he was a horse.

My milk spilled a bit – would he shout at me like Mum did when I was careless? I looked worriedly at his face, but Uncle Duncan didn't seem to care. He just jiggled me faster and faster with his face sort of twisting. I bounced up and down, hitting his bony hips and feeling very uncomfortable. I tried to make him stop, but he had his eyes closed by now and white spittle was dripping from the corner of his mouth. Suddenly he stopped with a deep grunt. Breathless, he plonked me back on the floor and gasped.

Then he turned to me and laughed. 'Now that was fun, wasn't it? But look at that milk you spilled.'

He shook his head, lips pursed. 'Don't worry, Michèle, we'll get a cloth. I won't tell your mum how naughty you were. It'll be our secret.'

After that I was sent round quite regularly. He would give me milk and biscuits. We would play 'horsey', but only if Aunty Flo wasn't there. I would inevitably spill some milk.

'We won't tell your mum. We don't tell Aunty Flo. It's our little secret, isn't it, Michèle?'

I nodded. I never told anyone what happened in that flat. I knew it was wrong, I knew it was bad. But I didn't dare say a word.

As my father became more seriously ill, he was taken into hospital for longer periods and I had to spend more time next door. I hated it when Aunty Flo was there. If Nicholas was with us we would play Snakes and Ladders, and if he wasn't they would show me their photo albums. But I hated it even more when Aunty Flo *wasn't* there. One day I made the slow trip up the stairs to the flat, dragging out every step, and Uncle Duncan opened the door in his kilt. Aunty Flo was also in hospital, having her hip replaced. My brother was at school. I was on my own with him.

'Ah, Michèle. Good. It's Burns' Day today. We'll have a Scottish party.'

I could hear Highland folk music playing as we climbed the stairs in the flat. Uncle Duncan had a large glass of whisky in his hand and his eyes were slightly unfocused. The music was too loud, it hurt my ears. Uncle Duncan stared at me intently, his eyes glancing all over my body. He stumbled a bit as he filled his glass again and took a long slurp.

'Do you want to try a dram, Michèle?' He laughed manically and held out the glass. It looked like cola so I took a sip, but choked as the whisky burned my throat. Duncan laughed again.

'Not your taste then? Ah well.' He tossed the remains back in one gulp.

He turned the music up even louder and I started to feel dizzy. He grabbed my hands and picked me up, swinging me round him. His bony wrists were holding mine tight but it didn't feel safe, it didn't feel fun. It wasn't like when Dad used to swing me, before he became ill. Duncan's mouth was open in a rictus of a smile and I could smell his breath, the sickly sweetness of the whisky overlaying decay. It seemed to last for ever, like some horrible nightmare. You know you're dreaming but you can't make yourself wake up, and every time you *do* wake, it's only to fall asleep and back into the nightmare once more.

Eventually he put me down, panting, sweat beading his sickly skin. I slumped on to the floor, the room spinning round me, the Toby jug faces leering at me.

But the respite didn't last for long. Duncan suddenly grabbed my hands and pulled me to my feet.

'Let's see if you can find out what's underneath a Scotsman's kilt, eh?'

He laughed and laughed as he twirled around the room like a madman, flashing his kilt up as he danced. I saw flashes of something that looked like another nose under there, another long bulbous nose on a thick stalk standing right up in the air.

'Let's see if you can play the Scotsman, lassie. Let me take your panties off and you can do some Scottish dancing too.'

I shook my head. 'I don't want to.'

He stopped for a moment and stared furiously at me. 'In my house you do as I say. If I say you're going to dance, you're damn well going to dance. Do you want me to tell your mother you've been a naughty girl?'

I could see something dangerous in his eyes.

- *Do as he says, Michèle.*
- *I know, Lucy.*

I shook my head mutely. He yanked off my panties and threw them on to the carpet. 'Now dance.'

I copied him, move for move, flashing up my dress as he flashed his kilt. The thing under his kilt seemed to be growing longer and longer, redder and redder. I knew this wasn't right, but I didn't dare say anything. He'd had a lot to drink and his mood was unpredictable and frightening, veering from laughter to anger in seconds.

He sat down, laughing and puffing as the music slowed its pace. His kilt was up over his scrawny chest. The thing was pointing in my direction. Abruptly he got up and switched off the music. My ears rang in the sudden silence.

'Let's play horsey before your nap,' he leered.

I wondered where I would sit, seeing as the thing was rising up from the centre of his lap. But he placed me lightly on top of it, so my bare bum was on his belly, and the thing was stuck between my bare legs. He started off slower than usual, thrusting me up and down on his lap and grunting as he muttered the nursery rhyme. I could feel the thing squashed between my thighs, pushing up at me as if it wanted something. Then he began to speed up, ignoring the rhythm of the rhyme, clutching me closer and closer. Suddenly the thing started to dribble and something like snot flew out all over my bare thighs. It felt disgusting, sticky and smelly, like the sea. I felt like being sick but I didn't want to embarrass him. So I pretended not to notice. Duncan stopped jiggling suddenly and flopped forward, crushing me. Then he sighed and fell backwards. The thing flopped on to my leg and then shrivelled and disappeared. We sat in silence. I was aware that this really wasn't right. I could sense it. He seemed angry with me all of a sudden. He wanted me to go. I had done something wrong.

- *Let's go, Michèle.*
- *Yes, let's, Lucy.*

I put on my panties, let myself out of the flat and quietly bumped down the stairs to the bottom and trotted as quickly as I could back to our maisonette next door.

The games with Duncan became part of my life. A horrible, frightening part of my life. Every time I clambered up the stairs to Uncle Duncan's home, I felt my heart sink, liquid dread seeping through me. I tried once more to plead with my father not to send me. He'd ask me why, but I couldn't say. I was too scared, too embarrassed. I felt that somehow it was my fault that Uncle Duncan played horsey with me; that I saw that horrible dribbling thing. I felt guilt and shame and fear. I knew that if I told anyone, Uncle Duncan would be angry, so angry. So I kept quiet and – to make it worse – Mum and Dad would tell me off for not wanting to see Uncle Duncan, when he was being so kind looking after me. So I was a bad girl whichever way you looked at it. Bad because I made Uncle Duncan do these things; bad because I let him; bad because I was letting my parents down by being ungrateful.

It slanted my view on everything and I can't remember

one day in my life when I wasn't aware of sex. I didn't get any pleasure out of it, though. I was never one of those precocious children who play with themselves from an early age. As I grew up, I couldn't understand why other children clearly didn't feel this way, didn't know these things. I can't really explain it, but I was so accustomed to it that I pretty well expected adults to be sexual around me – and they were. In fact, I was surprised if they weren't.

To the best of my knowledge, I was abused repeatedly throughout my young years. I found out years later that, when I was only a baby, my parents had left me and Nicholas in the care of Aunty Flo and Uncle Duncan while they went abroad – to Tangiers. It's absolutely amazing and shocking that they did this, given how Mum had found Duncan masturbating over me in my cot. Years later, when she told me about it, she said she had no idea that he was like that . . . that she had thought the incident in my cot had been a one-off, a stupid mistake. Why didn't her psychic powers warn her? I really don't know. It's something that has always puzzled me. It still does.

I have no idea what happened during that time when Mum and Dad went away – Lucy never said and the memories never came up during hypnosis. Really I am rather glad. I have enough memories of that man as it is.

Of course Duncan wasn't the only one. Around that time another neighbour, 'Uncle' Bob, also thought I was fair game. Did he and Duncan talk about me or was it pure coincidence? I don't know. The abuse here was more sporadic, but more intense. There was no concept of playing 'games', no pretence at being nice. He would simply grab his chances when he could. Often he would pop over 'to see Bruna' when he knew she would be out at work. He would put his head round the bedroom door to say hello to Dad, offering to make a cup of tea. He knew Dad wouldn't come out of the bedroom; knew he was safe to pull down his trousers and make me touch him right there in our own kitchen. On other occasions, he would offer, apparently so kindly, to take me back for tea or down to the shops for a lolly. He used to buy me the multi-coloured ones called Rockets and I can still hear him saying, in his flat London accent, 'Go on, Michèle. Suck that lolly. Good and hard. That's it, sweetheart. Suck.'

But worst of all was Connie. Mum had met Connie through work. She was tall and slim, with a very curvaceous figure. Her features were strong – her eyes were green, deep and penetrating; her large crooked nose dominated her face. Yet she was strangely attractive, and Mum found her rather wild personality and sense of humour quite compelling. Connie was married to a tall, striking man – with a handsome yet cruel face. He claimed he had been a mercenary in Africa and Asia and boasted freely about the horrible things he had done in the jungle.

He was a vicious, violent man and Connie often appeared with bruises and cuts. My mother was always worried about her, always trying to get her to go to the police, to press charges – but she wouldn't.

It seemed as if Connie was always round at our house. I suppose it started off as a safe place to go, but it worked well for Mum and Dad. Dad went into remission at several points and would return to work. Thrilled to have some energy back, he would whirl my mother around the room and take her out to parties or concerts. Connie would look after Nicholas and me. At first I was thrilled – anything was better than Duncan. But, as time went on, I changed my mind.

Connie was fascinated with Mum's magical apparatus – her incense and charms, her potions and amulets. I would often find her casting a circle, chanting and praying, surrounded by billowing clouds of incense. But there was a difference. My mother would pray to Jesus on the whole, sometimes calling on angels and saints. But Connie was turning bitter and her thoughts turned to darker powers.

'I have discovered the Black Arts,' she announced proudly to Nicholas and me one day. 'And I'm quite good at it.' She smiled unpleasantly. Then she pointed at me and my heart turned cold. 'You won't make old bones, Michèle. You'll die in a car accident when you're thirty-eight. Sorry, dear.' She laughed and I started to cry.

Nicholas and I were often dropped round to her house. The exact details are hazy in my memory and, to be very honest, I have never tried to recover them. I have always had flashbacks and images of strange people in black performing bizarre, horrible rituals. Often they would come as I was on the verge of sleep – images of people being tied up on an altar surrounded by black candles and of people being whipped. But then they would fade, leaving me feeling sick and terrified. However, Nicholas, being four years older than me, had much better recall. Years later we talked about Connie and what he told me made my blood run cold.

It wasn't much better when she came round to our house to babysit us. Nicholas said she had a really sadistic streak and would delight in being cruel. Sometimes she would cook boiled eggs and stuff them whole into his mouth, making him choke and gag, desperately trying to chew before he had to swallow.

I really don't remember how much I was involved; it's one set of memories I cannot recover. I think it was a survival mechanism. My mind simply blocked out the greater part of the horror. Thank God it did.

It does seems incredible that my parents had no idea of what was going on. But, once again, it seems that they were so wrapped up in their own everyday survival that it didn't cross their minds that the people who were helping them look after their children could be so woefully abusing that trust.

My mother had her own painful memories of childhood. Her father, Bruno Cumuni, was a violent man who regularly beat his wife, my grandmother Margherita. They lived in northern Italy, in a village called Cividale, and met when Margherita was only fourteen. My mother was conceived soon after this in the fields during the village wine festival.

When my mother was born it caused a huge scandal – nobody had known my grandmother was pregnant. Bruno's own family tried to garrotte him by putting a wire across the road where he rode his bike. But he was lucky. The moon shone brightly that night and, in the nick of time, he saw the wire and ducked. His family apologised to my grandmother, saying they were very sad she had to marry such a terrible man. It wasn't a happy marriage. Soon he wasn't only beating my grandmother, but my mother too. Mum once told me this tale:

'Every second day he beat my mother. One day my mother said to me to go to the inn and tell my father his dinner was ready. So I did, but he picked me up and threw me against the wall saying, "Tell your mother not to bother me when I'm drinking."'

My grandmother had eight children, five of which died as babies – many as a result of the beatings she had suffered while pregnant. One, however, was tossed into the air as a baby by my grandfather, and she banged her head on the ceiling and died. Another was lying in her cot by the stove when my mother raced in and knocked against the cot. The baby had a seizure and died. My poor mother blamed herself bitterly for the baby's death and lived with a huge guilt all her life.

As if there were not enough misery in the house, when my mother was about seven, she was raped by her father. In her own words:

'Your granny was screaming outside the door and when

she managed to get in, she put me on the table and looked at me. She cuddled me and was crying. We had a lodger upstairs and she heard what happened and went to the police.'

My grandfather – amazingly for that time – was found guilty of rape and sentenced to three and a half years in prison. He lost custody of the children and separated from my grandmother. My grandmother comforted my mother, telling her that she too had been sexually abused as a child. They clung to one another and wept.

So, as often happens, I was only the last one in a long line of abuse that stretched back over the generations. I also inherited something else: the ability to see beyond everyday life. From about the age of two, I started developing my psychic powers – with strange and startling results.

3

Healing Hands

Dad had been ill before I was born and it started getting worse when I was five or six months old. It was bone cancer, which made his bones incredibly brittle and caused him enormous pain.

Mum tried everything she could to save him. He went back and forwards from hospital for treatment, never knowing exactly what was wrong. It was a funny thing in those days – the doctors told Mum what the problem was, but left it up to her whether she told my father or not. She believed totally in the power of positive thought and so she always told him he was getting better. She used less orthodox methods too, taking him to the famous healer Harry Edwards who used not only hands-on healing but also remote healing (where the person doesn't even need to be in the same room – or even the same country, come to that). This went on for two years and I have reams of letters between my mother and Harry Edwards, reporting on his progress. Sometimes it seemed to be working – Dad would regain his energy and go back to work. Sometimes it didn't and he would relapse, retreating to his bed in agony.

In order to help him even more, Mum had trained in healing with the National Federation of Spiritual Healers. Now she ran her own healing circles too, as well as being a practising psychic and medium.

One day, when I was about two, she was running a healing circle in our living room and I'd been left to play in the kitchen. I was always being left to my own devices. It's a funny thing that, as much as Mum had professed to want children, once she had them she barely seemed to notice them. In reality she remained totally wrapped up with my father and with her own wild magical life. Nicholas and I were just the audience to her mad show.

I could hear murmuring through the closed door and as I peeked round the corner I could see about six people sitting around the room, including my mum sitting upright in one of the kitchen chairs and my dad slumped down in an armchair. I didn't know the others, but I wasn't remotely scared of strangers. I could tell that Dad was in pain, so I toddled in and walked straight over to him and placed my tiny hands on his head.

'Michèle make Daddy better.'

My mother jumped up, a concerned frown spreading across her forehead. I snatched my hands away and stepped back. She was worried that I would pick up my dad's pain as I was so young. She thought I wouldn't know how to channel healing through me, but instead would absorb it into myself.

'Eh, Michèle, leave your dad alone. Go on now. Off to play. We're busy, darling.'

But my father frowned and waved a hand as if to say no. In his calm cultured voice he said quietly, 'Leave her, Bruna. She takes away the pressure in my head. It feels better, it really does.'

Mum frowned again and watched me intently, to make sure I was all right.

I put my hands back on Dad's head. I could feel something passing through me, into him. It wasn't something I had inside me – but rather something that came from another place and just used me to get through.

'That's wonderful, Michèle. Thank you, darling.' He gave me a sad sweet smile and squeezed my hand. I grinned brightly back at him and happily wandered back to my toy animals in the kitchen.

From then on, I often used to 'heal' my father and he said it really helped. Mum recognised that I wasn't just copying her, but really did seem to have the gift.

'You are either a healer or you're not,' she told me. 'People say you can be trained, but really you either have it or you don't – all the training does is give you guidance.' She described it as like being given a road map. So she taught me the rudiments. You learned relaxation first of all, how to let go of the everyday cares and concerns and sink deep down into yourself. Then you opened the third eye to allow clairvoyance (remote seeing) and clairaudience (distant hearing). She insisted that, as a healer, I needed both clairvoyance and clairaudience so I could tell where the healing was needed.

'Maybe your mind will feel a pain here,' she touched her hip, 'and the pain belongs to the person you are healing. Sometimes your hands will move over a person and suddenly a voice will stop you and tell you they have pain there.'

My mother taught me healing almost by osmosis. I just watched and listened and practised what she told me. She stopped trying to keep me out of the healing circles and, instead, let me work on people. She told me that one time a man called Tom asked me to heal his leg, and that he said the pain vanished immediately. Another man, Graham, had twisted his ankle playing sport and, again, I took away the swelling and the pain. I even healed my mother, apparently:

'One time I was ill in bed with a migraine,' Mum told me, 'and you came in and took away the pain. I used to say to you, "Go and play. To play is important", but you would heal me and only then go to play. You were always a free spirit.'

It wasn't just healing that Mum taught me. She used the crystal ball with an uncanny degree of accuracy and would also read palms and tarot cards. I was always drawn to the tarot. It came easily – as natural as learning to walk, as easy as falling over. As a small child the tarot cards, with their bright pictures were fascinating to me – some so cheerful and happy, some so dark and ominous, all of them mysterious and magical. I used to turn them over again and again, just as other children might turn the pages of a favourite book. I don't remember Mum ever teaching me what each individual card meant: I just seemed to pick up the feeling, to know what they signified. To this day I can only use the Rider Waite pack – if you said to me, 'What does the nine of swords mean?' I wouldn't have a clue. I need to see those pictures, the pictures that have been part of my life since I could first put my fist around them. The beautiful Empress, the stern Emperor, the carefree Fool and the gruesome Devil. My favourite was always the Star and I saw myself as the Fool, leaping into the unknown with total faith.

I must have been about five or six when Mum told me to listen out for voices in my head. She said that, like her, I would start to hear the voices of my guides. But I was already hearing them. I'd been hearing them for years – well, one at least. Lucy's voice had been with me all my life and I talked to her as if she were right there, physically, by my side. It wasn't an external voice, more a telepathic connection. At that time I didn't question who Lucy was – she was just Lucy. She was my best friend, my ally, the other half of me. I certainly didn't know she was my sister; I had no idea she was my twin.

– *Don't tell Mum about me.*
– *Why?*
– *Best not. Not yet.*

Other kids had imaginary friends, but Lucy wasn't like that. I never saw her. She was just this presence, this voice in my head, this person who wasn't a person, closer than my heart. Sometimes when I think of her now I wonder what she would have looked like had she lived and grown up. Were we identical twins, or non-identical? Would we have looked the same, or very different? It's funny to think of someone looking the same as you. Would we have had the same character? I don't think so. I can't imagine Lucy playing up the way I did. But maybe, if Lucy had lived, I wouldn't have had to be so difficult. I wouldn't have pushed against the rails so hard. If. If. If. It's so easy to think things would have been different. If my twin hadn't died.

Of course if Lucy had been there I wouldn't have had to share a bedroom with my brother. When I think back I realise it can't have been great for Nicholas either – sharing a room with a toddler, and a girl to boot. The usurper who had stolen his security. But it was really grim for me. He used to hold my head against the wall and say, 'I'm going to smash your head against the wall.' So I'd wriggle like a fish or kick his shins and somehow escape. Mind you, I was no angel. I used to torment him until he chased me. I was so neglected that I couldn't bear to be ignored. I was either left alone or left with totally unsuitable adult people, like Duncan, Bob or Connie who were all continuing to abuse me and Nicholas. My brother was my only company, so if he ignored me I would wind him up until he snapped. One time he chased me into the living room, which had large glass doors. He cornered me and I backed, terrified, into the doors.

'I've got you now,' he said, smiling, his eyes dead and glazed. I flattened myself against the doors, almost willing myself to merge into them. He stood back and then gave me a short sharp push. I lost my balance and tumbled back. The glass was thin and I can still hear the horrible crack as it splintered.

– *Roll into a ball!*

Lucy screamed the words in my head. I did as she commanded, dropping like a stone to the floor and making myself as small as I could, as the glass rained down around me. Nicholas was worried – he was always sorry when it went too far. But it *always* went too far. I didn't move for ages. Then suddenly I screamed like a banshee and, with blood gushing all over me, I ran next door to our other neighbour (not Uncle Duncan, but a sweet kindly woman) and she patched me up. I still have the scars from that day on my shoulders – faint now but an unforgettable memory.

I suppose it could have been far worse – if it hadn't been for Lucy, if I hadn't rolled up, I might have been killed.

So, not only was I was being routinely sexually abused by my mother's friends and neighbours, but I was also being physically and emotionally intimidated and bullied by my brother. I don't think any of it really hit home when I was young. I just took each day as it came. I accepted that this was my life: I suppose I didn't know any different. I found huge joy in the simplest of things – a ray of sun glancing through the window; a pretty flower; learning a new game; or playing kick the can in the park when things were calm with my brother. I have always had the ability to be right in the moment, to revel in the sweet small things of life. So, although what I'm describing might sound awful, it was more a case of 'good things, bad things'. I never once dwelt on it; I never once thought 'poor me'. I learnt to love life and to value each and every second. Perhaps this was Lucy's first lesson to me? To understand the power of the moment and the beauty of life? Being alive has always felt so wonderful.

But I did wish people wouldn't touch me and I did sometimes wish to God that Nicholas wouldn't scare me. I wanted so much for him to love me. Nights were the most frightening of all, when we were together in our small shared bedroom. I was always trying to get into bed with my parents. Their bed seemed a haven of safety while the small room I shared with Nicholas was dangerous, very dangerous. So I would wait until I thought Nicholas was asleep and then lower myself carefully out of bed and start making my way ever so slowly to the door.

'Diddly doo di doo.' A very slow quiet voice came from his bed. It was horrible, sadistic really. As I crept towards the door, his voice would get faster and faster, louder and louder.

'Diddly doo di doo. Diddly doo di do.' There was something so creepy about it – he was communicating menace with rhythm, and I knew that if I got to the door he would shout out and grass me up. I wouldn't be able to sneak, unnoticed, into the safety and warmth of my parents' bed. I was trapped. So I'd walk back, shoulders slumped, and the voice would go quieter again, quieter and slower. It sounds strange but this was far worse than when he was chasing me or hitting me.

I don't remotely blame my brother. He was naturally a timid and quiet person, really it was a disaster for him being brought up by such a tempestuous mother. She simply didn't have the skills to bring up a child, any child – and certainly she didn't have the sensitivity to understand that she was bringing up an adopted child, an Asian child, a child who was, by rights, Muslim. She didn't have any concept that he might have needed to understand his roots, to retain his culture and heritage. She shrugged it off when the children at school bullied him and taunted him, calling him 'Paki'. In fairness she thought that, as she had adopted him (though, of course, never legally) he was Italian/English, and that is what everyone should believe. I passionately believed this too: he was my brother and he felt like my real brother. He still does. I couldn't wait to go to school so I could stand up for him, fight his battles for him. I watched him from the window, walking home from school, head hanging low, scuffing his shoes as he kicked the ground. Behind him, at a distance, came a gaggle of the other boys. If he was lucky, they ignored him. If not, they would be shouting taunts, throwing things, giving him a shove as they overtook. No wonder he came in with a face like thunder and wanting to take out his anger and misery on someone else, someone younger and supposedly weaker. I used to feel that if I could only place my hands on him and let the healing come through me (the way it did for Dad), I could take away some of the fury that raged inside him, the misunderstanding, the hurt, the pain. But of course he would never let me come anywhere near him.

I would have liked to have taken away the anguish inside my mother too. She was such a strange person. Everyone outside the family thought she was just so kind and caring, and she was one of those people who could never do too much for her friends, even for total strangers. She would give, and give, and give. People called her a saint. Yet when she closed the door, she transformed into someone quite different, a distracted, absent mother who closed in on herself. She had a violent irrational temper and could easily lose control, but she didn't direct it at me or Nicholas – at least not at this point. However, I do remember one exception. I must have been very small, maybe under two, and she had left me playing in the kitchen while she had a nap. I had felt lonely and crawled my way into her bedroom. My attention was caught by something bright glinting through the wardrobe door. It was a high-heeled silvery, strappy sandal. I quietly opened the door and discovered a world of shoes. They seemed magical to me and I got them all out, lining them up, trying them on as every child (or certainly every girl) has done throughout the history of shoes. She came in and, instead of laughing or leaving me to it, went ballistic. She shouted, she screamed, she threw the shoes around the room and even at me. I scudded back on my bottom, with my arms over my face, until the onslaught finished.

But when my mother wasn't being mad or bad, she could be wonderful. She was smart and funny and, of course, hugely gifted with psychic powers. I grew up in a house where the supernatural was as normal as eggs and bacon. I remember one conversation we had as we sat eating our breakfast:

'Pass the cornflakes,' said Dad, taking a gulp of coffee. Mum handed them over but she had a distracted look on her face.

'I went to Italy last night,' she said. 'It was ever so cold and wet. I don't understand it – it's August. It should be hot.' Nobody batted an eyelid. She regularly engaged in astral projection, sending her consciousness out to other places, while her body remained in north London. She liked the sea, and missed Italy, so she would often return in spirit, if not in the flesh. She said it soothed her.

Dad's bouts of illness came and went and, when he was in remission, he continued his work as a travel agent. I remember him coming home that night and saying, 'You were quite right, Bruna. The weather in Italy is atrocious right now.' She nodded vaguely. Of course she was right. She'd *been* there, hadn't she?

We knew all about her guides, the discarnate beings who

told her what advice to give her clients and who directed her when she was healing. My father humoured her. I'm not sure he ever really believed, although other people swore she was the most accurate psychic they had ever met. She also knew a lot about herbs – which ones could heal and which ones could harm – though she often believed in common superstition too. When I was a toddler, I brought in a dandelion and held it up to her.

'Brought you flower, Mummy. Pretty yellow flower.'

'No! Get that thing out of the house. It'll make you wet the bed.'

This is my first conscious memory of ever feeling emotional hurt. I had wanted to please her and had picked the dandelion with such love. I was aware that her reaction was strange. But I didn't take umbrage; I just toddled out again and placed it in a pot of water in the garden. When I came in, Mum and Dad were arguing.

'We should go to the zoo, with the kids. Like a good family, eh?'

'Bruna, I have to work. I can't just take off. Heaven only knows I can't work as much as I should.'

He had good days and bad days. Sometimes the pain was so bad it made him snappy. This was one of them, and after a few minutes of irritable debate he lost his temper.

'For Christ's sake, Bruna, shut up! We can't go and that's that.'

I marched up to my father and shook his arm sharply.

'Daddy! Don't you dare talk to Mummy like that. Don't you dare hurt her! I don't like it.'

She was unpredictable, difficult and often the worst mother in the world, but she was *my* mother and I wasn't having anyone – not even my father – shout at her.

I inherited so much from my mother, and I must have reminded him of her so much. I, too, was strong-minded, opinionated from a very early age. I was, if I'm honest, a precocious brat. I was just too strong. I had the same terrible temper, the same lack of control.

Looking back, I can't believe how I survived my early years. The level of tension in our house was sky-high. Mum and Dad would fight; Nicholas and I would fight. Mum and Dad would shout and yell at Nicholas and me one minute, and hug and kiss us the next. It was totally inconsistent parenting, and I never knew whether to open my arms or flinch from a barrage of bad temper. No wonder we couldn't control our own emotions. Mum was working like fury to make up the shortfall from Dad being ill and often unable to work. I barely saw her and, when I did, she was irritable and tired or wild and manic. Our neighbours were regularly abusing me and my Mum's best friend was a Satanist spiralling into paranoid madness. Really, it was a mad-house.

So when Dad told us that he was embarking on a business venture in Italy, and we would be going there for the summer, my heart positively lifted. Italy. Somewhere warm, somewhere different. Here, surely, we could be safe and happy? I could get away from my abusers. My family could relax and be normal. Couldn't we? However, it was in Italy that – once more – my life was to be in perilous danger. A danger not only physical, but also terrifyingly supernatural.

4

Bad Storm Coming

Italy was pure magic. We didn't go back to my mother's home village, Cividale, but to a place called Grado, not far from Trieste. It's a stunning island, set in the northern Adriatic, a place of healing since Roman times, where the sea water was supposed to have magical properties, and even the sand was considered specially therapeutic (due to the beach being totally south-facing and absorbing the maximum amount of sunlight). It was here, on the edge of the beach, in an area known as Al Bosco, that my parents were going to be running something called the Tentotel, a kind of upmarket camping site with luxury tents. It sounds odd but at the time, in the late 1960s, it was considered quite the thing and people rushed to stay in posh tents with their own bedrooms and bathrooms. As it was billed at the time, 'The Tenterrific Holiday!'

My mother and father actually made a great team. He was charm personified, the perfect host. My mother, on the other hand, was the practical one. Despite her tiny size, she was incredibly strong and didn't think anything of putting up tents, hauling gas bottles, taking the tourists out on excursions or driving a heavy bus. She never stopped. When she wasn't doing the grunt work, you'd find her talking to the guests, sorting out their love lives, giving them advice on their problems, listening to their worries and concerns. Everybody loved her. Her strength allowed my parents to carry on with the Tentotel even when my father had his sick spells. She carried the whole family on her back.

When she wasn't working she was rescuing someone or something. I remember the black mongrel she found in a ditch with terrible injuries. Everyone said it should be put down as nobody in Italy gave a damn about mongrels. The dog was passing blood in his urine and was desperately ill but Mum refused to give up on him. She sat up with him all night, healing him and soothing him. She mended him in spirit as well as body – the next day the swelling went down and he was fine apart from a broken leg. Mum splinted it herself, but it never set quite right and he used to dance around on three legs, following her everywhere, her devoted servant. This was the first of a line of dog rescues – there was also the Alsatian that nobody could get close to, because it was hurt and supposedly vicious. Mum sat and talked to it, with infinite patience, until it trusted her enough for her to get up close to it and deal with its problem.

It wasn't just animals. One day a man had a heart attack on the beach. In Italy at that time only the ambulance paramedics were legally covered to deal with medical emergencies so everyone else was too scared of being sued to get involved. Everybody crowded around but nobody dared touch him. My mother was disgusted. Without a moment's thought, she pushed her way through the crowd, knelt down on the sand, and banged life back into him. She didn't hang around waiting for thanks. As soon as the ambulance arrived, she simply rubbed her hands down on her apron and walked briskly away.

Everything felt different in Italy. Everything smelled different. It was a heady mixture of sea, pine trees, sun-cream, wood smoke and tent canvas. The supermarket at Grado had a particular smell too – a clashing scent of ripe fruit, the tang of tomatoes on the vine, the earthy saltpetre of coppa, the spicy pepperiness of salami, the fresh salty sweetness of the huge variety of fish and seafood. For some reason I was most entranced by the fact that they sold milk in cartons rather than the bottles we had at home. It was so different from the small shops in London, and I wandered round it as if in a magic world. I had the strangest feeling that any moment I might turn a corner and bump into another me – the same, identical person, someone lost and then found. When I think back, how poignant that was. If Lucy hadn't died, there would have been another child, another me. It was as if, at some level, I knew something, some*one*, was missing. Of course it never happened and really it was only a small sadness because here, in Italy, I had fun. So did Lucy. She didn't have to keep warning me, protecting me. In Italy there was no nasty Uncle Duncan. There was no Uncle Bob. There was no scary Connie.

I belonged in Italy. I was small and stocky, with lashings of thick dark hair sticking out all over the place like a cave kid. I had a dimpled face, large intense chestnut eyes and short strong hairy arms just like all the grown-up Italian women.

Plus I was the campsite manager's daughter. Princess of the camp, a bossy tomboy with an important role – and I was immensely, inordinately proud of my status. My brother was far too shy and uncomfortable with strangers to carve out a rival role as Crown Prince – he stuck to the shadows. But I blazed in the full sun. I made it my business to make friends and the whole campsite felt like one big family. Everyone was on holiday, everyone seemed happy, and they all had loads of time for a little girl with wild dark hair down to her waist, even if she did have a very feisty temperament. Of course, there was the odd ulterior motive – many of the women in the camp adored my father and thought that sucking up to a small child, his precious daughter, was a nominal fee to pay to get some of his attention.

But really that's a bit unfair. Children, in general, were loved and protected and played with (in a good way) and I revelled in the attention and the atmosphere of safety. Even at that young age, my intuition was finely tuned and I knew there was nothing to fear here. I saw much more of my parents too – despite the fact that they were working.

Even Nicholas and I got on better, with more space, more to distract us, more opportunity to avoid one another.

One incident, however struck a sour note. One afternoon my mother took Nicholas and me to buy an ice-cream from the tiny café on the beach. There were chairs and tables set around it on the sand, and quite a crowd of men sitting down, having a smoke and drinking beer. I took my lolly and carefully peeled away the wrapper. Then, like a good girl, I walked very self-consciously, aware of my audience, to place the wrapper delicately in the bin. Tiny dresses were in vogue for small girls and mine barely covered my bottom. As I bent down, my knicker elastic snapped and my frilly pink panties fell down around my ankles, exposing my baby pink cheeks. I stood stock still, barely believing what had happened. The men broke into a loud cheer and clapped, throwing money at me. My brother nearly fell down with a hernia guffawing at my mortifying embarrassment, tears of joy streaming down his face. I dragged the treacherous panties back up and stumbled, crimson-faced, to hide in the folds of my mother's lap, coins and lire still cascading around me. I was incredulous that she didn't save me.

But apart from that one incident, my memories are mainly blissful. The vast sky was always blue, the sun shone, and the days seemed endless and filled with light and love. My father and I would walk in the sea hand in hand, he in his red swimming trunks, searching for crabs in the water. Hanging on to his big safe hand, I felt protected and secure in his sturdy presence. Just his feet and mine, splashing through the shallow turquoise waters, seeking our prey. We would pluck them out of the water and put them carefully in my bucket, as blue as the sea, until the bucket was full of the blustery creatures, feisty crabs displeased with capture, throwing scaly legs up at my fingers, trying to escape. Then we'd walk slowly back up the beach to our 'bungalow' (to my huge disappointment we didn't have our own posh tent, but a wooden chalet). There we'd settle down to a supper of chicken risotto or some kind of fresh fish that my mother had already prepared. Ten to one, the crabs would escape at night, and one particular night a crab got into my parents' bedroom to wreak its revenge and Mum screamed blue murder as it nipped her toe. We all woke up in a panic, thinking she was being tortured – but when we saw the crabs scuttling across the floor we couldn't stop laughing. We laughed until our tummies ached while my father hopped and jumped, trying to round up the angry critters. My mother, meanwhile, stood perched on a swaying beach chair well out of reach of their claws.

Maybe because I felt so safe, maybe because I was naturally an inquisitive explorer of a child, I used to wander off all by myself. My parents were busy working and, to be honest, there wasn't the same fear then and children just wandered around freely with an unspoken rule that everyone kept an eye on everyone else's children. But I had an alarming sense of independence for a three-year old and would stride off, bold as brass, on my adventures. Anyhow, I wasn't really 'alone' as such – Lucy came with me. Usually I found myself wandering down the long path to the inviting sea where I could play happily for hours, little knowing that I had been missed and was causing a panic back at the campsite. I was always surprised to see frantic search parties scouring the beach and wondered what on earth they were doing – all that running and gesticulating. Then the pointing, and people racing up to me, heaving sighs of relief and asking if I was all right. It didn't seem to make a lasting impression, though, as, once the panic died down – I would be left alone again and inevitably wander off once more.

Each summer we were at Grado, I became more independent. By the time I was five, I had the run of the place. Anyway, Mum was far too busy to watch me all the time, and as Dad was getting weaker the majority of the work fell to her. Most of the time she was quite happy, knowing that the campsite acted like one big playpen, with hordes of childminders. But every so often she would allow herself to fall prey to conspiracy theories. One evening we had chicken for supper. I was sitting on the grass eating with an older child, Marisa. As the burning orange sun descended and the shadows lengthened over the grass, she showed me how to eat chicken bones. The rule was simple – only ever eat the bigger ones, and chew very, *very* carefully. Marisa was chic and Italian so obviously she knew what she was doing. But my mother caught us and slammed the plate out of my hand. Why was she making such a fuss? But make a fuss she did, screaming the campsite down, grabbing Marisa by the scruff of her neck, accusing her of trying to murder me. It took at least an hour to calm her down and, when peace was finally restored, we all went to sleep, sunset still barely kissing the watching hills. In my mother's eyes people were either totally good or totally evil – there was no middle ground. Everything was over-dramatised; each event was either a triumph or a disaster. She had no sense of proportion and her priorities were all over the place.

Still, despite that, these were good times. Happy times. But the shadows were gathering. As the summer progressed, my father wasn't so carefree any more. He spent more time sitting quietly, reading a book, or lying down inside the chalet. Looking back, it was clear that he wasn't fit to be working, but he wanted to keep everything the same for us. There were hushed conversations between him and my mother: urgent whispers; irritable exchanges. I would stuff my fingers in my ears – I didn't want to hear bad news. But bad news came anyway. My father had to return to London – he had to go to hospital and see his doctors. There was no choice. Mum, however, told us that he was going back on business; that his company needed to see him. I wasn't convinced: something was wrong.

He left my mother in charge of the campsite and, no matter that she was virtually running it anyway, she was uneasy at the idea of being abandoned.

'It's OK, Bruna, it'll be fine. Don't worry,' he tried to

reassure her. 'Anyway, I'm not leaving you alone. You've got Domenica to keep you company.' Domenica was my mother's third cousin who had just arrived to help Mum, ostensibly to keep an eye on Nicholas and me, and to prepare the food.

'Pah!' My mother nearly spat at him. '*Porco di dio!* Yes, she is a good worker; that's true. But she is a nasty type of person. She has always been that way.' Domenica was about sixty and had been a chambermaid in the Dorchester Hotel in London for about twenty years. I didn't like her – there was something odd about her, something that made me feel queasy.

My father smiled tolerantly. He was used to Mum getting strange fixations about people and things. He kissed her, patted us on the head, and got into the taxi. I watched him go, waving until the car turned a corner and disappeared out of sight. A shiver ran down my spine.

A heavy mood hung over the campsite after he left. A sense of unease. My mother became fidgety, jumping at the slightest noise. She seemed consumed with anxiety. 'Aunty' Domenica was unsettled too. She wouldn't look us in the eye and seemed to be glancing over her shoulder, as if catching sight of something out of the corner of her eye.

Soon after Dad left, strange things started happening. First of all the doors started unlocking themselves. If Mum locked the door to the bungalow at night, it would be open again in the morning. Mum shrugged it off, but Domenica seemed terrified.

Then we started to hear peculiar knockings and bangings at night. I was used to loud noises (anyone living with my mother would be), but these were sudden and strange. Nicholas and I were sleeping in bunk beds, in the same room as Mum's bed, and I noticed Mum had started taking her rosary to bed with her, and she'd lie there saying her prayers, turning the beads over and over.

Sometimes I would hear her, whispering, talking to the noises: 'Is that you? Is that my guides? Please pray for me, and give me strength because I have another heavy day in front of me tomorrow.' But she didn't sound terribly sure.

Domenica wasn't sleeping either, and she was becoming more and more pale and wan. One night she asked Mum if she could come and sleep in with her as she said she couldn't sleep in her own room. Mum agreed. That night, the knockings and bangings were even louder and I had to pull the pillow over my head, trying to get rid of the sound.

In the morning, when I woke, Domenica was sitting bolt upright in bed, her eyes staring wildly. She nudged my mother awake and started shouting at her:

'I will never sleep in this bed again. Never!'

'What? What's the matter?'

'I cannot sleep here.'

'But why?' My poor mother was still trying to wake up, rubbing sleep out of her eyes.

'Someone was wanting to push me out of your bed. I kept being pushed out of the bed.'

'I'm sorry.'

Poor Mum. What was she supposed to do? Anyhow, Domenica refused to sleep with Mum but she also refused to sleep on her own, so we lugged her bed into our bedroom, which was now ludicrously full of beds.

It didn't calm down Domenica:

'Bruna. Somebody is trying to push me out of the room. I am getting no sleep at all.'

'Eh, you're imagining it, Domenica. It's just your imagination. Nobody is trying to push you out of anywhere. Who would push you, eh? Me? The children?'

But she knew something was wrong. I did too.

One day, I was playing in the kitchen when Mum came back from the shops. She was looking worried.

'Something is wrong. Something bad is coming.' She was standing outside the chalet, sniffing the air. 'There's a storm coming. I can smell it. An evil storm.'

Aunt Domenica came outside and looked up at the sky. 'Don't be silly, Bruna. Look, there's not a cloud in the sky.'

But Mum was insistent. 'It's coming. We must warn the campers.' So we ran, Mum and Nicholas far ahead of me, with Mum shouting out to the campers:

'Get inside your tents! Shut yourselves in. Weigh down your things. A storm is coming. A bad storm.'

They laughed. The sky was as blue as cornflowers. The sun beat down. Yet, strangely, there was no bird song. No buzz of insects.

'What's happening, Mum?'

'It's a storm, a bad storm . . . How you say it? A *tornado*. Quick, back to the chalet. Run!'

We ran. At first it felt like a game but then, all of a sudden, the world changed. It was as if someone had taken a huge paintbrush and swiped it across the sky – in seconds the blue simply vanished and the sky turned a violent shade of purple-black.

Everything seemed to stop, as if the world were holding its breath, waiting for what would happen next. Then, in the distance, we saw an incredible sight – the ominous shape of a whirlwind spinning straight towards us.

I screamed. I think Nicholas did too.

Mum grabbed us and virtually dragged us into the chalet, slamming the door shut behind us and crashing the locks down, one, then two, then three. It was pitch dark in the chalet and we could barely see one another. Then a wild streak of lightning illuminated the room and I saw Mum, Domenica and Nicholas, staring wide-eyed, horror etched on their faces. The silence was ripped in half by the most ear-splitting crash of thunder I've ever heard. My heart crashed and I could hear the blood roaring in my head.

Then another sound, not so loud as the thunder, but even more scary. The tormented howl of the wind, as it threw itself at the campsite, whipping through the trees, plucking up tents and tossing them up in the air.

As another flash of lightning ripped through the camp-site, I looked out the window and saw the unbelievable sight of tents flying into the sea, clothing and suitcases tossed up into the air, as if some giant had picked up a pile of washing and flung it everywhere. It was like a grandiose scene from *The Wizard of Oz.*

Then the rain came. Deluging down, beating the tin roof of the chalet like someone going demented on the drums. The campsite vanished under an onslaught of rain, sheet after sheet lashing through the place, obliterating our view.

Mum dropped down onto her knees and clasped her hands together.

'*Madre di dio . . . salva nos –*'

She started off muttering to herself, but as the wind and rain got louder and louder, the claps of thunder closer together, her voice rose as if she were in a contest with the elements.

I glanced at Nicholas. I could just about make out his shape in the darkness. He was shaking violently and there were tears pouring down his face.

The thunder was right overhead now, and every clap seemed to make the chalet shudder. The flimsy chipboard roof shook and rattled. A horrible whining noise came from the windows, as if some demonic creature were trying to break in. It felt as if any moment the whole chalet would be picked up and thrown out to sea.

My mother stopped praying and stared wildly at us. 'We're doomed! We're going to be ripped apart and cast into the sea. The hungry sea. Our sins. Our sins will doom us.'

Both Nicholas and I were crying now, terrified as much by our mother's lack of control as by the madness of the wind.

'We're going to die!' she shouted. 'We're all going to die!' She looked around desperately, her eyes blazing. I was utterly petrified. She seemed so sure, so certain. I didn't want to die. I started sobbing even harder as she shouted:

'Pray! We must all pray! Only prayers of the innocent will save us. You children must pray!'

She ran over and shoved Nicholas and me down on our knees.

'Pray. Damn it, pray! If you want to live you have to pray, pray, pray.'

Aunt Domenica was on her knees now, turning her rosary over and over in her fingers. She was ashen.

Nicholas started the Lord's Prayer and I joined in, following him, my voice faltering over the words. 'Our Father, who art in Heaven . . .'

There was a horrible banging on the door. I thought it was a monster, a devil of the storm that was coming to haul us into the sea.

I prayed louder, 'Hallowed be Thy name . . .'

I was shivering with fear, my voice crashing in my head. All the time the storm raged around us, and my mother continued shouting anguished prayers in Italian. She only stopped to yell at the door:

'Go away! I cannot unlock the door. There is evil here. Run, run! Run away, and pray, pray for your souls. There is an evil spirit that is trying to kill us all. If you don't pray, we will all die.'

The windows were shaking now. Any moment I thought

they were going to shatter. I didn't know what was more terrifying – the demonic weather outside or the petrifying atmosphere inside the chalet.

I tried to shut my mother's words out of my head. If only Dad had been there. He'd have made it all all right. I kept praying:

'Thy Kingdom come; Thy will be done, on earth as it is in Heaven.'

As I prayed, I could feel a force building up around us. Nicholas and I chanted the prayer together, our voices getting stronger and stronger. I kept forgetting the words but Nicholas was shouting them now and my voice joined his. I closed my eyes to shut out the lightning but it still flashed inside my eyelids, blood red now instead of white.

As we drew near to the end of the prayer, the pressure inside the chalet was intolerable. I thought we had been picked up off the ground and were being hurled around in the storm itself. My heart was hammering, far too fast, and I could barely breathe. I panted out the last words.

'For Thine is the Kingdom, the power and the glory . . . .'

An inhuman howling was inside the chalet now. I stuck my fingers in my ears.

'For ever and ever. Amen!' We shrieked the final 'Amen' and hurled ourselves on the floor, clinging to one another.

At that precise moment the door was flung open – how I'll never know as there were two thick bolts on it. A woman's voice screamed, ear-splitting, as furious as hell, circling round and round the chalet. I could feel something gathering, pulling itself together, tormented and frustrated. But it couldn't hold, couldn't stay, and with one last anguished howl it threw itself at the door and screamed its way out, and then further and further, out to sea until it finally stopped.

Suddenly there was silence. As if by magic, the wind dropped and the thunder faded away.

We sat panting on the floor, staring at one another, as the darkness eased away and pale light filtered back into the chalet. Nicholas smiled uneasily, as if asking Mum if everything was OK. I looked at her, wonderingly.

Mum got up, brushed down her skirt and pulled the door shut. She turned to Domenica:

'I locked those doors earlier on. Did you open them?'

'You know I didn't. We were all here.' Domenica's voice was tiny and shaking.

'Then who opened them?'

My blood turned cold as Domenica sank her face into her hands and then looked Mum straight in the eye for the first time.

'Maybe it was that thing that followed me. It doesn't matter where I go, something has always followed me. Sometimes it will take a while, and I think I'm safe but then, after a little time, it will find me again.'

I stared at Mum. 'Mum, what was that? What was that thing that was inside the house?'

My mother wiped her forehead with her hand and pushed her hair back. 'An evil spirit, darling. A dispossessed spirit. It liked your Aunty Domenica. But it's gone now.'

She stood up, brushing down her skirt, rolling up her sleeves, rubbing her hands together. 'No need to worry now. It's all over. All over. Now we clean up, eh?'

Just like that, she slammed back the bolts of the door and marched out, ready to deal with hundreds of confused and frightened campers. Strangely, although the campsite was completely wrecked, our chalet wasn't even missing a roof tile. It was a lesson in the power of prayer. Mum didn't seem remotely bothered by it; she just went on as usual. Domenica left the next day. She barely spoke to us as she packed her bags; she didn't look backwards once as the cab took her away. We were hugely relieved to see her go, but Nicholas and I couldn't shake the events off so easily as my mother. He became even more withdrawn; his nerves edgy, jumping at the slightest thing. I was, frankly, petrified. I couldn't sleep and I no longer wandered freely around the campsite. I didn't dare go far from my mother, but shadowed her like a sad puppy, clinging to her heels. If the sky clouded over, I flinched. If a storm threatened, I trembled. At the first sound of thunder I would race under the table and hide there, with my fingers jammed in my ears. Even now I am still petrified of thunderstorms.

The campsite was closed – there were barely any tents left standing. We cleared up the best we could and then closed the Tentotel and went back to England.

I thought things would be better when we got home. I was wrong.

5

Daddy, Don't Die

We came back to England physically exhausted and emotionally drained.

Mum kept saying it was a miracle we had survived the storm and the evil spirits, that we should be grateful and give thanks, but it didn't feel like a miracle. I felt as if I had left all my happiness behind me in Italy. It was raining when we got back to England and our mood sank even further with the weather. The maisonette smelled damp as we pushed open the door and my heart plummeted as I saw a twitch at the curtains next door and Aunty Flo's thin pinched face peering through at us.

There were unopened envelopes piled up on the kitchen table and dishes unwashed in the sink.

'Naughty Dad,' I said, rolling my eyes like I'd seen my mother do.

'Leave your father alone. He can't help it,' said Mum sharply, her mouth a tight line.

The weirdest thing of all was that nobody ever mentioned

Dad's illness. Sometimes he seemed fine; sometimes he was weak; sometimes he was bedridden. Yet nobody ever told me or Nicholas that he was ill. I think it was how things were dealt with then – there was no concept of counselling, of preparing children for bad news. It was considered best to pretend everything was all right; to shield them from bad things. Of course, it was a foolish strategy – children pick up atmospheres and they certainly notice when their father is lying day after day in a darkened room. But we knew not to ask; we didn't dare risk one of Mum's temper tantrums.

So it was strange, but even stranger was that, even now, my father himself was totally in the dark about the nature of his illness. The doctors were still keeping my mother informed of everything that was happening, but nobody said a word to him. He colluded with this, leaving my mother to talk to the doctors, to arrange his treatment (both orthodox and alternative) and to monitor his progress. Mum told him he was anaemic; that he just needed to get rest and to get himself 'built up'.

Talking to my mother, once I'd grown up, I discovered that he had suffered terribly, first with bone cancer and then with leukaemia. But it didn't come as that much of a surprise. I used to listen to heard her talking with friends. I had always known it wasn't just anaemia. But I don't think that, as a child, I realised the extent of his suffering. Nor the strain it must have put on Mum – how she worked so hard to keep our family together financially; how she did everything she could to heal him psychically. She must have been utterly exhausted.

Those weeks after we came back are a fog in my memory. Dad was going backwards and forwards from hospital. Mum was working, cleaning both private houses and also the Spiritualist Association of Great Britain in Belgrave Square. When she wasn't working, she was trying to heal Dad or going with him to see the healer Harry Edwards. There was a strange atmosphere in the air, and it wasn't helped by the fact that, whenever they went off, I was sent to stay with Aunty Flo and Uncle Duncan, or sometimes to Connie's house. I wasn't sure which was worse. Why did my mother always put me in unsafe places? She was too trusting, too distracted – her mind on my father more than Nicholas and me. But also, I think it's really important to realise that psychics don't know everything. They can – and often do – have blind spots, particularly with very personal issues.

As I got older, the nature of the abuse with Duncan changed slightly. I was too big to sit on his knee so – instead – he would get me to touch him or have me lie down and ejaculate over my back. The smell of him made me gag and I still find it very hard to think back to those days, to what he made me do.

Connie made my skin crawl. She would stare at you as if she were delving into your soul, as if probing to find your weak spot, so she could use it against you. Both Nicholas and I avoided her like the plague if we possibly could. But if I couldn't avoid Connie, I would act tough, hoping she wouldn't engage with me if she thought I wasn't scared. It worked – to a point. Nicholas, however, was just plain terrified and it showed in every sinew of his being – and she loved his fear.

I was forced to watch, to see things no child should see. She was becoming more and more twisted, offering more and more degradation to her Satanic 'Lord'. She and her husband (and occasionally other friends) indulged in violent sado-masochistic sex with one another. Those images are etched on my memory – I have spent years trying to forget them, but they never go away. That kind of concentrated evil can take years to dissipate. Sometimes it never truly leaves.

Fortunately, because I had started school, I didn't need to be 'looked after' quite so much. But school brought its own challenges. I had been looking forward to going to school, to having friends, but the other children could sense I was different. They were nervous of me, they kept apart. I tried to make friends by telling their fortunes, reading their palms, but they didn't like it, they found it spooky. I suppose I did have a very strong personality. I was too much for them, even aged six. I had a strong sense of justice, of right and wrong, and it often made me over-react. Children copy their parents and my mother wasn't exactly a model of calm tolerance. Rather I learned from her that it was absolutely fine to go off the deep end over something incredibly trivial. On the other hand, I was so desperate for attention, I think I'd have done almost anything to have people notice me. I was so lost, so alone, so unseen at home. I was so desperate for love and attention. It made me hard to like.

One time I was in the toilets and some girl pushed me over. I was totally outraged.

'How dare you push me? I'm going home to get my dad.'

'You can't. You're not allowed to leave school.'

'I don't care. I'm going home right now.'

I did too. The dinner ladies tried desperately to stop me, but I pushed my way through and walked a good fifteen minutes home on my own. I found my dad, hauled him out, and dragged him back to school and into the head-mistress's office. Here I evidently told the headmistress exactly what I thought of the girl, of school, and of life in general.

I stalked out, marched up to the poor girl and said, 'The headmistress says you're a bad influence and that I should avoid you.' A few years ago, I found her on Friends Reunited – she said that the memory had stayed with her all her life!

My character was always strong, too strong, and still is today. I am continuously learning about moderation. But back then, I decided I'd give up on the girls. I refused to play netball or skipping or jumping elastic; I wasn't inter-ested in dolls and fluffy animals. Instead I played football with the boys. My mother wouldn't countenance chopping off my long dark hair so I yanked it back in a ponytail. In all other respects I became a little tomboy.

The contrast with Italy could not have been more marked. We moved from a world of light to a world of darkness; from a world of laughter and noise to one of hushed silence. The curtains were always drawn at Connell Crescent, the maisonette shrouded in a cowl of sickness and fear. Nobody talked about what was happening, but the wrongness was palpable: something awful was unfolding, you could smell it in the air. My father was a grey presence, a spectre who stayed mainly in the bedroom, only shuffling out from time to time to go to the bathroom or make a cup of tea. I tried to help him, but I could tell that my healing wasn't enough. It was like building a wall of sand against the inrushing tide.

Then, out of the blue, Mum said we were moving. I couldn't believe my luck. We were getting away from our tiny maisonette, away from Uncle Duncan and Uncle Bob, away from Mrs Click-Clack and her hobnail boots. We were going to live in what seemed to me like a huge house with an upstairs and a downstairs, a big garden. A house all of our own. I was going to have my own bedroom – away from Nicholas and his mind games. It wasn't far away, just a few streets, but to me it seemed as if we were moving continents. In my child's eyes, it also meant that things were going to be all right. My father would get well in this lovely new home. We would be a family again. The sun would shine once more.

In retrospect, it was pure madness. My father – whether he knew it or not (and of course at some level he must have) – was dying. We had no savings and he had no life insurance. But my mother's favourite uncle, Alfredo, decided to give Mum £700 for the deposit for the new house. Curiously Alfredo was the spitting image of my dad and was often mistaken for him. By a horrible coincidence, he too was dying and this was his parting gift.

I remember going there for the first time the day we moved in. The house felt huge. It was one of those 1930s terraced houses, Tudorbethan with a black and white triangle up by the eaves. It sat, square and solid, on the corner of Twyford Abbey Road. In front was a grass-lined street with conker trees nearby. It was closer to my school and there was a park at the end of the road with swings and a slide. I was in seventh heaven. It felt as if a huge dark cloud had lifted. I truly believed that this was the answer to all my prayers.

In the garden was a large apple tree. Mum and Dad were really excited. They had The Owl and the Pussycat tiles put into the kitchen and sang the song to each other. I was elated with this big bright house, and particularly with having my very own bedroom, albeit a tiny boxroom. No more sharing a room with Nicholas, no more arguing, no more fear. Everyone was happy that day. We laughed and ran around and planned to build a tree-house. We took pictures in the garden, my dad handsome as ever in his three-piece suit. Me clutching his big hand and feeling safe, although in the pictures I see a strained child looking more thirty than six. Hardly surprising, given that I had experienced things few thirty-year-olds or even sixty-year-olds have.

Dad got his tape recorder out and we sang nursery rhymes into it until I got told off for being too pushy and trying to jump my turn with Nicholas. I tried to blow a bubble to look cute, but my dad thought I was spitting at my mum and told me off. I was banished from the front room and felt outraged at the injustice of it all. However, it gave me some time to spend in my new room. I sat down on my bed and thought about my family. I always knew that, in some way, we were not a normal family; we lacked something I saw in other families. Some basic stability and normality was missing. I felt that this house represented a new start, with the promise of a happy ending. Things were going to be so different.

It's funny the way children's minds work. Because for that brief time I was so incredibly happy, I was convinced that, when disaster soon struck, it was my fault. I blamed myself totally and completely. I didn't deserve to be happy. It was twisted logic, of course, but perfectly typical of the way abused children think.

My mother never really had time to deal with the basics of life. For instance, we were told to brush our teeth but she never told us exactly how we should be doing it. She never checked. I was left to dress myself and my clothes were rarely clean or tidy. Mum was too busy looking after my father, working, and dealing with the stress of being mother, wife, nurse and sole breadwinner. From day one I never had her full attention or focus; she was always else-where, fighting for us to survive.

I don't remember the day my father was taken into hospital for the final time. One moment I remember him in his suit, all smiley and happy, holding my hand and playing games. The next he was reduced, objectified, a being in a bed in a horrible institution.

Just when it seemed it couldn't get worse, Uncle Duncan returned into my life. Mum went to see Dad in hospital a lot and we would have to go to stay with him and Aunty Flo after school. My heart sank as I turned the corner to our old street. If Nicholas was with me, it was OK. But frequently he wasn't. By now I was totally inured to the abuse: it was something to be endured, something about which I had no choice, something I didn't dare question. I was scared of Duncan, mortally scared. Not just for myself but because he said that, if I ever told my parents, something terrible would happen to my father. It was as if I held his life in my hands, as if I were responsible for his wellbeing. Being so young, I didn't question this – I believed it to be a horrible truth. So, if Aunty Flo wasn't there, I would simply head for the bathroom and strip off, waiting for Uncle Duncan. He liked to keep it in the bathroom so he could sponge me down afterwards; so he could wash himself and spritz hair-spray around to mask the smell of him.

But Aunty Flo knew, I was sure she did. On the odd occasions when she was there on her own, she would glare at me; ask me what I did when she was out; ask me what

Uncle Duncan did with me. I'd tell her we played games and she'd roll her eyes and curl her lip. 'What kind of "games"? I know his games,' she would say bitterly. But of course I never told. I didn't want to hurt my father. I was paralysed with fear about what would happen if I dared tell. Also, I didn't tell because I didn't for one moment think I'd be believed. Who would believe a child over an adult? Anyhow, maybe the adults knew – and let it happen, allowed it, approved of it. Like so many other victims of abuse I felt at least partly responsible for what happened to me.

I didn't understand that abuse damages children so badly – that it counts on the fact that children are trusting and dependent; that they want to please people and gain love and approval. I didn't realise that I wasn't the only one – I had no idea that other children suffered the way I did. Nobody spoke about it and I thought it was just me that was so disgusting, so horrible, that people did these things to me. I didn't realise that I was feeling what every child who is abused feels: fear, guilt, disgust at myself.

So seeing Duncan was horrible. But going to the hospital was even worse.

We went on the Underground to see my father in hospital. It was like descending into hell. On the way there, we got on the train at Park Royal, out in the open, the birds singing, no people. But the journey back was horrible. We plunged underground, into the belly of the earth, surrounded by unfriendly jostling crowds. I hated the sound of the Tube train approaching, like an angry dragon shrieking through the tunnel. As it roared into the station a cold blast of wind always knocked me back. It felt very unsafe, that journey. I would hide under my mother's coat, dreading ever going back.

The hospital was in Paddington and had a Victorian air, all tiled corridors like a giant toilet. I remember so clearly the nurses bustling by in their stiff uniforms, the cloying darkness of the dingy, endless corridors.

We struggled along, a sad little trio: my mother striding with her usual determination; I clinging on to my mother's hand; and Nicholas reluctantly tagging behind as if fearful of what might await us at the end of this tiled maze. Finally we reached a room full of see-through macs and clear plastic wellington boots. They didn't have a size small enough for me. Mum would pick me up and place me into huge clear wellingtons, wrap the see-through rain mac around me, and pull into place a mask that smothered my face. I still have a crystal clear memory, burnt into my mind, of standing by the coat hooks being pushed into the wellies. It felt so unreal. Wellingtons in a hospital? Weren't wellingtons for splashing in puddles?

'What are the wellies for?' I asked the sour-faced nurse.

'To stop the germs spreading,' she said, in an irritable voice.

I stared at her in horror. At six, I thought that meant we were trying to protect ourselves from my father's germs. It never crossed my mind that they were trying to protect him from ours. I swallowed hard. I thought we all were going to get as sick as my relentlessly sick father.

As we shuffled into the bright white room, I could see what was left of my father. He was grey and weak, his usually immaculate hair oily and limp, hanging over his drawn face. I didn't recognise him, something had already gone. He reached a bony hand out to me.

'Come and give me a kiss, Michèle.'

My mother pushed me forwards, but I recoiled in horror and fear.

'I don't want to catch it,' I mumbled, hiding behind Mum.

Tears filled his once steely blue eyes, now shrunken and red. He looked at my mother, his face crestfallen and defeated.

'What have I done to make her hate me so much, Bruna?'

My mother smiled reassuringly and made light of it.

'She is just a child, Michael. She doesn't mean anything by it.'

I was petrified that I could catch this disease that had sucked the life out of my father.

As soon as we left the hospital my mother reached into her coat pocket and pulled out her trusty Marlboro cigarettes. She struck a match, held it to the tip of the cigarette, and then tossed it to the pavement. She inhaled deeply on the cigarette, as if sucking comfort from it. I think it was the cigarettes that got her through, her only source of strength, her only company and support. Her family were all in Italy.

Dad's family weren't a part of our lives. Yes, she had loads of friends, but she was always the one who gave support; she didn't get much in return. She grabbed our hands and marched us to the Underground station, sucking back the pain and tears that threatened to overwhelm her. She clung to us as the train came in, fearful that we too would be snatched from her. That was the last time I saw my father. I can hardly bear the fact that my last words to him were fearful; that my last act was to flinch away from him. No matter that I was only six, my betrayal has stayed with me all my life.

As my father deteriorated, Mum obviously decided we shouldn't go back to the hospital. Life went on. I went to school. I played on the swings. I heard Mum talking to people on the phone. She would start off whispering, but would soon forget I was there and her voice would rise and I could hear things I wished I hadn't heard:

'It's nearly the end, Anne. How am I going to tell the children?'

Then one day I heard her say he had died.

'At least it's over eh? Poor soul, he's out of pain now.' There was a pause.

'The funeral? Yes, next week. Yes, of course. No, I'm not taking them. Eh, Santa Maria, a funeral is no place for children. No, I haven't told them yet. I know. Yes, I will. When the time is right.'

I didn't dare say anything. I didn't dare ask. Neither did Nicholas. We all sat and ate our meals in silence. Occasionally

Mum would seem to remember we were there and ask one of us something about school. We would answer monosyllabically and the silence would return.

Then, one day, my mother took me out into the garden. She pointed up to the sky and said, brusquely, 'Daddy is up there in heaven looking down on you.'

She came over to me and tried to put her arm around me, but I shrugged it off and walked away.

Was she totally mad? Was she a complete idiot? I knew my father was dead. I had heard her talking with all her friends, saying he was dead. I had heard about the funeral, about the crematorium, and I knew what it meant. They were putting his body in a box and burning it. But, in a funny way, I was glad she didn't say it. I suppose a tiny part of me kept hoping it was all a big mistake. If nobody said it out loud, if nobody said it to me, maybe he would come back. I could see him again, feel him again, hug him and bury my head in his chest, smell the wool of his jumper mixed with his after-shave. My real dad could come back, the tall good-looking one, not the husk of a stranger that had been in the hospital. But another part of me knew I wouldn't see him again. I didn't dwell on it; I didn't want to think about it. I blanked over that part of my mind, refusing to think about him, trying not to let any thoughts of him surface to the place where they could hurt. I was becoming very good at blanking off parts of my life. It was a useful skill.

The day of the funeral came and Nicholas and I were

sent packing for the day to Aunty Anne's. Aunty Anne was my godmother and she had two sons, one called Nick and one called Andrew. We didn't see them that often but I wished we could see them more. More than anything I wished that I could be looked after by them, rather than by Uncle Duncan or Connie or any of the other people that Mum so casually asked to take care of us. But they lived too far away. I always envied their life. They seemed to be this normal family that did normal things like taking the boys to football or off for picnics. Their house was always clean and there was always delicious food and home-made cakes for tea. There was something very different about their world. They were kind boys. They read *Just William* books to me to take my mind off what was going on. Nicholas didn't say much. He just sat on a chair in the corner and flipped through music magazines. He was more withdrawn and more openly upset than me. He was older and had had a very close relationship with our father – it was devastating for him. I tried to feel sad. I knew I *should* feel sad, but I was empty. I knew something had happened and that nothing could change it, nothing would be the same again.

When my mother came back from the funeral she was animated, high as a kite. She waved her hands around as she told the tale of how one of my father's mistresses, an American opera singer, had tried to climb into the funeral car to go to the funeral and how she had opened the car door and dragged the woman out by the hair. Always a drama – especially in times of pain. It was like she couldn't express her vulnerability: she felt she had to fight, fight to survive and stay alive. A good fight was better than drowning in her own sorrow. Anything rather than face the stark reality that she had a monumental task ahead of her, in this new house, alone with us two.

My mother had moved us into this big house, with no full-time job and no money saved. Now she was all alone, with no other support at all. I went back to school after a week or two and was immediately surrounded by a group of children, wanting to know why I hadn't been at school.

'Where've you been then?' one said. 'You been on holiday?'

'My dad died.' It sounded strange saying it for the first time.

I don't know what I was expecting. Sympathy? Acceptance? Acknowledgement at the very least. But they looked at one another, looked back at me, and then one of them started chanting:

'Liar, liar, pants on fire.'

'But he has. He really has. He died and they burned his body in a big fire.'

'Liar, liar, pants on fire.'

They didn't believe me. They circled round me, chanting nastily. I bit my lip and looked at the ground.

– *Ignore them.*
– *But why don't they believe me?*

– They're stupid. It hasn't happened to them so they can't believe it. Don't worry. I'm here.

Mum tried to comfort me too. In fact, for a few weeks after the funeral, she seemed to remember that she was our mother, with a vital role in our upbringing. She talked to us, hugged us, gave us attention. For once my clothes seemed tidy, my hair brushed and tied back, my bed made, my shoes shiny and clean. We ate proper meals and we drew close together, as a family. I clung on to this. Although my father had gone, maybe some good would come out of it all. Maybe we three could become this solid unit, this happy little family.

My mother, despite being so volatile, could be incredibly practical when the chips were down. She was also, as I've said before, unbelievably hardworking. Her action plan, following Dad's death, was to take up two jobs, cleaning during the day and doing auxiliary nursing shifts at night. In between she squeezed in psychic readings and kept up with her healing circles. She also advertised for a lodger. It was impressive and very brave, but it also left her wide open to trouble.

She had never been alone, never had to fend for herself. She had married while still a child really and my father, being middle class and proper, had always been a shield for her, even when he was ill. He was her voice of reason. Without him, the floodgates of bedlam soon opened. Nicholas and I were no longer enough. We had never been enough. My mother would talk to anyone and everyone. She was living in London, but treating it as if it were a small village in Italy. She couldn't say no and would help anyone who crossed her path. She befriended people from her healing circles; she scooped up any lame ducks who came to her for readings. The house was never empty. It was never just the family. If anyone needed to stay, she would welcome them in – even if she didn't know them from Adam. I can't think how many times I'd come home from school to find someone new sitting on the sofa, having tea with Mum; someone new sleeping in the spare bedroom. They'd come for a reading and touch a chord with Mum: she'd invite them to stay. They would be with us for a few weeks, become Mum's new best friend, and then something or other would come up and irritate her and she would have a screaming row and throw them out. For a few days, the house would be ours and then the cycle would start all over again.

On the whole, they weren't good people. They were nearly always troubled or strange in some way – needy, lost, damaged. A lot of them were literally living on the streets when Mum took them in. Inevitably (or so it seemed to me), a good many of them abused me.

At least eight of her lodgers abused me in the house, in our home. None of them stayed that long, so it was never long term – usually it would last for a few stray incidents or regularly over the few weeks that they stayed. One scenario that springs to mind was when I thought I was on my own in the house. I was going up the stairs to the toilet and directly ahead of me at the top of the stairs was the lodger's room. I don't remember his name, but he was in his late twenties. He was playing with himself, masturbating, with the door half-open. When he caught sight of me, he didn't bat an eyelid. He started chatting as if it was the most normal thing in the world for a man to play with himself in front of a child.

'Where are you off to?'

I didn't answer.

'Come on, come in. Hey, have you ever seen one of these before? Do you want to have a go at touching it?'

His voice was light and chummy, but underneath it lay an air of menace. I knew that he was aware that we were alone in the house. It was safest to do as he asked.

'There. That's good, isn't it?'

He stroked my hair.

The horrible thing was that these abusers made it all seem so normal. Yet at the same time I was in no doubt that this was something secret and bad. I always felt as if it were my fault, when of course it was them who created the situation. But children don't understand that. I felt so ashamed, so frightened. I always felt I was bad and that people only liked me or would pay attention to me if I did as they told me; if I gave in to their sick demands.

It's a strange and sad thing, but abused children seem to throw out an aura of availability; something that draws paedophiles like a magnet. But maybe the saddest thing of all was that being abused was about the only time anyone took any notice of me.

The brief period of attention following the funeral had vanished. Mum barely noticed us any more – her focus had swung away from us children and outwards into the wider world. She only talked to me if she was lonely; otherwise it was like we were living parallel lives in the same house. Nicholas would try to trip me up as I walked down the stairs or poke me hard in the ribs as I walked by. Our new house was never the happy refuge I'd imagined.

I kept out of Mum's way as much as I could. Somehow I couldn't bear to be near her, she felt so out of control, so unsafe. She couldn't offer me comfort; she seemed to have no idea of what I felt. I don't really think, in fairness, she knew how *she* felt. She was as lost as I was, as lost as most of the souls she brought home. Talk about the blind leading the blind – this was the lost leading the lost. She tried to help everyone, to comfort everyone – except her own family. The first person that crossed her path to bring *her* some comfort after my father's death was the window cleaner, a seventeen-year-old ginger-haired Irish lad called Jerry.

He was totally besotted with her and they began a tempestuous affair. She was forty-five at this stage, but still had her voluptuous Italian looks and an appealing child-like manner. Any vestige of interest in Nicholas and me veered away and we were left to fend for ourselves. When

Jerry came in, I think I knew it was the beginning of losing her completely. He was just the first of a string of totally unsuitable and unstable younger men. What with her lovers and her new friends, there was simply no time left to give to us. I don't think she meant it for one moment. I don't think she even realised that she was neglecting us, far from it. She loved us passionately, but we just slipped through the cracks of her overwhelming schedule. She was keeping so busy in an attempt to ignore her pain. She was also, ironically, determined to give us a better life – but by working so hard she effectively left us without a mother. Without any protection whatsoever.

6

So Lonely, So Lonely

Jerry didn't last long. He was too eager and too young. My mother left him heartbroken and went off instead with a man named Roy. He looked suspiciously like the man off *Playschool*, Zoë Ball's dad, and I kept asking him trick questions about the round window to catch him out. After him came a policeman whose name I have completely forgotten. All I remember about him was that he gave us Sheba, a gorgeous German Shepherd ex-police dog, who swiftly became my brother's new best friend. Where Nicholas went, the dog went. Sheba was probably my brother's equivalent to Lucy, a companion in the chaos. I loved Sheba too: she made me feel safe.

The time after Dad died was incredibly lonely. My mother wasn't around, and when she was she was laughing and giggling with one of her lovers or new friends. I hated it. How could she forget my father so quickly? How could she be so happy when he was dead? Why was the house so full of strangers all the time? Why did my mother seem to hunt out every mad and weird person in the neighbour-hood? Why couldn't she just be normal for once? I felt as if a huge black hole had opened up in the ground and I was tumbling down into it, being swallowed up by the thickest, densest feeling of gloom and despair. Lucy tried to keep my spirits up, but even she seemed overwhelmed by the darkness. Her voice seemed muted and sad.

My brother Nicholas still hated my guts and no kids would play with me – I even used to offer them money to let me join in their games, I was that desperate. My mother used to tell me she loved me, and I know she did in her way – but most of the time it didn't feel like it; it just felt like something you say because it's expected, like a reflex. I needed structure and rules, but got neither. I needed secu-rity and demonstrative love, but got neither. I needed to be heard and to be encouraged academically. But nobody bothered about my schooling. I was left pretty much to my own devices.

Mum often wasn't there when I came home from school so I used to sit on the doorstep and wait for her. Sometimes the old lady who lived across the road would call me over and we'd play Scrabble. Then Nicholas would come home from school, but he kept as far away from me as possible, which was a huge relief. So, basically, my home life was pretty non-existent. There was never any food in the fridge and I was always amazed when I saw other people's kitchens, with their well-stocked larders and fridges. We seemed to live on a solid diet of chocolate and chips. It sounds great but, trust me, the novelty palls after a while and you crave real food. Possibly that's why I loved the meals at my primary school so much. Real warming comfort food – I thought it was fantastic.

To be fair, Mum didn't have time to cook – she never stopped. However, on Sundays she did make an effort. Sundays were special and she would take great pride in her home-made apple pies, using the apples from the tree in our garden. They were probably soaked in lead because the garden backed on to Hanger Lane – and she always left whole cloves in, which tasted disgusting – but I didn't care. I loved this ritual. It was the one bit of normality in my life.

We might have moved away from Uncle Duncan, but we still went back there on occasions. I remember one New Year's Eve (I must have been about seven). I thought I was safe because we were all there, and Aunty Flo too. Surely he wouldn't do anything when my whole family was around? Uncle Duncan was wearing one of those joke aprons that looked like a kilt with a sporran. When you lifted a flap on the apron there was a bare bottom – a cartoon thing. He kept flashing it up, laughing loudly, spit flying from his mouth.

'Do you like that, Michèle? Do you want to see it again?'

I didn't dare say no. I laughed politely and nodded. He came closer and lowered his head so only I could see him and lifted the flap very deliberately, his tongue slowly – so slowly – licking his lips. His eyes didn't once leave mine.

Then he smiled – I could smell his breath, a horrible mixture of tooth decay and alcohol.

At that point Mum came in.

'What are you doing?' she asked.

'Just showing young Michèle what's under my sporran, Bruna, my darling.' He was so confident I couldn't speak. He turned round and, with a cackle, showed my mother the cartoon under the flap on her apron.

Mum was tired, I could tell, and getting irritated. 'Stop doing that. Flo wants you in the kitchen. Leave Michèle alone.'

Maybe at last she was realising about him. Then again, maybe not. Something really weird is that, out of the endless stream of lodgers we had, not one of them was a woman. Mum never rented her spare room to females; they were always men, only men. Did it never occur to her that she was putting her young daughter in danger? It seemed not.

The one good thing was that, around this time, Connie left our lives. She had been getting more and more insane until I think even Mum realised she was dangerous. Over the years Mum had tried to heal Connie over and over again. At first she was open to the healing and would let Mum lay on her hands but, as she become more hostile to the power of good, she refused. Mum would not give up, though, and would send her distance healing. She would also astral travel (where your spirit leaves the body and travels to other physical places) to check Connie was OK. Often, Mum would say, she found it hard to find her –

there were so many other people staying in her house. It was a large house – and not only did she have several lodgers, but she also took in elderly people who needed care. I dread to think what their lives were like.

Connie's relationship with her husband had deteriorated and he had become increasingly violent. Eventually she told Mum that she had had enough.

'Good. I'm glad,' Mum said. 'Are you going to go to the police? Are you going to divorce him?'

But Connie shook her head and smiled unpleasantly. 'I don't need the police any more. I can handle him myself.'

Mum asked what she meant and she said: 'Bruna, you choose your god and I'll pray to my devil.'

A few weeks passed and we saw Connie's husband in the street. He had always been tall and slim, but suddenly he had put on a lot of weight. He looked sick and strained, and several months later we heard that he had died. His weight had ballooned until he weighed a colossal 28 stone. The strain on his heart was too much and he collapsed suddenly one day. There was no apparent reason for the weight gain over such a short period of time and my mother became very frightened. She forbade us from going round to Connie's (as if we would unless we had to!) and the friendship ended.

Not that any of this made Mum more cautious. She was simply one of those people who would keep her door open for anyone – too trusting and naïve in many ways. As Madame Bruna, she had all manner of clients come to our small home. This was the early 1970s and the greatest sin was to be 'uptight'.

After my father died, I put on weight and at some point I had my long hair all cut off. I became very much a tomboy and a toughie, aggressive and forceful but never a bully. I hated bullies and I always saw myself as someone who stuck up for the weaker kids. I became a rescuer. I also wouldn't stand for any form of discrimination. I had an innate sense that we are all equal and all one. I remember being horrified at my mother's casual racism. One summer I hung out for a few days with a black girl called Sandra and Mum said, 'One of the neighbours wants to know why you got a black girl for a friend?' I couldn't believe that she was saying it. I hated injustice and was passionately idealistic. I just couldn't understand why the other kids didn't want to save the world and the animals or feel connected to the whole.

I used to fight my brother's bullies too which, sadly, made things much worse for him. If somebody picked on Nicholas and called him a 'Paki' or whatever (which he got a lot), I would weigh in. Of course this made him look even worse, as if was getting his kid sister (I was four years younger than him, remember) to fight his battles. Poor Nicholas. I would torment him to get his attention. Then as soon as he had turned his attention to me, he would inevitably beat me up and I let him. It became that weird pattern of negative attention-seeking – better to be beaten up than ignored. Just as I put up with being touched and made to touch, simply to have someone being nice to me beforehand and taking notice of me while it was happening. Of course, the rejection and turning away afterwards was unbearable, but it was all worth it for the sake of being someone, of being witnessed – even if it was for all the wrong reasons.

Even though they cut me out of their games and refused me their friendship, I felt terribly sorry for Nicholas, and the other kids. OK, I was separated from them, but they were separated from the whole of creation, from life itself. So, in a way, to my young mind, it was they who were lost and I who was blessed. I prayed fervently at that time, and I fully believed my prayers would be answered. I always knew I would be looked after by Spirit. I also believed that everyone was inherently good and that if people were bad or if they hurt others it was just because they needed love.

It was a pretty bleak time. Even Lucy seemed to let me down in some funny way. I was irritated that she wasn't more like a proper imaginary friend. I wanted her to be a separate entity, not just this disembodied voice in my head whispering to me. I used to hear people talk about imaginary friends and wished I had one, but all I had was this . . . this whispering.

So I turned in on myself. I discovered the local library and just read and read and read. When the library shut, I would come home and sit up in the apple tree, imagining myself being on the radio. I am sure this is one of my first cosmic orders that later came true as now I am on the radio a lot, and even had my own show. I thought about the future, figuring it had to be better than the present, and wondered if I might become an actress or a barrister. Justice was a huge pull but, above all, I was (and still am) fascinated by what motivates people and why we are here.

However much I wanted to be, I was never really going to be 'one of the boys' – there would always be a distance. Yet I inadvertently scared the girls by hanging out with the boys, playing kiss chase (on the boys' side!) and fighting with the boys. I used to act like The Fonz, one of my favourite TV characters, and I got a lot of stick for being Italian. Talking about reincarnation and ghosts and being able to see the future didn't help much either. I was simply the odd-ball with whom nobody wanted to be associated.

I remember one day sitting waiting for assembly and I started talking to the girl next to me about reincarnation. She thought I was mad and I was going, 'Don't be ridiculous. Of course we're all reincarnated and we were different things in past lives. Don't you know who you were?' Maybe I badgered her a bit too much, because she started crying and the teachers came and told me off for making things up, for frightening her.

At that point I was convinced I had been a soldier in a previous life, or something like that. I always had that kind of 'hero' mythology of saving people or fighting to save people.

Maybe because I was on my own so much, my psychic awakening was progressing in leaps and bounds. I clearly remember being at my Aunt Anne's house with Mum and my brother. We were watching some moon landing, or some other big moon event on the telly and I was having an argument with Nicholas and also Anne's son, Nick. Suddenly I turned round to my mother: 'I was alive during the war, wasn't I?'

'Eh? What are you talking about?'

'I remember being in the war. I was a baby and someone was running with me and all the buildings were on fire. It was you, wasn't it?'

'Don't be silly. You were born in 1966. The war had been over for years and years.'

It was so incredibly clear in my mind that I was totally gobsmacked by her response. I just knew I had been there. I started developing the power of prediction around that time too. I would 'see' natural disasters like earthquakes or big airplane crashes before they happened, and wasn't remotely surprised when they appeared on the news. It was a bit weird, but I don't remember it bothering me that much. I'd talk it over with Mum and she was pretty sanguine about it too. I was my mother's daughter in that respect after all. The supernatural was her currency – in fact, she was more at home in the world of the occult than in everyday life.

Mum was always giving me readings and asking me to read for her and her friends, even when I was only seven or eight. She knew I had the gift and I loved doing it – not just because it felt so natural, but also because it was about the only time we really communicated, when she listened to me, and gave me attention. I would have read the cards all day and all night if it kept her with me.

I was morbidly fascinated with her strange world and would rifle through her office trying to find bits of paper with spells and secrets on them, her magical stuff. One day I was thumbing through papers in her desk drawer and I found a pamphlet. Something about it intrigued me and I sat down on her chair and read with mounting horror:

A great chastisement will come over all mankind, not today or tomorrow but in the second half of the twentieth century . . . Satan will even succeed in infiltrating into the highest position in the Church . . . The great, great war will come in the second half of the twentieth century. Fire and smoke will drop from heaven and the waters of the ocean will turn to steam . . . Millions of people will die. Those surviving will envy the dead . . . The age of ages is coming; the end of all ends . . . go my child and announce it and I will assist you . . .

I knew it. We were all going to die. I'd had a terrible fear of death for as long as I could remember. A really awful, petrifying fear. Every time I left the house I was sure I'd never get back in one piece. I suppose it wasn't that surprising really given that my twin had died at birth and I had nearly joined her; that my father had died, and that even my mother had insisted we were all going to die horribly in the hurricane in Italy. This pamphlet, I later realised, was an excerpt from one of the infamous 'Fatima Secrets' that the Vatican held for decades. It received wide distribution in Catholic circles in the 1960s, but the Vatican neither admitted it was true nor denounced it as a fake. So huge numbers of Catholics were left in terrible fear that the end of the world was nigh. Huge numbers of Catholics – and also one small girl in west London.

I tried to forget the words of the Fatima Secret, but they burned into my brain. While I was fascinated by the other world, the supernatural world, I was also terrified of aspects of it. For instance, I never ever wanted to be a medium. I remember very clearly, when I was about seven, being given a choice about seeing spirits.

I was sick and off school with a chest infection. I was lying in my mother's bed, which had blue nylon sheets and a mustard-coloured nylon duvet cover. The bed was against the wall so I had my back to the door, while ahead of me was an arched window looking out on to the road. I had been ill for quite a while and was feeling pretty grim.

Mum came home from one of her cleaning jobs with a present from one of her rich clients. It was a small children's typewriter – old but perfectly functional. I couldn't believe it: I was over the moon. Immediately I held it I felt something surge through me. I knew it had meaning, but I didn't know what. I felt that the typewriter was part of my destiny. As soon as I touched it I could not wait to learn how to type. Part of the reason may have been that I had a clear memory of my father putting me on his lap in his office and helping me type my name. Maybe that was why I felt such a huge sense of comfort when my hands touched the keys.

I was too ill to sit up and type, but I wouldn't let Mum take the typewriter away. So she put it by the side of the bed and I lay looking at it, imagining the stories I would type. Maybe I'd be a famous writer or journalist. Later that evening, as it got dark, I had what can only be described as a visitation. One moment I was lying, slightly bored, wondering if Mum would come up with something to eat. Then, suddenly, I wasn't alone in the room. I could feel this presence. The hairs rose up on the back of my neck.

'Are you ready now to see us?' A voice sounded clearly in my head.

I was taken aback. I just lay there, very still, and thought about it. I could feel the presence there, waiting, on the edge of becoming manifest.

'No. Not really,' I said finally. Then, feeling I should be truthful, I added, 'I'm scared, but I don't want to be scared.'

I'll be honest, it was really terrifying. But it also felt what I can only describe as inevitable. Some part of me knew that this was going to happen one day and here it was. I knew in myself that if I committed at that point something would change in my life and I would have direct contact with spirits.

It may sound far-fetched. You might say it was the wild imaginings of an ill child, brought on by a fever. But it was very clear and real to me.

'Look at the bed,' the voice commanded.

I desperately wanted to shut my eyes and hide under the covers. I knew I was about to see something. And I did – the shadow of something started creeping above the covers. I panicked and shut my eyes tight.

It happened again. Again and again, maybe nine or ten times. But each time it got close to me and I saw the edges of it, I pulled back.

'No.'

I could feel that Lucy was there and that Lucy and the spirit were having a conversation, as if they were deciding which way I was going to go.

– *'She should see us.'*
– *She doesn't want to.*
– *'But she would be a remarkable medium.'*
– *She has another path.*
– *'But we need her.'*
– *She doesn't need you.*
– *'But we want her.'*
– *No.*

I was at a spiritual gateway and I almost feel as if my destiny was decided upon there and then. I was given the choice and I made it. I did not want to be a traditional medium – I didn't want to see dead people. It made me feel uneasy – it still does. I knew I wanted to write and communicate about life and spirit in a different way. There are many levels of spirit life, but I have always accessed the world of discarnate higher spiritual beings (you might think of them as angels or guides). Many people tap into this when they have transcendent spiritual experiences, or when they meditate or go into trance states. I can do it at will – it's simply like turning on a tap.

My mother, however, did allow the spirits through – and that exposed me to some truly terrifying experiences.

7

I'm Talking to the Dead

Mum didn't use the ouija board. Instead she would spread out letters around a circular table and place a simple drinking glass in the centre. She would gather everyone round the table, the lights would go low and the séance would begin.

Although Mum used to let me join in her healing circles quite happily, she was far more reluctant to let me attend her séances. Funnily enough, by not including me she made it more dangerous as I was left outside the circle of protection that she drew up around the room.

I would dread the doorbell ringing on séance nights. Sometimes I'd peer over the banisters into the hallway and see the people filing through – some faces familiar, some unknown. I would race back into bed and try to lose myself in a book, trying not to hear what was going on. For if I listened carefully, I could hear the glass sliding over the table; I could hear my mother's voice asking if there was 'anybody there'; and I could hear my mother's voice change from her familiar Italian lilt to other, unknown, frightening voices.

The problem was that the spirits, once summoned, didn't stay downstairs. It was as if they recognised something in me, a chance to communicate perhaps, and they would seek me out.

Sometimes kind spirits would be summoned and I would feel pleasant tingles of energy, playful taps and a warm feeling as if I were being gently hugged. But more often I would know it was a malevolent energy, trying its utmost to get my attention. I would hear strange knockings and scrapings along the walls and windows in my room. Sometimes it sounded like fingernails scratching down the window-panes; sometimes it sounded like claws scraping across the wall. I would hurl myself under the covers and pray my hardest. When that didn't work I would talk to Lucy, begging her help.

– *Make them go away, Lucy.*
– *I can't.*
– *You have to.*
– *It's OK. They can't hurt you. They can't touch you.*
– *But I'm scared.*
– *I know.*

After the people had all gone, Mum would come up and go to the bathroom to take off her make-up. I'd call out softly:

'Mum.'

'*Madre di dio*, why aren't you asleep?'

'Mum. There are people in my room. Spirits. They're scaring me.'

'Don't be so silly. There are no spirits here. They were all downstairs in the circle.'

'No, they're here and I'm frightened. They're making horrible noises.'

'Ah Michèle,' she sighed. 'Just wait a minute, eh? I'll fix it.'

She went downstairs and came back up again with a tray piled high. First she picked up a jar of holy water. She flicked it all around my room and bed. I jumped as it splashed me – it felt cold. Then she put that down and brought out some garlic which she placed all around the window sills and above the door. Finally, she sprinkled a line of salt right around my room.

I realise now she knew exactly what was going on, but didn't want to frighten me. She thought she could just kick all the spirits out after her séances if they made an appearance elsewhere in the house. But she was wrong.

I became more certain than ever that I never wanted to be a medium. Even though when I do readings now, sometimes spirits come through and give very specific messages, it is not something I encourage. I think that, once you open the door to be a messenger from the lower astral realms, it can take you over. I also think that talking to the dead can sometimes encourage people to live in the past. As I've said, I prefer to access higher forms of knowledge and I like to use my psychic ability to help people make the most of being here on earth, right now, living in the present. I sometimes describe myself as a 'soul coach' as I try to connect with a person's soul, to help them reach a higher sense of self-knowledge, to fulfil their full potential. Above all, to take each and every day and make the most of it – joyfully. I see life as a journey and believe we are all going home in the end. We have to accept the fact that, in a way, there is no such thing as death, just transformation; to know that there really is no separation between here and there. I have had cast-iron proof with visitations from spirits and that is enough for me. My job is to help people come into their power here on earth and to enjoy being here while it lasts.

For my mother, though, mediumship was just another one of her barrage of magical tools. She taught me palmistry and tried to teach me the crystal ball but I just wasn't interested in it. I didn't have much time for the tea leaves and all that either. I always wanted to look at it from an intellectual point of view and take it to the next level. I thought it was a bit uncool, to be honest, a bit Gypsy Lee. The tarot was something else, though: it was really accurate. I used to give readings for people and everything I said about their past was spot on. Often they would come back and tell me that my predictions for their future had been spot on too.

Mum would go in for weird Christian magic, chanting

psalms and burning incense. When she cast her spells under the vast six-foot-high painting of Jesus I knew they would work. I would go into her room to find a candelabra dripping with coloured candles. The room reeked of her magical oils. My mother's view of magic and religion were as complex as she was. On the one hand, she behaved like a Catholic yet she had rejected the Catholic Church – mainly because of the war atrocities she had witnessed in Italy and the inhumanity of the priest who had turned them away from his door. As I mentioned earlier, people were either good or evil, and treated accordingly – my mother could see no shades of grey. This extended to her relationship to me. I was either an angel from heaven or the devil incarnate. Half the time I didn't know who I was either.

She was an incredible psychic, though, and all sorts of people filed through the house or called her to them – MPs and other dignitaries, even foreign royalty. Unlike many psychics, she was very specific, very forthright and very accurate. Usually she didn't charge them, although most would leave her some money in an envelope. I knew how good she was because every prediction she made for me would happen within days or weeks. I think I take after her in this as my gift as a psychic seems to be mainly about immediate predictions of what is going to happen over the next few days, or maybe over the two or three months ahead.

When I think of her at that time, it's with a background of music. She loved music and the house rang with Glen Campbell, Tom Jones and Roy Orbison. She'd dance too, with whatever man she was seeing at the time. Sometimes it seemed as though our house was home to one big party, the living room full of people dancing and laughing and drinking.

No matter who she was seeing, life was always out of control. We had no set mealtimes, no set bedtime and, if I didn't want to go to school, I simply didn't. Mum would go to work and come home in the middle of the afternoon with a big bag of chocolate and biscuits, and that was it. Often she would bribe me with money to stay up late with her, to keep her company. She was obviously terribly lonely. There were no boundaries, no safety, no security in any of it. My way of dealing with it was to become mouthy and obnoxious – I'd never show vulnerability.

It got to the point where I couldn't stand her anywhere near me. I didn't trust her. I knew I wasn't safe. I think I must have known on some level that she was really just like a wayward, difficult, unpredictable child. It's a very scary thing for a child to be looked after by someone who is like a child.

I loved her and hated her in equal measures. I didn't want to be anywhere near her, yet I desperately wanted her to be a 'proper' mother, to look after me, to care for me, to love and protect me. But that was never going to happen so, from the age of nine, I handled my life by becoming totally independent. Yet I was still a little girl and, for all that I was a toughie, I was still terrified of death, and petrified of the dark. I was often left alone at night and I would lie awake in my small room, desperately waiting to hear Mum's key in the lock. Every time she was late in, I would be convinced she had been killed in a car accident.

But then 'death', 'dying' and 'kill' seemed to be Mum's favourite words. When Dad was alive she had been merely volatile, but now she was becoming increasingly extreme and aggressive. Maybe, with her poor English, she felt she couldn't communicate properly and so she'd just shout and be angry. Anger was her main emotion. She used to lash out, sometimes even hitting me with a wooden clog-type shoe, often for absolutely no reason whatsoever. She'd say 'I'm going to kill you!' at the drop of a hat and chase me round the room. If she dropped something while I was in the kitchen, I'd get the blame.

So it was little wonder that death seemed so familiar, so terrifying yet so alluring. It was the obvious answer to my loneliness. I used to sit in my little room, staring at the wall and wondering which would be the best way to die. What would it be like to be dead? Would I become one of those lost, angry spirits that roamed our house after the séances? Maybe Mum would pay more attention to me if I were a ghost. She might even listen to me. Would I go to heaven? Would I meet Dad? Maybe I'd meet my Italian ancestors, the grandparents I had never known? I'd be with Lucy and surely that would be wonderful. But what if I didn't go to heaven but to the other place? What if I went to a place where there was more abuse, where I not only had to witness torture and unnatural acts, but also had them inflicted on me? What if hell was full of people like Connie and her husband, of people like Uncle Duncan and all the other people who had hurt me? The thoughts whirled round and round in my head. Above all, I kept thinking how worthless I was. Nobody liked me. Nobody loved me. How could they? The more I thought about it, the more I thought the world would be better off without me. Lucy tried to talk to me, to cheer me up, but it was as if her voice were muffled, as if someone had pressed the mute switch on a radio. Most of the time I ignored her. I just pulled the bedclothes over my head and waited for her to go away.

Looking back, I was severely depressed and it's not remotely surprising. I had lost my father and any semblance of normal family life. Suicidal thoughts and attempted suicide is far more common than people imagine among children and teenagers. Some 22 per cent of depressed children will attempt suicide. Often the only reason they don't succeed is that they simply don't have access to the tools that would help them take their own lives. But one day I did.

I was at a kids' party – a very unusual occurrence for me. I think I was about eight or nine. All the other children were clustered in the living room, playing pass the parcel or something. I had been pushed to the side and told there wasn't room for me, so I wandered off upstairs. I wasn't surprised, I was always being pushed aside. It had been a miracle I'd been invited to the party at all – I think the girl's mother had felt sorry for me and tried to get her daughter to include me. It hadn't worked.

I wandered in and out of the upstairs rooms, thinking this was what a normal family home looked like. The parents' room was bright and pretty – with a bright flowery quilt on the bed and a dressing table with perfume bottles standing on a daintily embroidered cloth. The daughter's room was like something from a fairy-tale. Everything matched and everything had flounces on it. It was pink and fluffy and so, so soft. A line of Barbie and Sindy dolls sat on the window-seat. Teddy bears perched on the bed. She too had a dressing table, with a set of Pretty Peach cosmetics and a jewellery box that, when you opened it, played a tune while a ballerina twirled round and round. I felt a wave of depression and bitterness sweep over me. I bet *she* never had to worry about what she was going to eat. I bet nobody had ever made *her* play horsey, or made *her* touch a 'thing'. I bet her mother and father loved her and protected her and cherished her.

I felt sick as I stumbled out of the room and looked for the bathroom. It was a hot day and the window was partly open. It was a large window and underneath it was a wicker laundry basket. I listened to the muffled laughter from the room down below. It all seemed so stupid. What was the point? Nobody liked me. I had no friends and my brother loathed my guts. My mother kept saying she wanted to kill me, so why didn't I save her the bother and do it myself?

It was like something clicked in my head. It all seemed so easy that I was stunned I hadn't done it before. Why had I been so frightened?

'That's it. I'm going to kill myself. I'm going to jump out of the window.' I said it quite calmly, and moved slowly towards the window. I tugged at the sash and it opened wide quite easily, unlike the windows in our house which always seemed to stick. I stood up on the laundry basket and then slowly started to slide my legs out on to the window ledge.

I was sitting on the ledge, looking down, wondering how it would feel to fly through the air.

– *Michèle, no!*
– *You can't stop me, Lucy.*
– *Oh yes I can.*

I heard footsteps and then a horrified voice came from behind me:

'Oh my God!'

It was the mother of the birthday girl, who had come to find out where I was.

'Get away from the window. *Please.*'

I turned round. Her face was a mask of horror and I felt an overwhelming sense of pity for her sweep over me. She hadn't been cruel, she hadn't ignored me. In fact she had obviously seen I'd been left out and had come to look for me. It wouldn't be fair for her to have all the upset and the mess that my death would cause. Maybe this wasn't the right time or place.

So I did as she asked, numbly climbing down and allowing her to take me by the hand and lead me down to the kitchen where she plied me with cake and sandwiches. I figured her arrival at that precise moment had been Fate (or maybe it was Lucy nudging her): it wasn't my time to go. I remembered Connie, who had told me with such glee that I was going to die in a car accident when I was thirty-eight. Maybe that was my fate. Maybe I would have to wait. I didn't know whether I was relieved or disappointed. But the bottom line was: I didn't really care.

It was when I was nine going on ten that the trouble started in earnest at school. I was a smart kid, but I wasn't an easy pupil. I was incredibly opinionated and I used to question everything, interrupt the teacher, demand deeper explanations. When they tried to shut me up, I answered back and got angry. I used to get into fights all the time too.

I was a complete and utter nightmare, no doubt about it. But I wasn't always the instigator. Children can be incredibly cruel, particularly to someone who stands out, who doesn't fit the mould. They used to tease me horribly and call me 'Tubbydread' because I was chubby.

One day a new boy joined our class and smiled at me. I was a bit suspicious but, over the course of the day, he kept being friendly. We hung out a bit in the playground and talked. The next day when I opened my desk I found a love letter from him, asking me to meet him in the park. I was over the moon. Someone liked me. I could barely get through the day, I was so excited. I ran home and changed out of my school clothes and put on my best (and only) dress. I raced to the park. But he wasn't there. Just a pack of kids from my class, all pointing and laughing.

'Tubbydread! Tubbydread! Tubbydread!'

I felt sick. This couldn't be happening. How could they be so cruel? Why did they always pick on me? Why couldn't anyone like me and be my friend? I ran home with tears of fury and humiliation and misery pouring down my face.

Dear old Sheba was lying in the hallway in a patch of sunlight. As I crashed through the door she raised her head and thumped her tail. I don't know what got into me (maybe I was more my mother's daughter than I liked to think), but I suddenly wanted to show them what it was like to be scared. I wanted them to know how I felt.

'Sheba!' I yelled her name and she came, obedient and sweet-natured as ever. I slipped on her lead and raced back to the children in the park.

'Come to see your boyfriend, Tubbydread?' one of the boys laughed. 'Well, he doesn't love you. Nobody loves *you*, Tubbydread.'

I stood squarely and glared, my cheeks still streaked with tears. I yanked on Sheba's collar and she looked up at me.

'This is a police dog, OK? She's trained to bite people.' I gazed straight into their eyes and could see their uncertainty.

I knew that Sheba had the sweetest nature and wouldn't hurt a fly – but of course they didn't know that.

'She'll bite you if I tell her to. Who's going first? You could get rabies and die, you know.'

I moved towards them, filled to the brim with fury and misery. If they didn't move soon, I was going to burst into tears. I bit my lip so hard I could taste blood in my mouth. My hand slipped down to Sheba's collar and I saw them look anxiously at one another. One step further and then they ran, pushing one another out of the way as I let Sheba off the lead. But as they ran away I felt no joy, no triumph. Only a bitter knowledge that I had driven an even deeper wedge between them and me. I had lashed out through desperation, not really realising the consequences of my actions. I had achieved precisely nothing.

Mum was called into school after that. She was always being called into school. I was the bad one, the trouble-maker. She kept promising I'd behave, but really she had no control over me whatsoever. We had such a strange relationship. Most of the time she acted as if she loathed me yet, if the chips were down and someone else were threatening me, she would leap to my defence. One day I had been playing round the block when a neighbour I didn't know grabbed my arm and accused me of breaking her window. I had never seen the woman or her window before, but she dug her fingers into my arm so hard that it left a bruise. I ran crying down the street and my mother saw me and pulled me to her.

'What's happened? Who hurt you? You tell me now.' She was utterly furious. All her anger turned blissfully away from me and on to someone else.

The unfortunate woman made the mistake of walking past my mother in the street, on her way to go shopping.

Mum hurled herself down the street and spun the woman round. All five foot of my mother puffed up and screeching:

'Hey! What did you touch my daughter for? You ever touch my daughter again and I'll kill you!'

The woman, a tall willowy blonde in her fifties, towered over my mother and made the fatal mistake of underestimating her. Little did she know that Mum morphed into a Tasmanian devil when challenged. The woman didn't say a word, but simply slapped Mum round the face. Quick as a flash my mother took off her wooden shoe and started beating the woman about the head with it in a very unspiritual fashion. I had had direct experience of being hit with that shoe on many occasions and knew that it had to hurt.

'I'll teach you to slap me!' Mum shrieked. 'And I'll do it again if you touch my daughter again.' Eventually she decided enough was enough and let her go. The woman fled, clasping her hands to her head, horrified and sobbing. Mum finally turned to me:

'Now, Michèle, you go play. Don't you worry about a thing. Go to the park. I've sorted her out; she won't bother you again.'

I was shocked by the violence. I felt a strange mixture of pride for being protected and pity for the woman Mum had attacked as I could tell that she felt so sad and empty. I have sensed people's inner states all my life, from as far back as I can remember.

I went to the park as instructed, but felt uneasy. Something wasn't right. I turned around and walked slowly home, trying to figure out what it was. As I turned the corner I saw the flashing lights of an ambulance and police car. The woman's husband had come round and attacked Mum, knocking her unconscious and smashing out all her teeth. He was never arrested and they were both bound over to keep the peace.

The problems with men continued too and I was always running straight into trouble. It wasn't just a case of neighbours and lodgers: it was as if I were still a magnet to every undesirable under the sun. Given that Mum was working every hour of the day, she was rarely at home – so I was often left to wander around in the park or over to the canal, all on my own. It was the same situation as in Italy – weeks would go by when she would not be remotely bothered and then, all of a sudden, she would realise I wasn't home for tea and organise a huge search party or call the police. It was totally unpredictable, totally arbitrary. There were no rules and no reasons; she simply expected me to tune in and *know* when she was home. Of course the park and canal left me horribly vulnerable to yet more sexual predators. I recall one incident when a man who must have been in his late twenties started chatting to me in the park. He was really friendly and talked to me as if I were an adult. Then he started masturbating in front of me.

'It's totally normal,' he said, 'Everyone does it.'

In my experience that was true. But one afternoon he knocked on our door when my mother was in. I could hear his voice as I sat upstairs in my room. I couldn't believe he had dared to come to my house. How did he even know where I lived?

'Hi, Mrs Saunders,' he said, cool as a cucumber. 'I've just come to help Michèle fix her bike as she said it was broken. Can I have a word with her please?'

My mother was so distracted by whatever problem she or someone else had that she just let him in. I heard him come up the stairs and he came into my bedroom with a smile, locking the door behind him. Something in his manner had changed and I felt a chilling sense of genuine alarm. Without even talking he came over and pushed me on to the bed with one hand and pulled himself out of his trousers with the other. He lay on top of me trying to wrestle my clothes off. The way he did it alarmed me not only because my mother was in the house, but also because of the level of aggression. This time there was no pressure or charm to get me to do what he wanted; it was pure brute force. I could smell by his breath he had been drinking and I knew that that wasn't good. I kicked and fought, and hissed at him that my mother could come up at any minute. Suddenly there was another knock at the front door and more people arrived. Luckily this seemed to alarm him and he got off me. It was as if I were protected once more.

'Come out now and meet me in the park,' he said, his words slurring.

'OK, but just go.'

Of course, I never went to the park and avoided it for several weeks after that, quite terrified he would come and get me.

But the park wasn't the only dangerous place. Once I was with two other girls from school, walking by the canal. It was great because I was getting on with them and, for once, I felt included. We came across a man sitting on a bench, wearing a blue boiler suit. As we got closer, I realised he was masturbating over a porn magazine. Lucy gave a warning buzz in my ear. I knew what she meant – this man could be dangerous. But the other girls thought it was funny. They started giggling and teasing him, and I was so desperate to be part of the gang that I ignored Lucy and joined in. He loved it of course and came over and started talking to us.

The others were a bit worried about this and pushed me forwards, hiding behind me. His eyes ran me up and down and then he reached out and touched my chest, cupping my breasts.

'My, you're a big girl, aren't you?'

I smiled uneasily. The other two edged further back, but I stayed where I was. A normal child would have run, but I had been trained to be obedient, to accept abuse. It didn't occur to me that you could say no.

'Hey. Put your hand in my pocket and see what you find. Might be a nice surprise.'

I put my hand in the pocket, but of course there was nothing underneath and instead I found myself touching his erect 'thing'. I pulled my hand away and he went to grab me. All of a sudden I heard Lucy clearly in my head.

– Don't make him angry. Make an excuse. Tell him it's not safe here.

I held up my hands and made myself smile. 'Not here. Someone will see. Let's go somewhere else.'

'Smart thinking.'

'We'll see you under the bridge, in the bushes on the other side. In about five minutes?' I said.

'Yeah. Good idea.' He lazily scratched his crotch.

I walked slowly away, taking the other girls with me. When we got past the bridge, we started running like crazy. We ran and we ran and we ran. I lived miles away, about fifteen minutes further on than the others, and it was horrible running on my own, not knowing if he was following.

I wanted to tell someone, anyone – our headmistress, the police – but the others wouldn't let me. They refused to talk about it and just wanted to forget all about it. They were too embarrassed. Then, a few days later, another girl was touched up and nearly raped in the subway. It was awful. She fell to pieces and I remember the headmistress standing up in assembly and telling us about it, warning us that we must always report anyone suspicious. I blamed myself terribly for not telling – if I'd reported him, she wouldn't have gone through that. What made it even worse was that the others were really angry that I had even thought about telling. They stopped talking to me; they wouldn't play with me. So really, what was the point? I might as well have told the truth in the first place.

A few days later Mum got a new lodger. I forget his name. I watched him unpack his things in the spare room and he turned round and smiled lazily at me.

'Do you like playing games, Michèle? It is Michèle, isn't it?'

I didn't say anything. I just looked at the floor.

'Ah, I thought you did. We'll have some fun then, when your mum's out at work.'

When I look back I find it incredible that, while I was so desperate to tell the authorities about someone attacking other children, I never once thought about telling anyone about my own ongoing abuse. I was simply too numb, too depressed, too alone.

8

To Swing His Axe He Swears

Lodgers came and went. A few left me alone, but it seemed like the majority wanted something from me. Then Dennis came. At first he didn't really register other than that he had a beard and wore thick square bottleneck glasses. But quickly it became apparent he and Mum had something going on. Once again, he was someone who was much younger than my mother. To be honest, though, I didn't really think much about him. He was one of the ones who didn't seem interested in me and I was grateful for that – he was far too obsessed with my mother. One day I went out into the garden and saw them sitting on the swing-seat, holding hands.

'Eh, darling. Guess what? Dennis and I are getting married. We're engaged.' I looked blankly at them. 'Say "Congratulations" to us, darling.'

'Congratulations.'

What else could I say?

'Dennis will be your new father. We'll be a family again.'

I looked suspiciously at her. Could it really be possible? I wasn't keen on the idea of my father being replaced at all, let alone by such a strange man, but on the other hand I was desperate for normality. Maybe Dennis would make our family right again. I had this insane idea that we could maybe transform overnight into *The Waltons* or, even better, *The Little House on the Prairie*. I watched a lot of television and I loved those shows. Maybe he could calm Mum down, make her more rational, more normal. Maybe he could have some influence over Nicholas. Maybe if Mum married him, we wouldn't need to have all the lodgers. Maybe my childhood could become safe at last. I barely dared to hope.

It was a very short engagement. The wedding was held in the registry office and I was a bridesmaid, wearing a red velvet dress with white fur around the collar. I hated it, and as soon as I got home I ripped off the dress and ran to the park to play football.

Dennis was very different from my well-spoken civilised father. Dennis wasn't an educated man, nor well dressed and charming, but I grew to like him a lot. He always came home with some present or other – often the plastic butter-flies that came free in the packets of chocolate Ready Brek. Not that he'd spent any money – he just happened to work in the factory that made the cereal. He played Monopoly with us and, as far as I can remember, he was one of the few men my mother knew that didn't abuse me, that didn't make me do things that had to be secrets.

For a while it worked out OK. Mum seemed happy and

more relaxed. There were no more lodgers and Mum
stopped bringing stray people home to stay. As Dennis had
a regular job, money was a little less tight and she didn't
have to work quite so ludicrously hard. Mum was still
volatile, but it was directed more at Dennis than at Nicholas
or me. They would yell and scream at each other, then
collapse into each other's arms. I think they liked the
making-up sex. She still didn't have much time to take us
anywhere or do anything with us but, if she did, she would
more or less get me what I wanted, even if she couldn't
afford it.

One day we went to the school jumble sale and she
bought me two things I could barely believe. One was a
broken-down old piano. The piano didn't last three weeks
as Dennis had to sleep days and all I would do anyway
was bang away thinking I was a genius. The other was a
box of comics that held my heart and changed my life. I'd
never really been interested in girls' comics before – I'd
scorned *Mandy* and *Flo*, thinking they were a bit pathetic,
for sissies. Yet when I actually read them, the stories blew
me away. It felt like the box was full of hundreds of them
and they seemed like a treasure trove. Two stories in
particular really spoke to me. The first was 'The Four
Marys'. I desperately wanted to be like those four girls at
boarding school. Boarding school seemed safe, and justice
was always done. I could never understand why in real life
it wasn't the same as in comics and films. The second was
a story about a girl from a magical family, a girl who was

half-gypsy and could look into the future, a girl who cast spells and wanted to be a witch. Ironically, this made me feel normal. I actually believed these stories were true and that there were other families like mine.

The only problem with Dennis was that he loved to drink. In fact, he drank so much and so regularly he was obviously an alcoholic. Usually he'd become very playful and high-spirited when he was drunk, but sometimes he turned nasty. One night he turned very nasty indeed.

'*Porco dio*, where is he? I'm going to kill that bastard when he gets back.' Mum was shouting to herself as usual. I pulled the covers over my head, irritated but not unduly alarmed – she never talked normally if she could yell.

I could hear the key in the front door, sliding and missing the hole. A muffled curse followed and then the clink of the key dropping and skittering over the chipped tarmac by the door.

Dennis was coming home late, and quite obviously drunk after one of his infamous benders. Mum let him in, but was clearly not amused.

'Hello, gorgeous. Look what I got.' His words slurred into one another.

My interest peaked at this point. It was the day before my eleventh birthday and I wondered if perhaps he had got me a birthday present? So I slid out of bed, crept out of my room on to the upstairs landing and peered through the banisters. I could see him standing, swaying slightly, in the hallway below. In his hand hung a bottle of whisky, a brown bottle in the shape of an eagle. My mother stood, impassive, glaring at him.

'What is that flickin' thing?' Her eyes glared at the bottle while Dennis smiled lopsidedly and stroked the bottle. 'Where did you get that thing from?'

He laughed, failing to pick up the icy menace in her voice.

'Where – did – you – get – that – thing – from?' She said every word slowly and clearly, in her sharp lilting accent.

'Won it.' A big slack smile hung on his fleshy lips.

'Won it? How did you win it?' She spat out the words and her eyes were glittering. I could see her fists were turning white as she clamped them by her sides.

Dennis didn't perceive the danger. He was obviously still in that pleasantly inane state of drunkenness, where everything seems funny, everything a joke.

'I stripped, didn't I?' he slurred. 'Did an effing striptease for the whole effing pub. Showed 'em the crown jewels an' all.' He waved the bottle and shuffled from one foot to the other, as if about to dance.

She broke into a wild torrent of enraged Italian: '*Disgraziato*, you're making a fool out of me.' She called him every name under the sun, and then a few more, smashing her fists into him, slapping him, scratching at his eyes.

'Calm down, darling, it was just a laugh.'

Next, Mum moved so fast I couldn't believe it. One moment she was standing quite, *quite* still; the next she had snatched up a thick glass ashtray and lobbed it straight at him. It hit him right in the face and he yelled out in pain and anger, dropping the whisky bottle to the floor.

'You've knocked out my effing tooth.' He sounded as if he couldn't believe what had happened, his hand clasped to his mouth, a trickle of blood trailing down his chin.

As soon as he saw the tooth on the floor his manner changed. It was as if something evil washed over him. He turned away and calmly walked past my mother and out into the kitchen. I could hear heavy footsteps crashing over the floor and the creak of the kitchen door opening. He was going into the garden. There was nothing much out there, just a small patch of bald lawn, the old apple tree, and some concrete crazy paving dotted with dog poo. Sheba was cowering in the kitchen, under the table, keeping out the way. She had an animal's intuition that something was badly wrong.

– This is bad.
– I know.

I didn't need Lucy to tell me this wasn't good. Nicholas crept up silently beside me. He looked worried as well. Mum and Dennis were always rowing, always fighting, always slapping each other and breaking the crockery. It was a natural part of everyday life and we were pretty immune to it. But somehow this felt different. I ran silently away from the landing and into the bathroom, which looked out over the back. Nicholas followed me, peering over my shoulder. It was dark, but the garden was lit up by the light from the house. Nobody had bothered to draw the curtains.

The shed door was open. Surely he wasn't going to sleep in there? No. He lumbered out, one hand pushing the long greasy hair out of his eyes; the other dangling by his side, holding something with a thick wedge at one end. I screwed up my eyes, trying to make out what it was. As he came closer, the object swung into focus – he was carrying the axe he used for chopping up firewood. My heart gave a violent thud as he swung the axe into his right hand and pulled it up behind him.

'I'm gonna get you, bitch.' He walked back into the house.

Nicholas and I stared, wide-eyed, at one another as we heard the sickening sound of an axe chewing into wood.

We ran back out to the landing. I could hear pottery smashing in the front room. My mother would never merely shout if she could punctuate it with a smashed cup or ornament, and she was quite fearless. Then there was a deep cracking sound as the table split. God, were they going to leave us anything in one piece? The screaming intensified and I could hear our neighbours banging on the wall.

Suddenly there was an enormous crack and the sound of wood splintering.

'*Amore di dio*, Dennis. *Stop* it.' A new note had entered Mum's voice, one we hadn't heard before. I recognised pure rank fear. Dennis had slipped out of his usual persona into something far darker. It was as if he were possessed.

'I'm going to stop them.' I looked calmly at Nicholas. 'Wait here.'

'Don't be stupid. He'll kill you. He's gone totally mad.'

'It'll be all right. I've got to help Mum.'

He grabbed my arm but I knew he wouldn't hold me back. I shook off his hand and ran quietly down the stairs, jumping over the step where the carpet was frayed.

They were in the front room, the door pulled nearly shut. My heart thudding in my chest, I peered round the door. With a tingle down my spine, I felt a huge strength enter me and I went into warrior mode. My only concern was to get my mother out of that room, and I decided I would be like Purdy in *The New Avengers*.

It was a large room, knocked through from two smaller ones. The dayglo orange and brown patterned carpet was littered with smashed ornaments. Mum was standing, backed against the hatch to the kitchen, fending Dennis off with a chair. He looked completely crazed, taking wild swings at her with the axe. The alcohol was making him clumsy, but there was no doubt: he was going to kill her.

'Mum!' I couldn't help it. The scream burst out of me and she turned, sheer horror etched on her face, to the door. Dennis swung round too and for a second we all stood, as if freeze-framed. Then he lurched towards the door, towards me. I could see Mum standing frozen, her black hair thick like a helmet, her mouth red, her eyes shining with terror. I could smell Dennis – a thick heavy mix of sweat, whisky and a strange scent of burning rubber (like when the Hoover ring goes). I instinctively blinked as he hefted up the axe, but strangely felt absolutely no compulsion to move. I stood, four-square, staring straight into his face. For what must have been seconds, but felt like hours, we just stared at each other. He was breathing heavily through his mouth. Then he let the axe fall to his side.

'It's all right, sweetheart,' he slurred. 'Go back to bed. Your mother and me, we're just having a bit of a talk.'

'No!' I screamed, and started trying to jam open the door. It jarred into his leg and he frowned, pushing it back against me, trying to shut me out. But however much he tried, it wouldn't close properly – fear and fury were giving me strength far beyond my years and usual powers.

I had to get to my mother. I had to protect her. I kicked and rammed the door with all my might, but Dennis kept pushing the door shut. The other side of the door, Dennis did the same and we glared at each other through the crack. When I think back on it, the image that springs to mind is that moment in the film *The Shining* when Jack Nicholson is at the door with an axe – it was almost the same, and Dennis had exactly that demented evil look in his eyes. For a second I thought that I had pushed it too far – that I, too, was going to die.

But then time seemed to judder to a halt. I felt this strange feeling wash over me, as if someone were wrapping me in protection, cuddling me into a warm rug and holding me in safe, strong arms. A surge of total unconditional love swept over me – it was indescribable. I felt totally serene, totally calm. Glancing over Dennis's head I could see my mother, squeezing herself through the hatch to the kitchen. I knew that, if I could only keep Dennis here for a little longer, she could get away.

– Don't worry. You'll do it. I'll help you.

Lucy's voice sounded clear and calm in my head, and in that moment I knew it would be all right.

The love and peace washed through me like a big soft wave and I gazed deep into Dennis's bloodshot eyes. Instead of the fear and hate I'd had before, I now felt nothing but total love for this man, this poor crazy irrational being. He wasn't bad, just drunk, and taken over by feelings of rage and frustration; love and hate mingled together. He was a simple man, out of his depth. I couldn't believe how I could feel such love; such pure beautiful love – despite everything he had done, despite everything I knew he would revert to doing. He stared back, totally and utterly mesmerised, held by my eyes, and I could see confusion reflected in him. I was transmitting pure love, acceptance and peace to him and it held him for just long enough for my mother to clamber through the hatch, race through the kitchen and join me in the hall. She glanced at me and I nodded.

Lucy's voice echoed in my head.

– Go now. Go quickly.

I stopped pushing against the door and it slammed shut. Mum frantically turned the key and, luckily, it slid locked.

The moment of peace had passed; time speeded up once more.

'Get out. Run next door,' Mum yelled. Nicholas was pounding down the stairs and all three of us raced, Nicholas and I still in our nightclothes, to our next-door neighbours – whose door was wide open. The door slammed shut behind us and we stood, panting, in the hallway. As the blood stopped pounding in my ears, I could hear two sounds, two horrible sounds. One came from several streets away – police sirens, wailing closer and closer. The other came through the thin walls to the house next door – the sound of Dennis smashing what was left of our home. There was absolutely no doubt in my mind. This time, Lucy had saved *all* our lives.

The police took Dennis away and he was put in prison for several months. The next morning we went home, shaken, to salvage what was left of our house. It was around this time that I started having panic attacks. My nerves had been bad for years – hardly surprising, given the level of fear in our house. I would jump at the slightest thing and suffered from chronic insomnia. Again, it wasn't really surprising – going to sleep in our house was a dangerous undertaking. I never knew if I'd be woken by screaming and yelling from humans or scratching and whispering from spirits. Although most of my abuse had happened during the day when Mum was out at work, it also wasn't unknown for a new lodger to try my door – which I always kept firmly locked.

The axe incident curbed Mum's mania. We had come so close to being axed to death that it brought her to her senses a bit. She focused more on us and, for a short while at least, we became more normal. She brought us little surprise presents and made an effort to cook more. Nicholas and I became withdrawn. For a while we even declared a ceasefire on our hostilities – we had no energy to fight.

Gradually though, life returned to normal. Nicholas and I started sniping and then fighting again. Mum started shouting. A new lodger came and I checked the locks on my bedroom door. However, it wasn't all bleak. When I think back, I'm amazed that I carried on life pretty much as normal. I went to school, I did the tarot, I played music and watched TV. I prayed a lot as well – but not really in any kind of pious way. In fact, it was about this time that I started consciously practising cosmic ordering (though of course it wasn't called that then).

At this time I wanted a Chopper more than anything in the entire world. They were the 'It' bikes of 1976. I knew exactly the one I wanted, bright gleaming red. I imagined that bike in every detail; I could feel myself sitting on it; feel the breeze blowing through my hair as I flew down the hill, fast as the wind.

Logically, I knew Mum couldn't afford to buy me a bike. She was still working night and day and, without Dennis's wages, money was once again incredibly tight. I also knew that it would upset her if she knew how much I wanted it – so I never said a word. I never once let on how intensely I craved that bike.

Instead I would kneel down by my bed and pray passionately, endlessly, incredibly eloquently, to God. I believed totally in magic and knew that, if I wished and prayed hard enough, I could bring that bike out of my imagination and into firm tangible reality. One day I went out into the garden and picked a dandelion. Gently blowing the seeds, I watched them floating away on the light breeze. In my mind's eye I visualised them floating up to heaven, each and every seed carrying my wish for that bike.

'Give me a Chopper. Send me a Chopper.' I repeated it over and over again, almost in a trance, blowing the seeds, watching them meander away on the wind, visualising them as divine messengers each carrying my plea.

Then I felt something happen. I can't describe it, but it was as if suddenly the final piece of the jigsaw fell into place with a click, and I knew, I just knew, that my wish would come true.

The logical, rational part of my brain realised that it couldn't possibly happen. Yet one morning I woke up and there, at the end of my bed, it was – my bike. It was bright red, exactly the one I had wanted. A shiver ran down my spine. I had brought that bike into existence by the very power of my thoughts, of my intent, of my desire.

I found out later that Mum managed it by paying a tiny amount a week to a catalogue. But how had she known I wanted it; and that I wanted that one in particular? It was a clear case of asking, and the universe finding a way to make it happen.

I called that bike Red Rum, after the racehorse, and it was one of the happiest memories from my childhood. It wasn't just a bike; it became, in my mind, a horse, my faithful steed, something animate, something alive. It changed my life, giving me a blissful sense of freedom and also fuelling my imagination. It equally sealed my total belief in magic. Of course, 'Redrum' was the phrase repeated over and over by Danny, the boy in *The Shining*. He also writes it on the mirror and, seen backwards, it spells out Murder. Looking back, it's a macabre connection with the night of the axe. We were so very nearly murdered.

I couldn't help but imbue the things I loved with personality and power. I had the same feeling about my skateboard, which I also got at about this time. Both bike and board gave me confidence, speed and agility. I could whizz myself out of trouble, disappear in a whisper. Funnily enough, the bike and the board gave me an 'in' with the local kids. I used to ride or skate to Pitshanger Hill, a spot where loads of other skateboarders hung out. For the first time in my life, I wasn't seen as weird or odd. I was just another kid on a board. Another crazy kid who would make mad nollies or blowouts, pivots and plants, kickflips and grinds.

Dennis eventually came out of prison and wanted to come back home, but Mum wouldn't have it. The axe incident had shaken her too much, and she refused to answer his phone calls. She used to put a pillow over the phone as it rang and rang and ring. Finally, reluctantly, Dennis accepted it was over and they divorced. I remember being hugely relieved. At last, for once, Mum was being sensible, being a grown-up. I didn't imagine for one moment that she would remain single – it simply wasn't in her nature. But surely she couldn't possibly find anyone who could be as mad as Dennis. Could she?

9

Don't Do That, Please Stop It

Looking back, I was in a very traumatised place after Dennis. I became angry at the slightest thing and wildly defensive. I still couldn't sleep and Mum took me to the doctor, who prescribed Mogadon and Valium to calm me down. Amazingly, nobody suggested I see a counsellor or therapist. With hindsight I was probably suffering from post-traumatic stress disorder but of course it wasn't recognised then. You simply got on with it, coped the best you could. The drugs helped me sleep, but I didn't always dare take them at night – I was too scared of being caught unawares. The lock on my door had broken and Mum refused to fix it.

'Why you need a lock on your door anyway?' she asked.

'For privacy.'

'Eh, you're only a kid. You don't need privacy.'

But I did. I really did. I'd lie in bed and hear the creak of the stair. I'd see the door inch open. I'd hear the breathing of the new lodger – a man with a weak chin and a flat accent.

'You're a pretty girl, Michèle.'

I didn't say anything, just buried myself further under the covers, silently begging him to go away.

As an adult, I have often asked myself why? Why me? At the time of course, I did not know that once a child is sexually abused, he or she begins to accept it as normal. I didn't know that many men who would reel in horror at the thought of being described as abusers are nevertheless capable of this grotesque act. I didn't know that alcohol and opportunity are often the lethal ingredients that put an innocent child at risk. So 'why me?' begins to turn into 'of course me!' I was left alone with a string of men my mother – a terrible chooser of men – had in the house. There was no one to stop them and no one to tell me that I should complain.

Recently, in an attempt to understand my experience, I researched the subject thoroughly. I learnt that children who have been abused experience something similar to brainwashing and go into a state of 'chronic docile acceptance' of the abuse. For them it appears 'normal'. Tragically, as a result, they become easy pickings. The long term effects include attempted suicide, post-traumatic stress and uncontrollable anger. Victims often develop drink or drug dependencies, panic attacks and can be prone to self harm. A tough legacy indeed.

I seemed, as always, to attract the unwelcome attention of pretty well every man I met. In fact, the older I got, the worse it became – or maybe it's just that I remember more about it.

The abuse I experienced was a living nightmare, but even

as a child, I was under no illusions about these lodgers – they wanted my body and only my body. However, Nicholas messed with my mind as well as threatening me physically – and that was heart-rending. We had a real love/hate relationship. Sometimes he behaved like a proper brother; often he didn't. We stuck together a bit more after the axe incident, but not for long. We both felt so unsafe and so angry. We had lost our father, who had protected us from our mother's lack of boundaries. It was still a volatile and violent relationship though – inevitable really as Nicholas and I were both pretty unbalanced by now. I would wind him up, but he was becoming increasingly brutal.

Amazingly, my mother actually left me alone with Nicholas while she went to Italy for three weeks. I was about ten or eleven at the time. Did she really have no idea what was going on? I don't think she did. She was so wrapped up in everyday survival. My only memory of those three weeks is a feeling of fear so intense it's seared in my brain. Nicholas told me over and over again that his dream was to grow up and become so famous that he'd be able to have the luxury of ignoring me. He used to say: 'One day I'm going to be a big musician and you'll come backstage and I'm going to say to the bouncers, "Take her away, she's not allowed in here."' But he didn't ignore me. Not then.

One afternoon we were having a petty row. I could never give in, even if I was really scared. I taunted him until he chased me and finally cornered me in the hall. My face was pressed into the cream-patterned wallpaper and he said, clearly and precisely:

'I'm going to smash your brains out into this wall. I'm going to murder you and then I will go to prison and learn to play guitar.' He held me there for a split second, weighing up whether he should do it. Then he let me go. I knew that, on that occasion, he meant absolutely every word. Something in his eyes terrified me and it turned out to be a terrible foreboding.

As always, I fell back on other 'friends'. Lucy was still around, but mainly I spent the unrelenting summer of 1977 with Elvis. Elvis was God. Elvis made me feel safe. I loved him, every last bit of him, from his white-sequined jumpsuit to his black leather comeback cat-suit. *Blue Hawaii* totally mesmerised me. Eating bread and jam sandwiches, wearing my mismatched pyjamas, I would wriggle up as close to the screen as I could before it began to blur. If I could have clambered inside the TV and crawled into Elvis's arms, I would have been in heaven.

Why Elvis? Well, he was just how I figured all people should be. He was sensitive. If a girl was upset, he noticed; he cared. If a girl was spoiled or silly, he didn't hold it against her. He overlooked people's shortcomings and saw the good in everyone. Elvis could teach an unruly brat to become a real good person and, being an unruly brat myself, that was something I could relate to. He was the outsider who made good, and I could relate to that too. Nobody liked Elvis at the beginning of his films – he was the rebel without any friends. But, by the end of the film, absolutely everyone loved and accepted him. This was the dream I clung to, that one day my life might turn out like an Elvis film. I was an outsider too and all I really wanted was to be loved; to be seen to be a good person. I relied on Elvis to show me the way, and so I soaked up every frame of film. It brought me to life and taught me values that became instantly imbedded deep in my psyche.

Curled up in front of the telly I was normal. Elvis was the father I had loved and lost. Watching his films soothed me and they taught me really valuable lessons in how to relate to other people. Most of all I loved his goodness. The way he helped people and stood up for what was right. When I wasn't watching his films, I played his records on the tiny record player in my boxroom bedroom. I felt sure that we would meet one day and that, when we did, he would know me immediately. Elvis would be my friend. Elvis would understand me. He would look at me with his kind eyes and make it all better. He would know what to do. He was the one true constant in my life. Of course, looking back, the other thing that was interesting was that, just like me, Elvis had a twin who had died at birth. He had his own Lucy.

My personality, at eleven, wasn't any easier. I was still a fighter, a rebel and a free spirit who hated injustice. I was also, to be honest, incredibly irritating. I was far too intense. I would argue a point until I wore people down. That summer, of course, it was all about Elvis and I'd badger the kids in the park:

'Don't I look like Elvis?'

'No.'

'Yes I do!'

'You don't look anything like Elvis. Anyway, Elvis is a boy.'

'Look at my profile. I have the same profile as Elvis.' I'd turn my head to the side and tilt up my chin. 'In fact, if you look closely, I've got the same hairline and nose.' I pushed my hair up and thrust my face towards them. This would go on and on, until finally they would cave in, exhausted by the passion of my belief:

'Yeah, yeah, you look like Elvis.'

Satisfied, I would at last turn away. I thought I looked great. I was chunky and strong, with longish length hair, greased back. I wore a PVC 'leather' jacket with a tiger on the back and a gold cross around my neck. I desperately wanted to be popular, to be liked – but I still hadn't learned to keep quiet about the palm reading, the tarot, the spirits. I was never able to figure out why it didn't work, why I was always left out.

I remember waking up one Sunday morning excited about going to the park. It was 16 August 1977. I stretched lazily and clicked on my football-shaped radio. Then I leaned back and lay on my bed pondering if anyone would be around today. The strange stillness of Sundays struck me as I wriggled out of the orange nylon eiderdown I was entangled in. Elvis's '*Way Down*' was playing and I hummed along, relishing the warm feeling his voice always gave me. What a great way to start the day – with an Elvis song. Then my pleasure turned to horror with a stark announcement:

'The King is dead. Elvis died in the early hours of this morning . . .'

A chill flashed down my spine and I went completely numb. I ignored the news, flicked off the radio and got up. I put on my tatty flared jeans and went straight out of the house. As I walked to the park, I felt totally cut off and detached. When I look back, I can see it was exactly the same way that I'd reacted to my father's death. I refused to allow myself to feel any emotion; it was simply too painful. While other people would cry and sob and scream, I would retreat deep inside myself. There is a knack to it – you simply slam up a wall all around your feelings. Nothing can get out, nothing can come in. The more I've spoken to people who have been through childhood abuse and trauma, the more common I've realised it is to erect these barriers, to hide behind these walls. Unfortunately, there is usually a chink somewhere in the wall. Somewhere that the pain can seep through.

By the end of that summer the local kids had taken to hanging around one of the chippies. One day, as I came out of the chip shop with a portion of vinegar-drenched chips, I heard what I could only describe as Elvis singing. My mouth dropped open. I couldn't believe my ears. But there he was, a young guy singing a perfect impersonation of Elvis. He was good-looking with a subtle black quiff. He was also quite a lot older than the usual gang that hung out there. He told us he had won a competition and sung on the radio. I could easily believe it: even his accent sounded American.

We didn't question why he wanted to hang out with us, despite being so much older. We just liked having him around. In the evenings, he'd sing to us and I found him a comforting familiar figure. OK, he wasn't really Elvis, but he was 'next-best Elvis' and he filled the empty slot in my heart where true Elvis had always lived. I have to admit I was a bit jealous as well, as I'd been quietly deciding my future career lay in being an Elvis impersonator. After all, there was a gap in the market, wasn't there? But this guy obviously had a better chance of the job. In my heart of hearts, I knew I wasn't halfway as convincing as he was. OK, so my brother called me 'Deke' (a reference to Deke Rivers in *Loving You*), but really it was nothing about my staggering resemblance to the King, and all about winding me up as I was a butch little loud-mouth who couldn't sing.

One day I was kicking around as usual when next-best Elvis strolled by and asked me if I fancied a walk. I was over the moon and blushed vivid red. But I tried to act cool: 'Yeah sure, where do you want to go?' Walking up the road we must have looked an odd couple. I was a short stocky tomboy with scruffy hair, flared dirty jeans and a baggy red top. He was a smartly dressed, clean-shaven, rather pretty Elvis look-alike.

He sang to me as we walked along the road and I felt great. He seemed so different to all the other lads. Not only was he singing Elvis songs and had asked me to go for a walk, but he seemed incredibly cultured and intelligent.

Wandering along in the morbid summer heat, traffic trundling past at speed, we could have been in Memphis. I was in heaven. I felt safe, proud, accepted – and oh so cool. It was all going to turn out OK after all. Next-best Elvis was good enough for me. Another wish had been granted.

We crossed the road carefully and walked around the block a few times, circling the barren patch of trees we called the woods. He chatted about his plans and his future; he talked about nature and wanted to show me the birds that nested in the woods. I was a bit worried as a bunch of the tough boys regularly used to go there to kill pigeons and cook them over rough campfires. I hated what they did; it seemed so cruel and sinister. But he reassured me that no one would be there. He was right. We were totally alone.

Glancing around, he suddenly grabbed my hand. I was surprised that his hand was strangely small, the fingers narrow and thin. I remember my mother saying that a small hand on a man was a sign of weakness. But I didn't care. My stomach flipped over – this was like dating Elvis. How lucky was I? The age gap didn't matter – after all, there was a big age gap between Elvis and Priscilla, wasn't there? I could feel Lucy tugging at me, trying to get my attention, but I pushed her aside. This was *my* adventure. I didn't want her advice.

– *Get away. I don't like this.*
– *Back off, Lucy. Don't be such a stick-in-the-mud. Don't you want me to have some fun?*

She went quiet then, but I could tell she wasn't happy. I could almost imagine her rolling her eyes and turning away, hacked off with me.

As we got deeper in the woods he told me he had a special hiding place that was private and that he wanted to show me something. Even then I didn't get it. I'd been in so many situations with men who'd abused me sexually, but still I didn't realise what was going on. It sounds naïve, but it truly didn't cross my mind that his intentions were anything other than pure. How could they be otherwise? After all, he was like me, aspiring to be as Elvis was; to mirror his kindness and goodness, right?

We stumbled into a clearing, and he told me in his sweet lilting voice that he wanted to show me how to make a man happy.

'It's a good thing, sweetheart. It'll make your future bright and good.'

I frowned, but he went on, saying that learning such things was an honour. Above all, it was a secret. At this point a sense of inevitability and resignation took over. I had been here before, many, *many* times.

He unzipped his flies and pulled himself out. I stared at his penis with a blank expression. I started to bring down the walls, to go to my other place, but I'd been caught out. I'd left it too late to blank myself off completely. He took my hand and started moving it up and down his penis, telling me how good it was, telling me I was very good. All in that Elvis drawl.

'Now I want to show you something very important.' I felt the numbness descend again.

He sat me down on a tree stump and stood in front of me playing with himself, his hand rubbing up and down.

'Now just open your mouth and suck it like a lollipop,' he said. 'Everyone has to learn this, but it has to be our secret.'

I was deeply aware that this was not teaching me anything new at all. It was simply something horribly familiar and tedious. I didn't protest, though; I didn't say a word. Abused children usually don't. The shame and guilt and fear all become mixed up in a filthy tangled knot, one that sticks in your throat and prevents you saying anything. What would you say? There aren't words for describing things that tear you apart, body and soul.

'Hmmmmmmmmm, baby, that was good,' he said in his fake Elvis accent. 'Hey, I want you to take my younger brother out for a walk tomorrow, yeah? Do the same stuff, yeah? I'm sure you'll both get on just fine. Come on, we've gotta go now: I'm late for work.'

As soon as we left the woods he took off without a second glance. The emptiness and darkness streamed within me as I stumbled home. It wasn't so much about what had happened, but that it was the end of a dream. Things could have been so different, but he was just the same as the others and I was nothing. When I got home, I packed away all my Elvis records and tore down the posters from my walls.

– *OK, Lucy. You were right and I was wrong.*

I waited for her to say 'Told you so', but she didn't. Instead I felt her presence, silent but loving, gently stroking my face.

I felt so angry, so very angry. Not with him, though, but with me. I was so worthless. Once again I was the odd one out, the one who didn't have normal relationships. All I wanted was for someone to see me and like me for what I was, not for what I could give them in the way of sex.

In my young mind I muddled it all up with cosmic ordering, with creating your own reality. I had cosmically ordered my bike, Red Rum, and in some weird way I had summoned up next-best Elvis too. Elvis was dead and, through the power of my will, I believed I had manifested the next best thing. Except, of course, there wasn't a next best thing. I took the lesson out of this to be that Elvis truly was dead and I gave up all ambitions of being an Elvis impersonator.

Instead I started to have more and more sexual experiences. At first I didn't seek them out, at least not consciously – but after a while it did become intentional. I think in one way I was trying to punish myself, but in another it was a way of getting attention, and also a way of having control. It was a bit like being anorexic – I was controlling my body and also controlling how other people reacted. I would do anything anyone wanted sexually, except penetration – so I kept control. Then again, on some level, I think I was always hoping that a time would come when it would be different. When someone would say 'no'. When someone would just want to be with me without touching me or having me touch them. When it would be innocent. But it was hopeless. I seemed to give out the message in clear waves – 'Here, have me! I'm easy!'

It was fifteen years before I was able to listen to Elvis again. It was far more traumatic than all the other incidences of abuse because I had gone into it willingly, trustingly. I had really thought this was going to be different. It wasn't – and the little bit of trust and faith that remained in me was slashed to shreds.

But it didn't stop me hanging out with older kids. I found I got on better with them than with kids my own age. They weren't so judgmental somehow. At one point I started writing love letters to a young guy called Alan. He was about seventeen and, funnily enough, he fancied Mum. I separated sex and romance totally, and much of that time – both at school and at home – was spent gazing out of the window, fantasising about romance and love. I had massive crushes on both men and women, both people I knew and people on television and radio. I knew that it was 'normal' for girls to be attracted to boys so I tried very hard to find boys to fancy. Alan seemed ideal.

I used to lie in my room and conjure up fantasies of being with him, just hanging out, holding hands, chatting, sharing our dreams of the future. In my mind he was a good old-fashioned boy who was special and kind. Without realising it, I was slipping into the same mistake as with next-best Elvis.

Then, to my absolute and total delight, he made me up a tape – of his favourite songs interspersed with little comments, saying nice things about me. I was over the moon. He liked me, respected me. I was quite sure, quite convinced, that he was a million miles away from the grown men who abused me and the horrible Elvis look-alike. Just before my twelfth birthday Alan passed his driving test and offered to take me for a ride.

We drove along, chatting and listening to music from an old cassette player on the back seat. I felt very grown-up and very excited. Then he pulled over into a lay-by near some woods.

'How about you get into the back seat now?'

'Why?'

'Because it would be nice.'

'But I'm happy here.'

His tone changed. 'Get into the back seat. Now.'

I did as he said, moving the cassette player on to the magazine rack, feeling very uneasy. He jammed himself in beside me and slammed the door. The next thing I knew he was mashing his face into mine, squashing his lips against mine, ramming his tongue into my mouth. It hurt and I drew back, but he grabbed my top and started ripping it off. His hand plunged down my knickers and he was poking around, rubbing and pushing his fingers into me.

'No. Alan, no! Stop it. You're hurting me.' I was so shocked and upset. I really didn't think he was like that. It was far more devastating and I felt far more violated by him than by all the men who had been obvious about what they wanted. With the older men, the adults, there was something inevitable about it. This was just what men did. But Alan was only seventeen. I'd had a romantic vision of him, and he'd ripped it apart. Looking back, it was interesting that this was the first time I'd said 'no'. I was simply so shocked, so horrified. I had got it drastically wrong once again.

He came to his senses and pulled away his hand, nervously patting my shirt as if he could mend the rip. Then he sat panting, looking down at his hands in his lap:

'I'm sorry.'

'It's OK. Can you take me back now?'

'Sure.'

We got back into the front seats and he drove off. He was so nervous that he hit the island in the middle of the deserted road, nearly turning the car over. I never saw him again.

When I got home I felt pretty sick. Why couldn't men just like me? But it seemed that, having got to eleven, I was fair game. I had thought there was a difference between the people who were the 'abusers' and just used me for sex, and people like Alan, who I had thought was a proper person, who liked me for being me. But it seemed there was no difference at all. They were all the same.

I was obviously getting a reputation as soon afterwards I bumped into an older guy in the park who worked with Alan. He pulled me into the bushes and started unzipping his flies. I had a horrible sinking feeling: he was going to rape me and there would be nothing I could do. No way was I strong enough to fend him off, and if he succeeded, I would be badly hurt. But Lucy didn't seem too worried.

– *It's OK. He's not a bad guy. Just tell him no. You'll be OK.*

'No. Please. I don't want to. I'm only eleven.' I stared up into his eyes and saw the uncertainty. 'Someone would see anyhow. You'd get sent to prison.'

He seemed to make a decision in his head and slowly zipped up his trousers. He gave me a little push, and I ran off. Lucy got it right again.

It's strange, but being sexually abused felt like the only time I was ever seen. The only time anyone really saw me was when I was pleasing them. Even if it lasted just ten minutes, it was a focus; it was the only time anyone ever looked me straight in the eyes. It did untold damage to my psyche, though, and my panic attacks and insomnia were getting worse. Mum took me back to the doctor who simply upped my doses of Valium and Mogadon. He did ask why I was in such a state, and Mum said our home life had been difficult, that I hadn't got on with my stepfather. He nodded sympathetically – he had heard all about Dennis. What he didn't know was that my next stepfather was going to be even more dangerous.

10

Sympathy for the Devil

My mother met her third husband, Russell, on a train coming back from Heathrow. I wasn't that surprised. She struck up conversations with everyone and anyone. If she was on a train platform and there was someone way down the other end, she would make her way towards them, sit down and start chatting. Once she even cornered Judi Dench on a plane. I can just imagine that encounter. Mum would have had no concept of giving a famous person space. She would have raced right up: 'Hello, darling! I think you're fantastic. I love your films and I watch you on TV . . .' And so on. Bless her, Judi was charming to my mother and they got chatting, about life, where they lived and, above all, their children. It turned out that Nick and Judi's daughter shared the same birthday. Every time I see Dame Judi on the television I remember her kindness to my mother.

Even at fifty, Mum still had that disarming child-like charm that made her irresistible – to everyone, but particularly to men. Russell was much younger than her – about thirty-four when they met. He was a plane engineer at Heathrow and had one leg shorter than the other from a motorbike accident. He was a good-looking man with thick brown hair, a full mouth and slightly protruding eyes, but there was always something odd about him. I had a bad feeling about Russell from the word go, and every last bit of my intuition was screaming for her to walk away from this one.

She fell hook, line and sinker for Russell. It was strange, but her intuition, her powers, totally abandoned her when it came to men. But she told me later on that they had fantastic sex – quite kinky and adventurous. It was the first time in her life that sex had been really satisfactory for her and I think she fell in lust more than love. Although she would treat me like an adult in so many things, she wouldn't listen to my advice. Opinionated as ever, we used to fight all the time. I tried to warn her, reminding her about Dennis, about how badly wrong that had gone. I asked what Dad would have thought, but she simply said he would have wanted her to be happy.

As with all her relationships, this one escalated quickly. They were married within weeks and Russell moved in. Lucy and I watched him bringing in his things.

– *What are those magazines?*
– *Pornography. Dirty pictures.*
– *Oh, not again. Do you think he's going to want me to do things to him?*
– *No. I don't think so. Not this one.*

The magazines – an extensive collection of porn – went up in the loft. Mum wasn't keen on porn, but Russell was encouraging her to be more wild and adventurous and she didn't complain about them. Then I watched him bring in his guitar and I was pretty excited about that. He had been in the Air Force at one time and was obsessed with planes, trains and cars. Over the next few months he accumulated a load of junk cars and our back garden (which wasn't much to begin with) began to resemble a junkyard. It drove Mum mad.

At the beginning, it was actually OK. Much to my surprise, he didn't want to molest me. It's a funny thing, but the men she married seemed to be pretty much the only ones who didn't harm me sexually. In fact, we had some good fun. He had long nails and would sit and play the guitar for hours, though I have to say I found that pretty boring. His absolute pride and joy was his brown and white Mini Clubman car and sometimes he'd take us all into the West End to the cinema. I loved it.

He and Mum were pretty happy – or so it seemed. They went off to France together, leaving me and Nicholas alone again. Needless to say, I wasn't happy about that. Our usual warfare intensified, but I was becoming bigger and stronger now and Nicholas couldn't intimidate me quite so much.

But the honeymoon period didn't last that long and Russell swiftly became moody and uncommunicative. It turned out he had a history of mental illness (something he'd conveniently forgotten to mention before the wedding), and he could also turn from moody to violently angry in seconds. When he lost his temper the veins in the side of his head would bulge and throb.

One day we all went fishing by the canal. I hadn't wanted to go, but Mum had insisted it would be nice for us to go out as a family. He and Mum were walking in front, hand in hand; Nicholas followed and I was lagging behind, kicking stones.

'Hey, keep up.' Russell glared at me.

I ignored him and bent down to pick up a stone.

The next thing I knew he had hauled me up – one hand was grabbing my shoulder, shaking me; the other was jabbing a finger in my face.

'Keep up, you stupid brat!' He shook me like a terrier shaking a rat.

'Hey, leave her alone!' Mum weighed in. For all her faults, she was always very loyal to me, and if Russell had a go at me or made any negative comment about me, she would turn and attack him. This gave me huge comfort; it made me feel that, despite everything, she still loved me.

Little things like this started mounting up, creating an atmosphere of unease and fear. What would set Russell off next time?

One day I was being unusually helpful, clearing a backlog of ironing in one of the upstairs bedrooms. I don't know why, but something must have distracted me and I left the iron, face-down, on the carpet. The next thing I heard was

Mum racing up the stairs and the horrible smell of burning wool. She was furious – the carpet was new and the room had only recently been redecorated. She screamed and yelled. I screamed and yelled. Then we both went our separate ways. But when Russell came in, he went berserk:

'You stupid little bitch! How could you be so bloody stupid?' He started smashing up the house as Mum and I cowered by the front door. It was like the night of the axe and Dennis all over again. Russell tossed the glassware out of the cabinets and threw the furniture around. He even ripped the electric plugs out of the walls. Mum and I ran out the door and down the road to one of Mum's friends. When we went back, the place looked like a tornado had hit it. Most of our home went in a skip – it wasn't even salvageable.

They started rowing more and more, and much of the tension in their relationship was probably down to me. I had turned from a troubled child into a nightmare from hell. In fact, my mother thought I was, quite literally, possessed.

All the local kids loved horror films and were avid fans, often sneaking into films like *The Omen* when they were supposed to be seeing *Star Wars*. It was pretty easy in a multi-screen cinema. They would buy a ticket for a U- or A- rated film and then, when the film had started and the lights had gone down, sneak down the corridor one by one and slide into the back rows of the darkened cinema to see the X-rated film. They never invited me to join in, but one day I contrived to bump into them and they couldn't avoid me. They were off to see a double-bill of *The Exorcist* films and I was desperate to see them too.

'If you don't let me come in with you, I'll grass you up,' I said. 'I'll follow you and tell the cinema people what you're doing.'

They looked at one another doubtfully.

'Of course,' I paused, smiling sweetly, 'If you let me come with you, you can all come back to mine afterwards.'

That clinched it. They knew there were no rules in my house and one of the older boys wanted to fool about with his girlfriend. I was in.

The film absolutely terrified me. Unlike the others in our group, I had had direct experience of the supernatural and the demonic. I knew, from my own bitter experience, how easily spirits can get out of control. I also felt incredibly lucky that nothing worse had happened to me, although I remembered with a shudder all the scratching and scrabbling and the occasions when I had even felt my bed shaking. I really wanted to slope off on my own, to digest what I'd seen, but a promise was a promise. So we all traipsed back to our house and came in to find Mum doing one of her periodic cleansing routines. While other mothers used Jif and tap water, my mother went in for full-on spiritual cleansing and used *bona fide* holy water. We watched her going round the kitchen flicking the water in all the corners.

'I bless this house. Evil be gone,' she said, her fingers

flying out. A couple of drops landed on me and, just for a joke, I clasped my hand to my arm.

'It burns! It burns! Aaghh, what is that? It burns!' I said it in the possessed voice of the girl from the film. I thought it was hilarious, but of course Mum hadn't seen the film and she didn't get the joke at all. Instead, she completely freaked.

'She is possessed! She has evil in her!' she shrieked and poured the entire rest of the bottle all over my head. 'Something has possessed my Michèle! Be gone, Satan! Leave the child!'

On she went, screaming and shouting and yelling curses at the devil. I just stood there, calmly, waiting for her to quieten down, but the others were petrified and ran screaming from the house, convinced that my mother was entirely mad and certainly possessed by the devil herself. I glared at Mum and then went flying after them, trying to calm them down, to tell them that she was really OK, just a bit crazy. I could see what would happen. Once again, kids would turn away from me because of my mother. I deeply resented the fact she wasn't normal and that other kids thought our family completely mad.

After that, our house swiftly turned into hell. Mum wouldn't drop the idea that I was possessed and Russell would pick fights with me over the smallest thing. Pretty soon I had become the scapegoat for everything that went wrong, and he stopped calling me by my name and referred to me as 'The Thing' or 'The Freak'.

This cut me deeply because I felt it was true. I thought I was a 'thing'; I was a 'freak'. I figured he was just telling the truth. I felt I was totally and utterly worthless, an abomination. I felt totally unlovable, totally unattractive, totally useless. By now I had developed a full-on eating disorder too (something very common in abused children). I wouldn't eat for ages, and then would binge on chips or chocolate. It was as if I were punishing my body with food.

I didn't take it lying down though. I was always winding Russell up. Once I nicked his beloved Air-Force uniform and turned it into a punk jacket, which didn't go down remotely well. Sometimes Mum would turn on me herself, but more often she would try to defend me and they would have howling, violent rows. Of course he could never even think of winning against my mother so he turned his anger and hatred towards me.

School wasn't much better. By now I'd left primary school and was at Twyford High. At first, I thought I'd reinvent myself, become good, do my best. But it didn't last long. I had a reputation as a tough nut and I suppose I gave them what they expected, what they seemed to want.

One good thing was that about this time I started making a few friends. I had toughened up over the years and was now a fully fledged 'bad girl', and so I hung out with the other bad girls. Lots of them were much older than me and had left school, or were simply bunking off all the time.

One I remember in particular was a girl called Jennifer.

The moment I saw Jennifer I felt connected to her. She was always boasting about sleeping with men, older men. She didn't seem to feel any shame or embarrassment about it. I admired her self-confidence, her assured air. I also thought she was very gorgeous. I started spending a lot of time around at her house in Harlesden, frequently staying over. Russell was still being vicious to me and it was heaven not to have to endure his taunts and tempers. Jennifer's parents both worked and weren't there much – we had the place to ourselves.

We'd lie in her bed talking about kids at school, about who we fancied, who we didn't. Jennifer was dismissive – she said she only fancied older men. But, to my intense surprise, she also said she fancied me. I was over the moon. I had felt some chemistry between us, but hadn't quite believed it as Jennifer was always talking about men. She gazed at me very intensely and the next thing I knew we were kissing.

It was fantastic. I felt a huge surge of love for her, a deep emotional attachment. At last everything seemed to make sense. I loved girls.

But then it turned rough. Jennifer was a damaged soul, very wild, very violent. Loving her was not a gentle initi-ation, but yet more violence. That night with Jennifer I finally lost my virginity in the technical sense. She was very rough, ripping my pyjamas, tearing at me. I actually felt my hymen break and there was quite a lot of blood. I was hugely shocked, but I let her carry on as I preferred it to having boys or men touch me. I was twelve.

Jennifer got me into some dangerous situations too. One day an older, bearded guy came round to her house and she introduced me. She was smiling and flirting with him and I thought I ought to go. But suddenly, she whirled round and said, 'I've got to go out. Michèle, you'll look after him, won't you?' Without a backwards glance, she grabbed her coat and vanished out the door.

The man smiled at me. 'How about we go for a walk? It's a fabulous day.'

I didn't want to go, but felt I had to. I was supposed to be looking after him, whatever that meant, so I nodded and we walked out. We talked as we walked and he seemed OK at first. We got to talking about animals and I said I wanted horses when I was older.

'I'll buy you a horse.'

I looked at him quizzically.

'I will,' he continued. 'You're so beautiful. I'll do anything for you.'

I stared at him and noticed he was shaking. His eyes kept darting over my body and I could hear Lucy sending warning vibes.

'I really want to touch you.' His eyes had gone blank and his tongue flashed out over his lips. We were standing by some waste ground and I backed up against the railings. His hand reached out and slowly he moved it up under my T-shirt to touch my breasts. I flinched, but he didn't take it away.

– Get ready to run.

– OK.

I heard footsteps coming round the corner and the click of a dog's claws on the pavement.

'Someone's coming,' I whispered. It was enough for him to whip out his hand and I didn't wait around. I ran.

After that I became more wary of going round to Jennifer's. When I told her what had happened, she simply shrugged.

'He would have got you the horse,' she said. 'What's the big deal?'

I was amazed at her casual attitude. Fortunately perhaps, it wasn't long before Jennifer was sent to a children's home – she was too wild, too out of control. I confess I was quite relieved.

My brother's friends also started taking notice of me about this time. Instead of running away, like they'd always done before, now they were constantly climbing up to my bedroom window. I would be asleep and then get woken up by a persistent *tap*, *tap*, *tap*, and in they would sneak. Boys, even a few years older than me, were no threat to me though. For all their posturing, they were very insecure, very unsure about their bodies, about their sexuality. They'd want to mess around, to kiss, to fumble, to fondle. I didn't really mind as long as they didn't want to go any further. It seemed as though Mum was, once again, oblivious to it as she never caught them and never said anything.

Or maybe she did know. The final straw between us came one day when she came to the corner near the chippy to get me. I was hanging out with a bunch of kids and, right in front of them all, she said:

'What you hanging about out 'ere for? You like a common prostitute or slut or something?'

I was totally mortified. It cut me to the quick because I thought it was true. It brought up a deep shame in me. Whenever I misbehaved after that she would call me a slut, whore, anything. After this incident, if she called me names, I would let rip in return with all the swear words under the sun. It became a bloody battle. She hit me and beat me and I screamed blue murder. I didn't take it all lying down by any means – I gave as good as I got and was very aggressive back.

School became increasingly isolating, but there was one interesting development. I developed a crush, like many girls do, on my English teacher. Miss O'Connell looked a bit like Sigourney Weaver, and drove a blue MG sports car which I thought was the coolest thing in the world. I would rush along the corridors in my grey school skirt and Doc Marten boots, eager to get a seat at the front of the class. English was my favourite subject as I loved to read. It had always been my escape and at the time I remember I was reading Émile Zola and Marge Piercy. I was incredibly lovesick, and I used to fantasise about Miss O'Connell on the bus going home, gazing out of the window.

The emotions were so overwhelming that one day I

decided I simply had to tell her, and I wrote her a passionate love letter. It was the day before the school broke up for the summer holidays. The air was muggy and thick with tension. I paced up and down outside the staff room. I was frustrated as I knew how geeky I looked in my school uniform. I could never keep my socks up and I always looked scruffy, no matter how I tried. But convinced that love would conquer, determined that love would find a way, I clutched my letter to my chest.

'Can you tell Miss O'Connell I need to see her?' I asked the geography teacher as he went in. He nodded curtly and shut the door behind him.

I could see the blue MG parked outside through the window, so I knew she hadn't left, but she didn't come out. Her best mate, Miss Mukherjee, came out instead and told me she had left. Odd, I thought.

'Miss? I know you are friends with Miss O'Connell. Can you give her this letter for me?' I lowered my voice, 'I'm in love with her and I can't keep it to myself any more. Will you tell me what she says?'

She nodded vaguely. 'Yes, Michèle. I'll give it to her. Now run along home or you will miss the bus.'

'Promise you will give it to her today? I've left my number on there if she wants to ring me.'

I spent hours on my knees praying to God to make her love me. I went to church every day. But she never called. During that long hot summer I finally realised that I was only attracted to women and decided to come out. Far from being traumatic, it felt liberating. I was suddenly free from the attention of all the men now as I simply told them: 'No, I only like girls.' I told my mum, but she didn't take a huge amount of notice. I think she thought it was a phase I was going through and left me to it.

It was fantastic. A whole new life. I spent every night hitching around London, from club to club, and the rest of the time going to tons of rallies and political events. I was on a mission. I truly believed we could save the world with our passion. I was meeting like-minded people for the first time ever and I felt at home with myself. I never once thought I was in danger – I felt invincible and protected, and never thought twice about hopping into a stranger's car or on to the back of a motorbike. It was all one huge adventure.

My favourite author was Marge Piercy and my all-time favourite book was her classic novel, *Woman on the Edge of Time*. I must have read it ten times or more – wherever I went, the book went too – until it was confiscated at school. It's a story about a Chicana woman living in New York in the 1970s. Violence and mayhem surround her and she is committed to a mental institute where she is visited by a person from the future who lives in an equal society in which discrimination is unheard of. It is a utopian fantasy about a woman considered mad who is, in fact, deeply psychic. Could I relate to her? You bet!

Somewhere along the line, I forget where, I heard about a meeting. It was being organised by a group who wanted to start a radical magazine written by young women for young women. I made my way to the meeting in Goodge Street and signed up immediately to join the collective. I was wearing pink cords and had very short cropped hair and eyebrows that had been plucked to oblivion. The magazine became *Shocking Pink* – a groundbreaking feminist magazine and a bit of a style icon of its time. I think that someone at *Spare Rib* was involved in urging it on and helping with distribution. It was a huge success and ended up being sold nationally all over the place, even getting into W H Smith, which wasn't bad going for a small magazine with such a radical stance.

I was a rough, tough working-class girl with a mountain of chips piled on both shoulders and barrel-loads of opinions. The other girls were middle-class young women who'd been to university. Jasmin Defoe (who went to my school) and I were, at thirteen, the youngest. It was the start of my education in many ways and taught me more than school ever did. I wanted to be as clever as those older girls. I wanted to learn and understand and write.

There was none of that 'you're a child' rubbish here and Jasmin and I were welcomed as equals. We all set to work with a vengeance and came up with some brilliant ideas. I was thrilled when I was picked to be in a photo love story with a twist – about a girl coming out at school.

I joined anything and everything, even an improvisation group of older middle-class women that was called 'Contradictions' where they'd run around screeching and yelling, banging tambourines. One was quite a well-known jazz singer called Maggie Nichols.

Of course I was still very much an outsider because I was so different from the rest of them. But at least here my differences were not only tolerated, but people actually spent time patiently trying to understand me. They were happy to encourage and fuel my desire to learn. They also thought it was great that I was psychic and could give readings. It was the 'in' thing and I had an edge. I would have to argue my corner fiercely when it came to religion, though, as some people were die-hard socialists and thought spirituality was the scourge of the earth. But even that was wonderful. We were all trying to create Utopia in our own way and I loved it.

There were drugs and drink, all-night parties, solidarity and hope. We took magic mushrooms and I would regularly get drunk every night and end up back at one of the squats my new friends lived in. I was a thirteen-year-old living the life of a twenty-something student and it was fabulous.

Often I'd hitch back home or, if I was too drunk or it was too late, I'd simply crash out at a complete stranger's house. I was totally oblivious to the dangers. Well, anywhere felt safe in comparison to my real home. Sometimes I'd even leave home in the middle of the night, to escape the terror and violence that were endemic there. Once, I found myself walking down the Seven Sisters road at 11 p.m., having run away from another ferocious battle at home. I was heading for a squat I'd been to several times before which always felt safe and humming with life. The road was deserted and, unusually, I started feeling a bit nervous. When I got to the squat, it was empty. Everyone had gone out to an all-night party. I broke in and sat up all night reading another favourite Marge Piercy book, *Vida*, consumed with fear and panic. I stayed a few days, but there wasn't enough food – everyone was surviving on rice flavoured with an Oxo cube.

My new life didn't go down too well at school. When I could be bothered to go, I was becoming increasingly difficult, obstreperous and rude. I interrupted in class and refused to follow the school rules. None of it seemed right or fair – nobody but me seemed to care about the state of the world, about racism and sexism or homophobia, and animal rights. I got hauled up in front of the headmaster time and time again, on any pretext the teachers could invent. The final straw was my hair. I had two-tone hair (but then so did many other kids) and the headmaster complained. I lost the plot and called him a 'sexist pig', and that was it.

When I was fourteen I was expelled from school. Mum wasn't that surprised – she had been warned enough times about my behaviour. But, as always when the chips were down, she stuck up for me. She was furious with the school and went to see the headmaster, asking why *I* had been expelled but not the other children with wild hair? He fudged the issue. because he didn't want to admit the real reason for my expulsion – that I was gay.

Shocking Pink had been going great guns and getting lots of publicity, so my expulsion made the news. I was snapped by a hidden photographer coming out of one of the collective's houses eating a Double Decker in my red Harrington. The picture appeared on the front page of the *Acton Gazette*. It even got on the BBC news, and reporters turned up at the house trying to get a story. I was blissfully unaware that this was any big deal and took it all in my stride. My diary for 3 December 1980 says: 'Today a *Nationwide* reporter came round asking questions and wanting to take pictures. Judith rang me from Edinburgh and said my name was on the radio and I was expelled for being a dyke. I'm going to Newcastle on Monday (expenses paid) for a television interview. I'll be a star yet (what with Janet Street-Porter and all)!'

I was invited to meet Janet Street-Porter, we talked about 'yoof' culture and I was filmed for a children's TV show. Later that night, staying in a big smart hotel, I couldn't sleep. I had raided the mini-bar and I lay on the huge bed listening to the radio, hearing that John Lennon had been assassinated. It gave me pause for thought. Even *I* knew I was burning too fast, too bright, packing two lives into one. I felt the need to live every single minute to the max; in some strange way trying to make up for Lucy dying.

But, although I had had more experiences than any fourteen-year-old girl should have had, I was still an innocent. I was incredibly trusting, always believing the best of people. No matter what I did, I felt safe, that I could come to no harm. That was a potentially lethal mistake.

11

You Don't Have to Put on the Red Light

A loud knocking and shouting woke me up from a deep sleep. I squashed my face into the pillow in a vain attempt to block out the sound. I hadn't got in until well past 3 a.m., having hitched back from a late-night club in Warren Street. But, even so, I was quite relieved to have been woken. I'd been in the middle of an incredibly vivid dream – flashes of colour, a bus crashing, splintered glass, people screaming. I was used to nightmares; in fact, I had only ever had one good dream in my entire life – about Barbara Streisand and a pool party in Hollywood! I ran through the crash dream in my mind as I stretched slowly, listening to my mum's raised voice in the background.

'It is not your appointment now. It is later. You have come on the wrong day.'

Because my mother could not write English properly she was always getting her appointments confused. People would turn up for a reading and she would insist they had the wrong time or day. The more she said 'no', the more they wanted the reading. She screeched and raved, but nothing put them off. Amazingly, they tolerated her – maybe they instinctively realised she was really just a child who would in time calm down. Eventually, she usually did.

I grabbed my favourite black corduroy dungarees and pulled them on over a white T-shirt. Not bothering to wash my face or brush my hair, I padded downstairs to see what all the fuss was about. I just caught the back of a dark-haired woman disappearing into Mum's office. Oh, OK, just another client.

Stifling a wide yawn, I wandered into the front room. Perched on the settee was a stunning young woman of about twenty-five. She was fishing around in a large black handbag with long slim fingers, bright red nails scratching about. She looked up, fixing me with large almond eyes.

'Is she your mother?' She nodded towards the office door. I nodded my head. She smiled ruefully. 'She's pretty terrifying. And I haven't even had my reading yet. I was so scared that I let my friend go first.'

'Don't worry about her. She's always doing that to people. You'll love her. Everyone always does.'

She rummaged a bit more in her bag, then looked up. 'Have you got a light? I can't find my lighter.'

I grabbed a box of matches off the sideboard, striking one and lighting the cigarette resting between her bright-red lips. She looked a bit like a Middle Eastern version of Kate Bush. I was used to all sorts of people appearing in

the front room, but they weren't usually this young or interesting.

I turned on the telly: it was the news.

'I had the weirdest dream about a bus crash last night,'
I said musingly, 'it was so vivid.'

As I spoke the words, a crashed bus appeared on the
screen as if by magic. I was pretty surprised as, although
I was used to my dreams coming true, they don't usually
happen that quickly. I slid a look at the woman, worried
that she might think I was some kind of freak, but she
didn't bat an eyelid.

'You're like your mother, aren't you?'

'Yeah, I suppose. It makes me not want to go to sleep
as I'm always having nightmares about plane crashes and
wars and stuff and then it happens. I don't like it.'

Most of Mum's clients ignored me; in fact, most people
ignored me, full stop. But this woman was chatting in a
very familiar way and I began to feel shy. My cheeks were
burning and I curled up into a chair, absentmindedly playing
with my foot. She told me her name was Manna and asked
me mine. She quizzed me about my life and seemed really
interested, particularly in my psychic abilities.

'It's a gift you've got,' she said, nodding fiercely. 'Never
look a gift horse in the mouth.'

It was all a bit weird somehow and I mumbled something
and headed out into the kitchen, feeling uncomfortable and
out of place, even though it was my home. I didn't come
out until I heard Mum's door squeak open and her voice

saying goodbye to the other girl, and inviting Manna to go inside.

An hour later I was out in the garden, staring up at the sky from my apple-tree eyrie. The tree only had two branches you could sit on and I used to feel guilty sometimes that I was hurting the tree by clambering over its branches. Surely it wasn't really strong enough? The tree always felt sad, but also kind somehow, almost as though it knew it provided a necessary escape for me. Did it put up with its own discomfort so it could comfort me? I was musing about that and daydreaming about becoming a radio DJ when the glass back door opened. I looked up and it was the girl with the red fingernails. My face flared red; I was instantly embarrassed by all the dog poo on the crazy paving and the fact I was sitting up a tree at my age.

'Pssssst, Michèle, come here,' she hissed. Curious, I jumped out of the tree as nonchalantly as possible, but still managed to land unevenly. She opened her big black handbag and pulled out two bags of pills. She took out two tablets, one blue and one a two-tone capsule. I recognised the blue one – it was speed, I'd had that in the past. The other I had never seen before. She held them out like sweets as I came close. Once again I felt my cheeks flare.

'Take these and hide them. Don't take them until I tell you to.' She gave me a broad smile and touched my arm. 'Don't worry, your mum told me all about you. I know you like girls and I do too. I'll give you a call and we'll go out sometime.'

My mouth dropped open, but I tucked the pills into the top front pocket of my dungarees. She nodded approvingly, gave me a quick flash of a smile and with that she was gone. Wow, how odd, what did she want to go out with me for? I knew there was something not quite right about it all, but I didn't want to question it too far. 'Never look a gift horse in the mouth' indeed, I mumbled to myself as I bounded back into the house.

'Bye bye, *dahling*,' my mum was waving her and another dark-haired girl off from the front door, her new best friends.

One evening a few days later the phone rang. Mum was at work and I grabbed the grubby white phone from the kitchen wall: 'Hello?'

'Hello. Is that Michèle?'

'Yeah. Who's that?'

'It's Manna, darling. Have you still got those tablets I gave you?'

Oh my God, was it really that girl calling me?

'Yeah, sure, they're right here in my pocket,' I said, patting my dungarees.

'Good. Right, we're going out, so take the blue one and in about twenty minutes the car will pick you up. Have you got a skirt?'

'Uhhhh, I never wear skirts and look, I haven't got any money at all. I can't afford a cab or anywhere posh.'

She paused for a moment, as if she were thinking. 'Don't worry about that. I'll pay for the cab and I'll also get you dressed when you get here. I think you're about the same size as me. OK, I've gotta go, so just jump in the car and get here quick. We'll have a blast.' Click – she hung up.

I danced around the kitchen, but I was also horribly nervous. How could I possibly fit in with her friends – they must be so different. She seemed pretty posh. I rushed up the stairs, two at a time, and washed my face and brushed my teeth.

'Hey, Nick,' I yelled at my brother. 'I'm off out. That girl called, the good-looking one from the other day, and asked me to go out with her!' I was still incredulous. Nick just grunted and went back to plucking his guitar. On reflection, this was highly insensitive of me as he had never had a girlfriend and here was his fourteen-year-old sister bragging about a date.

A taxi hooted outside. Fishing out the blue pill, I grabbed a glass of water and swallowed. I had taken plenty of pills and didn't think twice about it; it never crossed my mind that it might be dangerous. My heart was already thumping as I jumped into the car. We arrived at her basement flat in Earls Court and she answered the door, immaculately dressed in a dress with a very low-cut back and wearing perilously high heels. I immediately felt horribly self-conscious, still wearing the dungarees she'd seen me in last time. They were my favourites, but suddenly they seemed gauche and rather childish.

'Hi,' she said, with that flash of a smile. 'Come in quick, we're in a hurry. Let's see what fits you.'

We moved swiftly into the living room where another

woman, blonde with a stern face, sat tapping her foot and sucking on a cigarette. She looked me up and down.

'Hey, this is Michèle. Michèle, this is Paola.'

'Hi.' She said it flatly, without any vestige of a smile.

'Don't mind her, she's got her period,' said Manna. 'Come on, this is my bedroom. OK, try these on.'

She flung various dresses at me, flimsy silky numbers, and I batted them away in horror:

'Seriously, I can't wear these. I've never even worn a skirt in my life,' I said, lying through my teeth.

Manna bit her lip and looked through the wardrobe. 'OK, try these. You'll look great in these.'

She tossed me some soft black leather trousers and a beautiful white silk blouse. I undid my dungarees and slowly pulled off my clothes, feeling very uncomfortable as she just sat staring at me. The floor was covered with discarded clothes, but she kicked them aside and chucked me some heels. I stared at them and looked at her in horror. I never wore heels.

'Don't argue. Put them on, darling.'

'Where are we going?'

'I've got to meet some friends. It's a bore, but just be nice to them, then we can be alone later. OK?' Her eyes looked a bit weird, still almond and perfectly made up, but sort of unfocused.

The taxi was still waiting outside. I reckoned it must be costing her a fortune, but I was concentrating too hard on walking in heels to worry much about anything else.

We drove off and pulled up outside an absolutely huge hotel somewhere off Hyde Park. She opened her bag to get out some change for the taxi driver and I noticed two huge bags of pills – really huge, supermarket carrier bags half-full. I knew that having that amount of drugs was not good. If we were stopped, we would be arrested and it would be serious. My eyes were like saucers and my heart was thumping even faster – firstly because of the speed, then because of nerves, and now through sheer fear. This wasn't right at all.

I could feel Lucy draw close, but the drugs were making me unable to tune into her; I could feel her tugging me but I couldn't hear what she was saying.

Manna and I walked slowly up the hotel steps towards the huge swing doors where a uniformed doorman was waiting. She bent down and hissed in my ear:

'Don't say anything. Sometimes these bastards don't let me in.'

I didn't know what she was talking about, but I kept silent and we walked past the doorman without incident and on into the lobby. Deep-red carpet stretched in front of me, overhead were vast crystal chandeliers, and there were several glass coffee tables dotted around the space, each surrounded by a cluster of low-slung armchairs. There was a soft buzz of conversation, the clinking of glasses, and somewhere I could hear a piano playing.

Four Middle Eastern men walked towards us as we crossed the carpet. They looked annoyed.

'There you are,' said one of them, a solidly built man somewhere in his fifties. 'You're late.' He looked me up and down and raised his eyebrows slightly, turning back to Manna. 'Who's this?'

'This is Michèle. She's a new friend of mine.'

The man took my hand and kissed it. I stifled a giggle. All four of them stared at me very intently.

'Hello, Michèle. It's very nice to meet you.' His accent was very strong and it was hard to make out what he was saying.

I felt distinctly uncomfortable. I didn't have a clue what was going on. Why were we meeting all these men? We climbed into a large black limo and drove off to a club on the King's Road. This really was way out of my comfort zone, continents away from the clubs I usually frequented. The club was covered in mirrors and there were silver trays full of unusual foods. The music was foreign too and I was the only one there who didn't look Middle Eastern. We drank, and the men took it in turns to dance with Manna. When no one was looking, she would hold my hand under the table. Hours passed and I was getting seriously bored.

Every so often, Manna would whisper in my ear, her voice getting progressively more and more slurred: 'We will be alone soon, don't worry.'

Everyone was speaking in a different language and dancing and singing; Manna sat on various laps, and was laughing. One of the men stared at me and tried talking. He had a very open face and big, kind, brown eyes.

'You're not like the other girls, are you?' he said. 'I want to contact you after tonight. There is something very sweet about you and, you know what, you are not meant to be here.' He stared at me intently and pushed his phone number into my hand.

Finally, it seemed they had had enough drinking and dancing. As we got ready to leave, Manna took me into the toilet and hugged me.

'Thank you for coming, Michèle. You saved my life. The other girl couldn't come and these are my best clients.'

Clients? I suddenly began to feel very stupid – and not a little anxious. I was starting to get the general gist of the situation. What would happen next?

We went back to the imposing hotel and I was terrified we were going to be stopped and the drugs discovered. We climbed into the huge mirrored lift to go to their room. I felt nervous and hot, my mind was racing, and I wasn't feeling right at all.

The four men sat on a couch in front of a glass table and kicked off their shoes. The room was enormous and looked right out over Hyde Park. It was more like a flat than a room – a massive suite. They began to take powder out of a paper package and cut long lines of it on the table. Leaning over they snorted it, one after another, using a rolled-up £20 note. Then they offered me the rolled-up note. I shook my head. Even though I couldn't understand the language, I could tell they were all having a heated discussion about me as they were gesticulating and kept looking over at me. It seemed as if they were arguing about what would happen next and they were pretty much split down the middle. The nice man and another one were shaking their heads while the other two were getting angry. The older man smacked his hand on the table, letting loose a fine mist of cocaine.

Then, all of a sudden, he threw up his hands and stalked out of the room. The nice man smiled at me and grabbed both me and Manna, pushing us towards the door. As we reached it, he shoved a large envelope in her hand and waved his own hands, as if to swat us away.

'Get her out of here.'

Manna turned to him in amazement. 'Are you sure?'

'Yes. She is too sweet, too young. There is something different about her, take her home.'

As we climbed into a taxi, it was nearly morning. The early sun was kissing the city with a golden pink haze. I was shattered. All I wanted was to get away from that place.

We held hands in the car and she stared at me, her eyes glazed and with a faint sheen of perspiration touching her face.

'You *are* sweet, aren't you?' she said, patting my cheek.

We got out of the taxi and walked into her flat. The sour-faced blonde was still up and, if it were possible, was looking even more sour-faced than before. She didn't even bother to say hello.

'Go to bed, darling,' said Manna. 'I'll join you in a minute.'

I climbed into her bed fully clothed. I was utterly exhausted but my mind was racing. I knew now that she was on the game. Plus, the bag of drugs was still freaking me out. This was way out of my league. I could hear her arguing with the blonde. Suddenly Lucy was in the room, in my head.

– *Michèle, get up* NOW! GET UP, WE HAVE GOT TO GET OUT OF HERE!

I grabbed my own clothes and quickly changed. I could hear the women mumbling and, as I got closer, I heard Manna say in an urgent hiss:

'Let her go. She's no use. Really. She really is innocent.'

'No. He'll be here any minute. He can decide. We can make loads of money out of her; the punters love that fresh-faced look.'

Lucy's energy was shoving me forward.

– *GO NOW! YOU ARE IN REAL DANGER HERE!*

As I turned to pass the living room I saw the blonde with a band around her arm, a needle poised, just about to enter her vein. She and Manna both looked up, startled to see me.

'What is it, darling? Go to bed. I'll be there in a minute,' Manna said.

'No. Actually I gotta go,' I said.

Manna staggered towards me as I reached the front door. I was petrified that she would stop me, but instead she pushed me gently out of the door and shoved a ten-pound note into my hand.

'This is for the cab. Take the other tablet when you get home. It will bring you down and make you sleep. Now, listen, Michèle, this is important. Never call me. Never come here again. Now go, quickly.'

I could see the blonde trying to get up from the sofa, telling Manna not to let me go. But I was out of the door and up the street without a backward glance. I hailed a passing cab and breathed a huge sigh of relief. That was seriously weird.

In the cab I talked to Lucy.

– What was that all about? Didn't she like me?
– She liked you a lot, Michèle, but she is very lost. There was great danger there. There was a very bad man coming. That was the worst danger you have ever been in. You must not take drugs. I can't reach you if you take drugs.
– Maybe we should save her?
– You can't save her; she has to save herself.
– Maybe I can call the police if she is there against her will?
– Michèle, in a way you did save her and she saved you. You gave her a gift – you showed her that she can still do the right thing. She let you go. She saw your innocence and that gave her part of herself back.

– *I don't understand. I just feel so empty and alone.*
– *Michèle; you are never alone. I am always here. Now go home and get to sleep. You will feel better later.*

I slumped back in the taxi and breathed a sigh of relief. It had been a close shave. I had been lucky. But would I be so lucky next time?

12

Don't Drown on Me

The night at the hotel had given me a fright, but it didn't put me off going out – quite the opposite. I figured as long as I stayed away from posh hotels and dodgy women in fancy clothes, I'd be fine. After all, anywhere was better than home.

Life at home was – if it were possible – spinning even more out of control. Russell and my mother were arguing all the time. My brother Nick wasn't speaking to anyone but Sheba, the dog – he had withdrawn entirely, drinking in his room. I was a torrent of anger and frustration. I had decided that I was now a fully fledged adult. I was used to parenting myself; I didn't want to be controlled in any way. This led to running battles. If I wasn't staying away in squats overnight, I was following in my mother's footsteps and turning our suburban home into a hostel for all the waifs and strays I met in the night.

Russell simply couldn't handle it – his idea of taking a parental role was to punch me in the face. I would retaliate by fighting like a banshee. One day he beat me up so badly in the street, punching me again and again in the head, that my mother took me to Acton police station. But they wouldn't press charges because in those days it was considered 'a domestic'. He didn't always come out on top though. On one occasion, as he punched me, I managed to get in a hard kick to the balls and he needed hospital treatment.

It was mayhem. If one person wasn't screaming and battling, another would be. Then Russell lost his job and my mother went back to providing for everyone again by working day and night. He just hung around the house – he was such a slob, he never cleared up, he never cooked, he never did anything. I hated him. He hated me. *Quid pro quo*.

I regretted the bad energy between us, but I couldn't find any way of stopping it. It gradually escalated over time to the point where I am sure he would have killed me if he could have done. In fact, he did try his hardest. The funny thing is that I wasn't really frightened of him even though he was a big man and a violent one. I could see that he was not really grown up; he was more like another child or adolescent. What I hadn't factored in was the fact that even children or adolescents can be dangerous when they get spiteful.

I used to borrow Russell's extremely small red bike to go to the shops, and I would often cycle over the Hanger Lane gyratory system to get there. Even then it was a busy road system, with cars, buses, lorries and trucks thundering along. Mum would have been horrified if she'd known I cycled it – but then she never thought to ask how I got to and from the shops. She never knew that I borrowed the bike. But Russell did. It drove him mad and, because it drove him mad, I delighted in taking it.

One day I was cycling along the road, humming to myself, when suddenly the brakes packed in. No matter how hard I clamped my hands down, nothing happened. I started panicking a bit as I was going downhill quite fast. I started gathering even more speed. I dipped my toes to the ground, trying to slow myself down, but that made the bike start to judder and so I picked them up quickly, looking ahead, wondering what I could do. The road was – amazingly – pretty quiet. But that couldn't last. If I could just hold on until the road began to rise – in about half a mile – I might be OK. Then, just as I'd reassured myself a little, the handlebars started shuddering in my hands. I gripped them more tightly, pulling upwards to try to secure them, but – to my intense horror – they fell off.

The whole bike started wobbling uncontrollably, veering all over the road – I couldn't steer, I couldn't do anything. For one horrible moment I thought the bike was going to lunge into the middle of the road or even over the central reservation, but incredibly it didn't. It felt as if a giant hand grabbed the whole bike and twisted it round so it hurtled on to the hard shoulder. Then it simply fell apart, like a bike in a cartoon. Both wheels fell off, one skating into the road. The frame went one way and the saddle the other.

I pitched forwards and skidded along the road. I rolled into a ball and covered my head, convinced that this would be the end. I could hear the thunder of traffic which, suddenly, seemed to fill the road. But it passed me by. Cautiously I opened one eye, then the other – and couldn't believe where I was. The bike was scattered in a pile of pieces over the hard shoulder and road – but I was in one piece, right up against the crash barriers. I was winded, scratched and bruised but, amazingly, not seriously injured. As the cars shot past and a huge truck trundled by, feet away, I knew what a narrow escape I'd had. I wasn't surprised, though. I knew I was protected, always protected.

I didn't dare go home without the bike so I spent a dangerous twenty minutes dodging traffic to get all the bits and tack it together again. I limped home with the bike in pieces and, by the time I got there, I was absolutely mad.

Russell was out the back, tinkering with a car. He looked up as I walked in and smiled nastily. 'You been in the wars?'

I was livid. 'You absolute bastard! You unscrewed the bike. I could have been killed, you nutcase!'

He just carried on smiling. 'Maybe that'll teach you not to take my things.'

I couldn't believe it – he really had tampered with the bike, knowing full well that I would take it, realising that I'd ride along a busy stretch of fast road. Mum cottoned on pretty quickly and was livid: a huge row erupted. I can remember clearly taking my turn to smile. I loved it when she defended me. I felt she belonged to us, not to him, and so I was happy to alienate him whenever I could. Poor Mum. She tried so hard. Caught between the devil and the deep blue sea.

But as Russell became increasingly violent, so I became increasingly anxious. I couldn't sleep at all, the panic attacks were getting worse and my doctor upped my Valium yet again. He seemed quite happy to accept that I was under strain and pressure because I didn't get on with my step-father. He did try to get me to go to counselling but that was a disaster. The counsellor was too young and inexperienced – she had no idea what she was dealing with. I hated talking about my life and was sullen and unresponsive. The whole experiment petered out with relief on both sides. I had a social worker too – in fact, several. They came and went with monotonous regularity as none of them seemed to be able to control me or help me. My diaries at that time are nearly incoherent with the pain and misery I was in. There were wrangles going on over my schooling. I hadn't had any for ages and finally it was decided that I would have a home tutor. This wasn't too bad and I actually enjoyed learning – when I was in a fit state to do so.

I had found out, by a little experimentation, that combining my prescription drugs with alcohol gave me a wonderfully out-of-it feeling. It was the answer to my problems. I started drinking and popping pills like there was no tomorrow.

Really, when I look back, I'm surprised I'm still here. I

used to take four or five Mogadon with several pints of lager. I thought it was normal. In fact, what's really revealing is how I thought most of my life was normal. I certainly didn't think it was bad – at the time. Because I only had black eyes or bruises, I didn't think it was any big deal. I had been hit all my life but, even now, I don't see myself as someone who was beaten. I knew my mother and brother, at least, didn't really want to hurt me. I knew my mother loved me.

To be fair, she was also terrified for me but, as always, she expressed her fear with anger – or rather extreme rage. We made the Osbournes look like the Waltons! I stormed about the house raving about the injustices of the world, racism, sexism, any 'ism' that existed. I must have looked a fright to her with my punked-up hair, leather jacket, DMs and a myriad of badges shouting 'Rock against racism' and 'End the arms race'. I was a million miles away from the carefully dressed teenagers of her Italian adolescence. No way would I be going to dances dressed in pretty frocks, with neatly groomed hair and slingbacks. I was like an alien creature to her. She would do the tarot for me over and over again, hoping it would show a better future, praying that I would change. Then she'd yell at me and I'd run away. She'd come chasing after me, waving the tarot deck, screaming at the top of her voice: 'You are in danger; you get killed in the night!'

Yes, I stayed out all night. Yes, I slept with women. Yes, I even hitched all the way up to Scotland for a party. But frankly, the main danger I faced was from my mother's own unguarded emotions. Many times she really terrified me and I honestly thought she would kill me. I knew she was acting out of frustration, but she was totally out of control. In fact, no one in the house had any sense of self-control and things soon took a turn for the worse.

The bathroom was a place of refuge, a small oasis in a house simmering with discontent. It was quite a large room, with a long mirror across the opposite wall to the bath. There were two windows and a scraggy pink carpet on the floor. It was usually the one place in the house where I could get a bit of peace, where I could lie back and daydream about saving the planet or indulge fantasies on the latest crush I had on a tennis player.

There were no locks on the bathroom in our house and people were quite free and easy about going to the loo if someone was in the bath. One day I was lying in the bath, mesmerised by the bubbles, and chatting to Lucy in my head about the injustices of the world and how we could change it. Every so often I'd talk out loud, imagining I was being interviewed on television, using the soap on a rope as my pretend microphone. Then, suddenly, my mother barged in, giving me a start.

'Who are you talking to?'

'Nobody.'

'You're talking to someone. What are you doing, eh?'

'None of your bloody business. It's a free country, isn't it? I can talk to anyone I want.'

'You tell me! Who are you talking to?'

'It's not a police state, is it?'

It soon escalated into a row, with both of us screaming names at one another. My mother was towering over the bath (as much as her five-foot frame would allow), bellowing at me. My way of handling her intense anger was to bellow back as loudly as possible.

'Leave me alone, you witch! Get off me!' I yelled.

'*Disgraziata! Cattiva!* I'll kill you!' Suddenly, without any warning, she lunged forwards and grabbed my shoulders, pushing me under the water and holding me down. I remember watching it as if it were a film – all of a sudden I was no longer in my body but floating above it. I could see myself from above being held under. I think Lucy must have taken me out of myself to stop me being scared – it was like a form of astral projection, the kind you hear about when people are in hospital and suddenly find themselves floating out of their bodies, watching themselves being operated upon by the surgeons. All I could see beneath me was my mother holding me under the water and me flailing about in the bubbles, coming up for gasps of breath and then being held under again. God, it all seemed so pointless. So this was how I was going to die, degraded, naked in the bath? Each time I came up for air and she pushed me under, a part of my love for her died.

Then, as quickly as it had begun, she suddenly stopped and stalked out shouting a smattering of Italian insults.

I managed to jump out of the bath through sheer

adrenaline but my legs immediately collapsed under me and I sat on the soaking wet carpet, shaking and shivering. I didn't even have the strength to pull a towel around me. It felt as if some line had been crossed and I felt distinctly unsafe. Before that moment, I didn't think my mother could ever really harm me. I knew without doubt that she loved me, but she had become seriously unhinged. Her irrational outbursts were due partly to my wayward behaviour, but I was too far down the path to stop.

After that, it just got worse and worse. I used to ram a chair against the bathroom door to keep her out, but I no longer took long lingering baths. I didn't dare. So next my mother took to chasing me with a carving knife, calling me an evil slut and the devil's child.

'I wanted a child too much and you are my punishment,' she would yell, over and over again.

Luckily for me, Mum wasn't a very fast runner. We'd be having a row and she'd run off. I'd hear her racing to the kitchen in a flurry of expletives; listen to her pulling open the cutlery drawer, and grabbing the large carving knife. Then I knew I had a matter of seconds to race up the stairs, before she stormed out of the kitchen, knife in hand, hot on my heels.

'I'm going to kill you, you *cattiva*!' My mother was a force of nature and had the strength of a man, so I would hurtle into my room which, fortunately, was the first door at the top of the stairs. I would wedge myself against the door, sitting on the floor with my legs pressed against the wall as a barrier, and push with all my might so she couldn't get in.

She would try ramming the door first, but our strengths were pretty equally matched. I may have been young, but I was pretty strong. Then, when she realised it was jammed shut, she would start stabbing the door with the carving knife, all the time screeching and cursing. I knew that, even though she wouldn't mean to hurt me intentionally, if she had got in she would most likely have accidentally stabbed me to death. So I held firm and focused my eyes on the posters on the wall: Virginia Wade holding up her trophy at Wimbledon; Gary Numan, dressed as an android for *Replicas*. I'd chant the lyrics to myself to stay sane, trying to drown out her attack.

When she finally gave up and went away, I banged my head against the wall, sobbing, not knowing what to do. My bedroom door was slashed nearly to ribbons, great stab marks and holes gouged out of it. How long would it hold up against these attacks?

I knew I had to get out for good or something terrible would happen. Mum was finally totally out of control, and so was I. She was at her wits' end. She had a violent unstable husband and was trying to hold together enough work to keep up a large mortgage and a family of four. It was simply too much. But it was too much for me too. Mum had always been volatile, always unpredictable, but when the chips were down she had always stuck up for me, been on my side. Now she wanted to kill me. I can't describe how devastated I felt. It was as if my soul had been wrenched in two. I adored my mother, but now I could barely look at her. It was the final betrayal. I was totally numb, sitting in my room, rocking backwards and forwards, unable even to cry.

Before long I was offered at place at Brookfield Close children's home. It felt like a miracle.

13

You Can Check Out Any Time You Like

Heading toward the children's home I felt relief wash over me. I sat back in the social worker's small blue car and felt as if I could breathe for the first time in years. No more drama, no more knives, no more Mum, no more Russell, no more Nick.

I stared up at the place that was to be my new home. It was a small, modern square building with a character-less, soulless air. It looked so normal, so ordinary, that surely it had to be safe and boring – and safe and boring was just what I needed. It sounded like heaven. As I walked in, I noticed a table tennis table. There was also a music room and a TV room. My spirits lifted – actually this could be fun. Safe *and* fun? My prayers really had been answered.

I was introduced to someone called Lesley who worked there and she seemed nice enough. I made it clear from the off that I was an adult and was used to living freely and that the one thing I couldn't handle was rules. She smiled reassuringly.

'Don't worry about it. We try not to burden you all with too much restriction. But obviously there have to be a few rules – for your own safety. I'll explain as I show you round.'

Secretly I was quite pleased to have some boundaries and I got the feeling I would like the place. There weren't a huge number of other kids staying there – maybe six. As we climbed the sparse white stairs to my room it never occurred to me that these people could hold any power over me. I still felt totally autonomous.

What I didn't realise was that this place would strip me down and draw out all my pain, the pain that had been bubbling under the surface for years and that had now tipped into self-hatred and rage. I felt as if I were standing on the edge of a precipice and that nothing was real. Primal and feral, I reacted to the slightest thing with adrenaline. I was stuck in survival mode with my foot rammed on the accelerator.

I had barely settled in when more new kids arrived. They were younger than me, three Asian sisters who were so terrified they were visibly shaking.

'Who are you? What you in for?' I asked the older of the girls who seemed about my age.

'I'm Shelina. Our mother left us and we don't know where she is,' she said bleakly. One of the younger ones started to cry.

I squatted down to look her in the eye and smiled reassuringly.

'Don't worry. I'll look after you. No one will mess with you while I'm here.'

I always knew how to resolve other people's feelings and make them feel safe. It gave me a focus to avoid my own feelings.

A couple of other kids that lived in were a bit older. Dan had ginger hair and glasses and was about sixteen. He was a white Rasta and always had reggae blaring out of his room, next door to mine on the top floor. He had been in a children's home for years and was petrified that soon he would have to leave and make his own way, on his own. He was sensitive and ground his teeth a lot. Pat was also older, quite good-looking and tough as old boots. She gave me a long hard once-over to ascertain how tough I was in comparison to her, whether I'd give her any trouble.

Playing the hard nut was an act for me as really I was a total softie. But it was a role I had played so well for so long that everybody believed it. Nobody messed with me – unless they were seriously insane.

The first night Pat made the mistake of snatching the remote control off Shelina. I asked her to give it back nicely but she said no – so I launched myself at her like a missile. We scuffled, I got the remote off her, and tossed it to Shelina.

I stared evenly at Pat: 'Don't mess with them, they just lost their mother.'

I suppose she had previously been top dog, and was now testing me as she didn't like this upstart coming in and interfering with her control. Like many bullies, she caved in as soon as I showed her that I wasn't going to take her nonsense. After that the bullying stopped and, in fact, we became firm friends. She showed me how to climb out of the fire escape if I wanted to get out without anyone knowing, and so I settled into this routine without much bother. It all seemed like some great game. I still went out to clubs and discos; I still met up with all my *Shocking Pink* friends. It was simply a welcome holiday from home.

It didn't take me long to figure out that it wasn't just the kids who had issues – all the staff did too. I didn't particularly mind – in fact it merely confirmed my suspicion that I was an adult and their equal. How did they think they could help me when they couldn't even help themselves? Rachel was allocated as my key worker. This wasn't the best idea under the sun as I was a radical lesbian and she was a fanatical Christian who gave me the impression that she thought all lesbians were evil and would burn in hell.

Jamie was also a fan of the Bible, but in a different way. Jamie was young and funky; totally gorgeous. She was so trendy she reminded me of my older friends, so it felt quite odd that she was a member of staff rather than one of us kids. She loved the same music as me and we often had deep conversations about the end of the world; she

would read to me from the book of Revelation in the Bible
and warn me that I should always be on my guard, for the
anti-Christ would be coming any minute.

She used to let me and Dan go to her flat at night when
she was on night duty and we would all sit around doing
tarot readings, or she would read bits of the classics to us.
Dan was totally fixated on her. He used to ask me to talk
to her on his behalf as she let me into the flat on my own
at night more than him. Jamie and I often chatted on
through the night until dawn. I would read her tarot and
we would both do the I Ching for one another, figuring
out what the rather arcane messages the ancient Chinese
oracle gave us were meant to represent. There was a strong
bond and affinity between us and I loved her literary
knowledge. I started to read more of the classics on her
recommendations. She also introduced me to fantasy and
sci-fi novels, in particular the Stephen Donaldson trilogy
about another outsider, a man with leprosy who stumbles
into an alternative reality. I could totally relate to his anger
and feelings of being ostracised, of being 'unclean'.

As I got to know Jamie, I realised that she was more
like us than I had realised. She confessed that she'd had
a nervous breakdown the year before. I loved that she
wasn't perfect, that she wasn't trying to be all grown-up
and distant. It felt like she understood us, that she understood me.

One morning I noticed she had two plasters over her
wrists.

'What happened to your wrists?' I asked.

'Oh, I cut myself.' She blushed and pulled her blouse down over her hands. 'It was an accident. I dropped a milk bottle.'

'Come on, Jamie, you can tell me. I'm not a kid, you know. I know what they are; you tried to kill yourself, didn't you? I thought you were all better now?'

'I wasn't trying to kill myself, Michèle, I promise.' She looked terrified. Her eyes were darting all over the place. I knew she was lying and she knew I knew. Finally she grabbed my arms and looked intently into my face.

'I just cut myself because it releases tension. Promise you won't tell anyone.'

I looked at her carefully and then took her hands and gently released them down to her sides again. 'OK. I won't tell anyone but you have got to promise me you won't do it again. All right? You're a very special person. Dan and I think you are fantastic and you've really helped us.' I had one of my instant flashes of knowledge, and smiled broadly. 'Life will bring you great things. In fact I see you being a mother in two years and having a really happy life.'

She grinned widely at the last bit. She desperately wanted to be in love and get married.

'Thanks, Michèle. I won't do it again, I promise. So please don't worry and don't tell anyone.'

When I went to bed that night, I couldn't sleep. I often couldn't sleep – that was nothing new. But that particular night I couldn't stop myself thinking about all the times I had been touched and what a bad person I was. The thoughts wouldn't stop spinning round and round in my head, that I was horrible and unlovable and that everything my mother said to me was true. Perhaps I really was evil and bad and worthless. I hated myself for being so aggressive and tough when all I wanted was to make things better for people. I kept messing up and I hated the way I looked. I felt like I wanted to explode. I was so tense I could see the veins standing out on my arms. My jaw was clenched tight and I was breathing shallowly, almost panting, hyperventilating.

– *Why is it like this, Lucy? I will never be loved, nothing will change, no one understands me. I feel so lonely.*
– *You will come through this. Calm down, it will be all right.*

I sat up and started playing with the empty glass of water by my bedside. Tossing it from one hand to the other, it suddenly occurred to me that maybe if I cut my arm it might help to release my tension. After all, Jamie said it helped her. Did I really believe it? I don't remember. I was just so desperate, so pent-up, I thought I had to do something or I would spontaneously combust. So I smashed the glass before Lucy had a chance to guess what I was up to and stop me, and quickly cut into my arms time and time again. The blood welled up immediately and I watched in amazement as the bright red drops dripped down my arm.

It didn't hurt, but it looked dramatic and, yes, it did lift something. I was amazed. WOW, this works. I was so delighted that I felt I had to go and thank Jamie. It wasn't her shift, so I went along to her flat and knocked on the door. When she opened it, I smiled brightly and showed her my arms as if offering her a present. The cuts weren't that deep, but I'd made lots of them so there was blood everywhere.

'Jamie, you were right, it does get rid of the pain!'

I was delighted, so pleased with myself, but Jamie just stared at me, horrified. She grabbed my arms, checking to see how deep the cuts were. She seemed relieved to discover they looked more dramatic than they actually were.

'Go to bed, Michèle,' she hissed. 'Wipe down your arms and put some plasters on them, and we'll talk in the morning.' She was looking anxiously up and down the corridor.

I did as she said and went to bed, puzzled and hurt. I'd only done what she had told me she did. Why wasn't she supporting me? Why wasn't she pleased?

After that, when I cut myself I did it in private. I never told a soul.

14

Suicide Is Painless

The children's home wasn't really the safe refuge I'd imagined. As soon as the staff went to bed, the games began. If
Dan wasn't threatening to kill himself with a razor blade,
someone else would be having a crisis, sobbing or screaming.
The atmosphere was always tense and heightened. So many
problems in such a small square footage meant we lived on
constant red alert and rarely got any sleep. It wasn't good
for the nerves, but it was a great way to slim. I was barely
eating and lost weight at an alarming rate.

I still saw Mum. She didn't really come to the children's
Home, but I went back to her place quite regularly. Nothing
really changed; there were still huge arguments, still loads
of shouting and slaps. Nick and I were still at loggerheads
– one time we had a fight and he pinned me to the floor
and held a cigarette to my face. I screamed and thrashed
around, feeling the heat from the tip. Then he just laughed
and let me go.

I hadn't been in the children's home long when I went

back to my mother's house for Sunday lunch. It all started out all right. I was telling them about things that had happened at the home. Mum was telling me about some new client. Then Mum brought out dessert – that old staple, apple pie. She served up a slice and handed it to me.

'No thanks. I'm not hungry, Mum.'

'You got to have some pie, Michèle. You're too thin.'

'I'm not hungry.'

'So you don't want my pie?'

'I'm not saying that . . .'

'You don't want my food? You reject my food?' Her voice started rising higher and higher, louder and louder.

'For God's sake, Mum, it's just a slice of pie.'

'But I cooked it especially because you like it.' She was screaming now. Suddenly she just flung the whole pie, in its Pyrex dish, on to the table and stormed out.

I got my coat and left. Would nothing ever solve the problems we had, Mum and I?

Back at the children's home the girls were convinced that there was a poltergeist on our floor and, given that poltergeists are attracted to disrupted adolescent energy, there probably was. Who knows, it may even have followed me from Mum's house. Things would mysteriously vanish and then reappear in different places. More scarily, doors would slam shut (when there was no draught) and stuff would be smashed to the ground. One day we watched in amazement as a heavy vase literally moved up off the side table in the hallway and then paused for a moment, wobbling, before being hurled at the wall. It was nothing new to me and I wasn't unduly bothered but the others were terrified and, inevitably, they turned to me to sort it out.

'C'mon, Michèle, you know about this stuff. Can't you exorcise it or something?'

So one night we snuck down to the kitchen and I pulled out a large bag of cooking salt from the cupboard and found a head of garlic in the fridge. I sprinkled the salt all around our beds and covered the window ledges with garlic just like my mother had done at home. It seemed to do the trick, for the poltergeist stopped throwing things around and calm was temporarily restored.

It was supposed to be a safe, secure house, but the security was hopeless. Like I've said, we would regularly sneak out of the emergency fire escape. But, of course, it worked the other way round too – all sorts of people could sneak in. Dan had a Rasta friend who was older than me and very charming. We all went to the pictures once to see *Flash Gordon* and he sat next to me. Halfway through the film I found his hand reaching out for mine. I didn't mind – I just held it back. People thought he was all big and tough but really he was a very gentle guy. But I just couldn't seem to get it over to him that I simply wasn't interested.

He didn't live at the home, but often sneaked in to see Dan. One night I was fast asleep (a rarity) and he came into my room, climbed into my bed, and started to touch me underneath my T-shirt.

'Get off. Leave me alone. I don't fancy you. I'm gay, remember?'

'You're not gay, Michèle,' he whispered huskily, 'All you need is a real man. A man like me.'

'No, I don't. Leave me be.' I sleepily removed his hand and gave it a pat. He gave a sigh and planted a kiss on my forehead and quietly padded out of the room. If he had pressed me I probably would have slept with him just because he wanted to, but he was a sweet guy and thankfully he didn't push it at all. He was just a bit vain and was truly puzzled – he really couldn't understand that I wasn't attracted to him. Such encounters happened all the time and I took it in my stride. After all, I was used to it. It was just another form of self-harm – only one that cut much deeper than superficial scars. However, it did make me slightly nervous about who else could get into the room. The more I thought about it, the more I realised that basically little had changed in my life. This place might have the veneer of safety and security, but really it was no safer for me than anywhere else.

The lack of sleep and the fact that I hadn't eaten properly for months was also beginning to take its toll. I was a bag of nerves and more defensive than normal, if that were possible. All my feelings were right out there on the surface as if someone had peeled my skin back, leaving me exposed to the elements. So I wasn't in any fit state to deal with what happened next.

I had only been at Brookfield Close a few weeks when

I met Brenda. The place was quite deserted that day, and Pat was helping me dye my hair half white, mucking about as she did it.

'This looks half ginger to me, not a whiter shade of pale,' I said, looking in the bathroom mirror. 'I think you've done something wrong. Are you sure you mixed it right?'

'Yeah. It'll be fine. Anyway, what's wrong with ginger?' She laughed and flicked a towel at me.

Lesley stuck her head around the door.

'Hey, Michèle. Come out a minute. Brenda wants to meet you.'

Brenda was the deputy head, who had been away on holiday when I came to the home and so I had never met her.

I swaggered along to the staff room, laughing, with my head covered in a towel.

'Hello, Michèle. I've heard so much about you – you're quite the little celebrity! I loved *Shocking Pink*. I'm a feminist myself.'

I looked up and gazed into the most compassionate china blue eyes I had ever seen. She seemed filled with softness and love and I was instantly struck dumb. I literally couldn't speak. I fled the room.

Bursting into the girls' room I shouted at the others, 'You never told me she was so amazing. She must think I'm a total idiot. I couldn't say a bloody word.'

'What you on about?' said Pat. 'She ain't all that.'

I just shook my head and wandered off to my room in a daze. From that moment on Brenda was my main focus, my entire life. I used to write her poetry endlessly . . .

rays of blue love shimmering through a mist of kindness,
personalities step forward, minds intertwined,
all this energy preoccupied with this love on my mind.

Or I would go dodging behind cars when she went home on her evening shift to make sure she got to the station safely. It was the perfect distraction from my problems and a great way to experience love, even if it was a one-way street. She was very tolerant of my teenage crush but it must have been tough to have such an intense adolescent idolise you to such a degree.

One cold January day when we were having lunch, one of the dinner ladies said, 'Brenda, what would you like for dessert?'

'Ohhh, just give me Robert Redford covered in cream – that'll do,' she laughed.

It was only a light-hearted remark, but it felt as if a dagger had been plunged into my heart. She wanted a man. I felt as if my life had come to an end in that second and, stifling a sob, I fled the table. Just like Mum, I over-reacted: I had no sense of moderation at all.

I ran from the building and out into the dingy streets, tears streaming down my face, barely noticing where I was or what I was doing. Eventually I ran out of steam and stopped, heaving for air, outside a chemist shop. It was freezing cold and I could see my breath coming out in gasps. On impulse I walked in and bought a packet of Dodos. It was a bronchitis medicine people used to get high on and it had a similar effect to the amphetamine speed. I walked slowly back to the children's home, thinking hard.

What was the point of going on? It was all just futile. I couldn't erase the past and the future felt bleak. There was nothing for me there. By the time I got back to my room I knew what I was going to do. I walked in, shut the door, lay down on the bed, and swallowed the whole packet before Lucy could say a word.

– Michèle, what have you done? Get help now.

Lucy's energy was vibrating in my head, buzzing furiously. She was petrified.

– No. There's no point. I'm tired of it all. I don't fit in anywhere. Russell's right – I am a freak. No one will ever love me.
– Michèle, listen! I promise you that isn't true.

We argued in this way for what seemed like hours. Lucy was getting more and more distressed, trying harder and harder to persuade me to get help. I was becoming more and more insistent that I had made up my mind.

– You should be pleased. I'm coming to join you.

– I don't want that.

– You don't want me? You don't love me either?

– I didn't say that.

– You have a great future ahead of you. You will do so much with your life. You will be happy and help people and live in the country. You will have huge success. You will have anything you want. Don't give up now.

There was a long pause, before I said, very firmly.

– I don't believe you.

Then something really scary happened. Lucy's voice disappeared. I felt her energy just fade away. This was awful. It had never ever happened before, especially not in the worst of times. What if I died and Lucy wasn't there to meet me? What if I died and I was even more alone?

Three hours had passed since I had taken the overdose. It had to be too late now to do anything, didn't it? I headed unsteadily for the staff room and stood swaying by the door. Lesley looked up.

'What's the matter, Michèle? Are you OK?'

'Lesley. I've taken too many Dodos.'

At the hospital I was raw with fear. There was still no sign of Lucy. Perhaps she had broken some kind of code by telling me my future? Perhaps I had broken some code by saying I didn't believe her, by trying to take my life.

Whatever the reason for her absence, it was clear something had happened. I knew without a shadow of a doubt that I didn't want to die. Yes, my life was miserable but I was petrified of not living.

'Am I going to be all right, Lesley?'

'I don't know. Wait until we see the doctor.'

'Lesley, I'm not going to die, am I?'

'Wait until we see the doctor.'

She wasn't remotely reassuring. I think she was simply totally fed up with me and all the trouble I caused. I stared blankly into space and prayed I'd be OK. Prayed that Lucy would come back.

The doctors and nurses weren't exactly sympathetic either. I sat miserably in a tiny cubicle with a torn green curtain, feeling like hell. A nurse tore the curtain aside and shoved a paper cup with a clear liquid under my nose.

'Drink this.' She thrust the cup into my hand. I turned my head aside.

'Don't you know there are people here with real problems?' she said in an icy voice.

'I'm not drinking that crap.'

'If you don't drink it . . .' She paused, a deep furrow appearing in her forehead, her mouth set in a furious thin line, and then she slowly waved a long piece of plastic tubing in the air in front of me. 'Well, we will have to give you a stomach pump. That involves holding you down and forcing this tube down your throat.'

That didn't sound good. 'Are you sure this is necessary?'

'Yep. Your choice.'

No contest, I went for the liquid. It tasted as bad as I thought it would and it wasn't long before I started retching. The nurse handed me a plastic bucket without a word and turned to Lesley.

'This should teach her a lesson. I don't think she'll be in a hurry to go through this again.' She laughed bitterly and stalked out.

I heard Lesley talking with one of the other staff. They were debating whether to call Mum but decided against it.

'I don't think she was serious about it,' I heard Lesley say. 'Let's just play it right down.'

For the next twelve hours solid, I threw up. They had put me on the geriatric ward and I felt guilty for disturbing the old ladies who were moaning in their own pain and suffering. I tried to retch as quietly as I could. The next morning, when I felt better, I talked to the old ladies and brought them all cups of tea, apologising for causing them such disturbed sleep.

'Don't worry, duck,' said one old girl, giving me a pat on the arm. 'I was a rebel at your age. Things will get better for you. Don't you worry.' She chatted to me for a bit and it made me feel much better. Then a harassed-looking doctor came into the ward and ordered me back to bed.

'What have we here, young lady?' he said, poking my sliced arm with his ballpoint pen.

'Nothing,' I scowled.

He sat on the end of the bed and started making notes.

'I need you to answer a few questions. Did you seriously intend to end your life?'

I was savvy enough to know that the answers to these questions could either have me released, or have me sectioned and thrown into a mental asylum.

I shook my head slowly. 'No. I was just upset. I just accidentally took too many.'

'Why are you in the children's home?'

'Because my stepfather is a total nutcase who likes to beat me up.'

'So why did you harm yourself?'

'Look, stop treating me like I'm a nutter. I'm as normal as you and it was a spur of the moment mistake, all right? I don't need a psychiatrist or nothing.'

He wrote a few more notes and moved on. A little later Lesley came in and we headed back to Brookfield Close. I felt as bleak as it is possible to feel. Dead inside. My thoughts whirred round and round, an endless cycle of self-loathing. I hated myself so much. Over and over I told myself how stupid I was, how mad I was, how my ridiculous self-destructive act could have led to me losing Lucy for ever.

My suicide attempt seemed to mark a turning point at Brookfield Close. Life limped along, but it felt like the end of an era. Shelina and her sisters had been sent back home and Pat kept disappearing – she was barely there. Dan was the only one left of the old crowd and so I was

stuck in this big white box with few friends. Jamie was
confused about her on-off relationship with a guy called
Robert who also worked there. She was distracted and
didn't spend so much time with me, although we still had
occasional nights at her place where I did her tarot and
she did my I Ching. Robert found my connection with
Jamie confusing and – quite obviously – threatening. One
night Pat and I were having a trivial argument – nothing
we wouldn't have sorted out on our own. But Robert came
crashing in and cornered me in my room, pushing me up
against the wall and yelling in my face:

'You are not an adult, Michèle. You are still a child, for
Christ's sake. Get that into your thick head!'

In a funny way I respected what he was trying to get
across but, at the same time, I felt he just didn't get it. I
felt that his anger was based on caring, though, and that
felt horribly familiar.

My visits home continued to be unsuccessful. Mum kept
begging me to come home. Russell kept sneering at me,
taunting me for being 'delinquent', a 'hopeless saddo', a
'psycho nutcase' – which was pretty rich, coming from him.
I couldn't decide which was worse, home or the children's
home.

Even though there were fewer kids now, the staff seemed
more on edge than ever. Brenda and I had good and bad
days. Sometimes we would walk through Gunnersbury Park
together and watch the boats. One day she picked me an
ivy leaf and gave it to me (I put it in my diary and treasured

it). We talked about socialist politics and feminism: I was in heaven. Other times she kept her distance and didn't speak to me at all. I knew she was a softie, though, and that it was me who had caused the rift – my intensity was too much. She was kind and concerned but I had put her in a corner and I had left her no space to help me.

There was the odd surreal moment that lifted the mood, like the time we were sent by a charity to see Cannon & Ball at the London Palladium. I thought they were distinctly unfunny, but at least I got to buy a pair of bondage trousers from Carnaby Street. But on the whole you could never get a handle on the home. One minute you were treated as an adult, the next a child. It was incredibly confusing. For instance I was allowed to go to a disco in King's Cross on my own (travelling on the Tube) providing I was back by 1 a.m. Yet, on the other hand, I got hauled over the coals for doing my laundry!

I actually really liked doing laundry. It was novel for me and I found it curiously relaxing. I'd sit and read a book while the clothes dried, spinning round and round, the rhythm of the machine punctuating the silence. The laundry was down in the basement and it was normally a great place to be alone, to have a bit of peace and quiet. One evening I was sitting, watching the laundry spin round, letting my thoughts wander. It was like a form of meditation and I was feeling pretty deeply relaxed for once. It was 9 p.m. when the door opened and Ben, a member of staff, came noisily in.

'Michèle, it's lights out in five minutes. Can you finish up now and get to bed?'

I hadn't had many dealings with him but he seemed nice enough, reasonable. I nodded and smiled.

'Yeah, sure. I'm just waiting for this to dry – it shouldn't be too long now.'

'No. Michèle, turn it off and go to bed now.'

'Yeah. Just give me a minute.'

The next thing I knew he stepped sharply towards me and tugged me by the arm. I pulled my arm away and a struggle ensued.

'I said I'm coming in a minute,' I shouted.

'Now!' he said, and I noticed small beads of perspiration forming on his forehead. He reached out with both hands and grabbed me under the arms, accidentally brushing my breast. Before I knew what I was doing, I punched him in the nose. I must have hit him square on as his nose exploded and blood was dripping everywhere. He dropped my arm and staggered back. I didn't waste a second. I shot out the door and raced through the hall and out of the main entrance. I was totally freaked out. I hadn't meant to hit him – it was purely a reflex – and I was terrified I would go to prison.

– Lucy! Lucy! Where are you?

I yelled out for Lucy in my mind as I hid behind some cars just out of sight. No answer. This was getting weird.

Lesley came out, shouting to me.

'Michèle, it's OK. Come back in – nothing's going to happen.'

She waited, listening.

'Michèle. If you stay out there we will have to call the police. We won't have a choice.'

I weighed it up, wondering if it was some kind of trick. But Lesley was looking really concerned. I decided to trust her, and so I slunk out from behind the car.

'I didn't mean to hurt him. Honest. It was just a reflex.'

She smiled reassuringly. 'Look. You can apologise to Ben in the morning. Now get to bed.'

In the morning I apologised to Ben. It all seemed to be over and forgotten. But I found it really inexplicable that he had grabbed me like that. More odd still was the fact that Lucy didn't come when I needed her. I knew something was wrong but couldn't put my finger on it. Something had changed.

I tried hard to fit in, to do what I was told, but I was sick and tired of the seemingly arbitrary rules. They just felt so silly, so pointless. I still wasn't sleeping or eating properly; I still felt miserable to the pit of my stomach. My panic attacks were getting worse. I would have this paralysing terror that I was going to drop dead at any moment. I could barely breathe – it was as if the oxygen had been sucked out of the air around me. Everything would look different, as if I were floating up a long way away from the ground. A sense of impending doom permeated my mind and body. I would become rigid with fear and hide under my duvet, trembling for up to two hours, waiting for normality to return. I think I knew that I was spiralling into self-destruction with no parachute. My diaries at that time were filled with thoughts of death, of suicide, yet also packed with terror, with fear of what death would be like.

One day I had a row with one of the care workers who had always disliked me. Out of the blue, she accused me of throwing a rock at her. I was absolutely incensed with the injustice of it, as it simply hadn't happened. Why would an adult and a care worker say such things? I barricaded myself in my room and refused to talk to anyone. I just sat on my bed and methodically slashed my arm, slowly, carefully, hoping it would clear my head.

Brenda was on duty and I desperately wanted her to understand the injustice of it all. But she resolutely refused to talk to me – no doubt fearful of another intense reaction. Every time I heard footsteps on the hallway outside, I peered out through the crack in the door hoping it would be her coming to talk to me. But I waited hours and hours, the blood drying in thick rivulets on my arms. At last she did walk past, but by then I was so furious that I shouted out:

'I know you're not interested. So why don't you just get lost then?'

Her brilliant blue eyes, now cold as ice, gazed back through the hole.

'I can't get lost, Michèle. I work here.'

I slumped back on the bed and sobbed, realising the futility of it all. This was not a place of safety with equal friends, but a prison. I realised then that the time was coming when I would have to leave Brookfield Close.

There was a meeting to decide what should be done with me. Brookfield Close was really a holding centre and, on the whole, kids were passed on to other institutions. I idled by the door waiting to hear the outcome.

The head of the home didn't appear very often. He was a short, bearded man and looked just how you would expect a social worker to look. He wore brown corduroy trousers, woolly jumpers and Hush Puppies – and he had a thick bushy beard. We hadn't had much contact and my only impression of him was that he seemed pretty harmless. Now he poked his head around the corner and beckoned me in.

'Come in, Michèle.'

I walked in and took the seat he offered me at the large round table. I glanced around at Brenda, Lesley, Rachel and Ben, but they didn't catch my eye.

'Well, Michèle,' he continued. 'We have come to the conclusion that the best thing is for you to leave here. We're recommending you go to a secure unit in Northolt.'

A secure unit? What on earth? But there was more.

'You will be on the boy's floor. It's a precaution as we feel your sexuality may influence the other girls.'

I jumped to my feet and slammed my hands on the table:

'Are you mad? You want to put me on a floor with only

boys? No way! And you think I should be locked up? You're all more nuts than me! The bloody lunatics are running the bloody asylum.'

I stalked out without a backwards glance and phoned Mum.

'OK, I'm coming home,' I said. 'But there's a condition – you have to realise that I'm an adult and not a kid any more.'

She was delighted. 'Yes, come home, darling. This is where you belong.'

The head of the home tried one last time to talk me round:

'Think about it, Michèle. We can help you. We can do what's right for you.'

'Yeah right. Off to a boys' lock in? I don't think so!' I retorted.

I packed up all my stuff and shoved it in the taxi. It was great to watch the home disappear out of the back window, but I couldn't help feeling some trepidation about going back to my mother's. I had been away for just three months, but it felt like years. I knew that neither Nick nor Russell would be exactly pleased to see me.

15

Sniffing the Glue

Sure enough, the veins in Russell's forehead started to pulsate as I walked into the front room. He glared at the telly and didn't say a word. The place felt weird. Smaller somehow. Mum held out her arms and stroked my hair as I hugged her. She was very relieved that I was home. I knew she loved me, and my being away had made her realise just how much. But all the same, some invisible cord had been cut.

We were both keen for it to be different, a new beginning somehow, and so I didn't make a fuss when she told me it had been arranged for me to start at a new school – Brentford School for Girls.

I was – as always – optimistic and excited. I loved new challenges and once again I hoped it would be a fresh start.

I walked in on my first day, wearing DMs with the school uniform, a broad smile on my face and with my bag stuffed full of *Shocking Pink* issues to hand out. The whole class froze. It was like that scene in *An American Werewolf in London* when they go into the village pub and everyone stops what they're doing and their jaws drop. I looked around, feeling pretty put out. Some of them stared right back while others dropped their gaze and became overly interested in the contents of their desks.

'What's up?' I said. 'Have I got my skirt tucked in my knickers or something?' I slid into a desk next to a girl with sleek brown hair. 'What's going on? Why's everyone staring?'

The girl stammered and stuttered and looked frankly terrified. Eventually I got it out of her. The head had warned the class that I was coming – and had given them chapter and verse on all my issues. Just great. So that was the end of my nice fresh clean start.

It was supposed to be a 'nice' school but the girls were no angels, no different from any others really. They smoked behind the fence and in the toilets. A fair few of them were sniffing glue too.

I hadn't been there long when I came across a gang of them huddled behind the toilets.

'What are you doing?' I asked.

'Sniffing. Want a go?' One of them held out the glue and a plastic bag.

'Nah. I'm not into that.'

'Scared? It's only glue. It's not like it's heroin or anything,' said the girl with the bag.

'Thought you were supposed to be this big tough-nut hard girl,' said her friend with a sneer.

I know it's pathetic, but I didn't want to look weedy. I

tossed down my bag and sat on the ground. I snatched the glue and glared at the girls.

'No big deal,' I said.

I breathed into the bag and the most incredible feeling immediately overwhelmed me. It was so intense – a sudden rush to the head that sent me reeling. It was incredible, truly incredible, and then, even better, I blanked right out. While other people might crave the rush and the high of drugs, it wasn't rocket science to realise that my drug of choice would take me right out of my life. To a place of total nothingness. It was escape, a blissful escape – and so easy to get.

After that we sniffed regularly but, as with all things, I went further and crashed harder than the others. It wasn't long before I was hauled up in front of the head. Once again I was being expelled. No matter that it hadn't been me that had started the glue-sniffing. I was cast firmly in the role of bad girl, and everyone naturally assumed I was the instigator and a bad influence. So I left the school, but I didn't give up the glue.

One drag on that plastic bag and I was gone. As I sucked in the vapour, my brain would freeze over in a fog of chemical hell. I was not a pretty sight, eyes glazed, dribbling, becoming increasingly incoherent and then passing out. But I didn't care. I was out of it, floating off somewhere else, somewhere peaceful. Sometimes I'd sniff up to a litre of glue a day. Sometimes I combined it with alcohol. Add to that the fact that I was barely eating (my eating disorder had got worse and I would go days without food), and I really was dicing with death.

Time after time Mum would find me passed out, in a catatonic state, and would have to call an ambulance or haul me into a taxi and race me to Central Middlesex hospital. I would wake up in the casualty department, angry and disoriented, and demand to go home. I had no idea of the danger I was in or the pain I was causing my mother. I was oblivious to everything.

I had lost the way and very nearly didn't come back. Then Fate stepped in – or rather my guardian angel did. One day I had been to Ealing Broadway – to the pictures – and I was walking alone down the road. I looked up and found myself outside a church. It was very old, Gothic in style with huge towering, forbidding steeples – stern but beautiful. I had passed it thousands of times before and, like all things familiar, had never even noticed it. Suddenly Lucy hissed urgently in my ear:

– *Michèle, go inside. Go inside the church and have a look round.*

I couldn't understand why she was making me go inside a church in broad daylight. It wasn't even a Sunday. But Lucy didn't come as much as before and I knew this was significant. She must have a reason for it and it was good to have her 'on-side' again, so I pushed open the big wooden door. I found myself staring down a beautiful forest of graceful arches. It smelled of frankincense. Mum always burned incense when she was doing her magic and spells, and there were always plumes of smoke coming out of her office. So it felt familiar, welcoming even.

In the far corner I noticed there were hundreds of candles burning; they drew me like a moth, and I walked slowly and with as much reverence as someone in bondage trousers could manage. On the wall, next to the huge table of candles, there was a board absolutely covered with pieces of paper. I remembered Mum telling me about this sort of thing – they were prayers for people who were sick or in trouble.

It was so quiet that I could hear my breathing and the slight rustle of my trousers as I walked slowly towards the candles. No outside sounds penetrated the peace – not the traffic, not the shoppers. As I got close enough to read the messages, my mouth dropped open. There had to be literally hundreds of scraps of paper there, all in my mother's inimitable scrawl; hundreds of scraps of paper pinned to the board, virtually illegible writing in broken English:

'pleez sava ma daurter Michell, God protct her and save er from di glue'

'pleeze sava Michelle, look afta er and stopp er takin glue'

'pleeze pray fo may dauter Michèle, she needa help'

They were all prayers for me. The writing was passionate and fierce, the pen almost gouging through the thin scrap paper at times. She could read, but she could barely write her own name, never mind mine. When we went shopping I had to write her cheques as she couldn't even write numbers. So to have done this was a massive feat for her.

I could not believe it. Lucy and my mum were trying everything in their power to save me. Tears streamed down my face. My heart ached and I was totally confused. I had thought Mum didn't care about me at all and here she was praying for my very survival. It was a miracle that I came into the church. I stood staring at the prayers and the flickering candles for a long time. Silent, just breathing it in.

– *Thank you, Lucy.*

When I got home I rushed in and hugged Mum.

'What's that for?'

'Nothing. Just cos I love you.'

I stopped sniffing for a few days and I really wanted to stop for ever. But the fights and violence crowded back in. The glue had made me paranoid and my temper was out of control. By now I was smashing things at home and getting into endless fights with Mum, Russell, Nick – anyone really. It was just impossible to resist the chance of escaping reality, and it wasn't long before I started sniffing again.

Mum tried everything, asked everyone she could think

of for help. But nobody seemed bothered. Even my social worker brushed it off as a phase. Finally, out of sheer desperation, Mum decided to take me away from London altogether. She arranged for us to go to Italy to stay with her sister, Aunty Pina, in the hopes that a change of scene and atmosphere would wean me off the glue. I hadn't been to Italy since the tornado incident, but the place was in my soul and I jumped at the chance of going. I was spaced out on the plane, but as soon as we landed I felt something lifting. Italy was like a sigh of relief. A warm blanket of comfort enveloped me the instant I smelt the air. I took in all the sights and smells: the policemen with guns, the signs in Italian, the heady scent of garlic, lemons, tomatoes and warm sun. Everyone was like me – dark-haired, demonstrative, a bit too loud, waving their hands in the air, laughing loudly, shouting greetings, arguing passionately. There was no polite whispering here; this was the land of the large. Shouting and yelling were the normal way to interact. No wonder I felt instantly at home.

Aunty Pina wasn't at the airport to greet us, so we got a taxi to her block of flats in Udine. It was a five-storey-high white block, built on small stilts. It resembled a council block in a way, nothing fancy. It sat four-square, solid and reassuring, on the outskirts of town, overlooking a cornfield. It had survived earthquakes without a wobble and it had a good feel, a grounded safe feel, about it.

Pina looked nothing like Mum. My mother was dark and exotic while Pina was fair-haired and pinched-looking, rather plain. Mum looked ten years younger than she was while Pina looked ten years older, even though she was the youngest. The family barely spoke any English and I can't speak a word of Italian but we managed with a sort of pidgin English and lots of hand waving and gestures. The sisters seemed pleased enough to see each other although Mum had warned me on the plane that, in the past, Pina had always been jealous of her.

We sat down to lunch in the tiny kitchen, a small portable telly blaring in the corner. Lunch was thinly sliced ham, pickled onions, peasant bread and cheap red wine. I was a fussy eater (when I could eat at all), but it tasted divine and I refused to eat anything else for the whole of our time there.

It was a small flat and a bit of a squash. It was odd and yet familiar. My cousins were Manuela and Lorenzo. Manuela had been in a terrible car accident and nearly lost her life. She had been walking along a pavement when a drunk driver hit the curb and smashed into her. She had got through it all, but was more or less made up of steel pins that were keeping her together. She was outgoing and blonde and quite a strong character. She had a great sense of humour and, even though we spoke different languages, she made me laugh. Lorenzo looked just how a Lorenzo should: dark and stocky and very Italian. They were very sweet to me. Manuela must have been in her early twenties, while Lorenzo was about nineteen.

This was such an unusual taste of a totally different kind

of family life. I loved it. I met the local kids and hung out. At first they really seemed to like me, which was great, but it was not long before they started finding me odd. I was too forceful, too full-on, too in your face. Italian youngsters seemed much better brought up than any of the kids I'd known in London. They didn't rock the boat. I wanted to talk about politics and the injustices of the world: they wanted to listen to music and talk about who they fancied. They ended up thinking I was a weirdo.

Part of me longed to be like these kids – normal. They were very traditional and they all seemed so happy and studious. Back at home I would have scoffed at kids like that, but however boring and safe their lives were, they seemed happy in a way I patently wasn't. I think they found me interesting at first, something wild and different, but the novelty soon wore off and I was left to my own devices. Mum was making an effort, but she was still very temperamental. We would argue about what to watch on the telly and she would end up slapping me hard round the face. I know she didn't mean it – in fact, she had been trying with all her might to make things right between us – but we were just two strong characters. I would never back down; the more she hit me the louder I became, petulant and precocious to the end.

One day she drove me up into the mountains to meet a famous psychic and witch. He was called Stephano Aldo and she wanted to ask him if he could put a spell on me to make me behave and turn my life around.

I had met him once before in England and he'd seemed OK. But out here in the mountains, he seemed slightly sinister. He dressed all in black – black jeans, black polo neck, black boots. His wife was beautiful and blonde but was, apparently, visited every night by aliens who took over her body and spoke through her.

Aldo yawned widely and apologised, saying that the alien visitations were actually a real hassle as he had to sit up and transcribe what they were saying and so, consequently, he got easily tired during the day.

His wife didn't look like an alien to me, or even the kind of person that might channel aliens. She was the spit of Catherine Deneuve and was actually really nice and very interesting. She took me to one side after lunch, and told me that all people are bisexual.

They were the oddest and most exotic pair I'd ever met and I was intrigued. While Aldo dressed in black, the entire house was white – white-painted walls, white marble floors, even white furniture. He stood out against it like a big black shadow. The only colour came from the books – there were wall-to-wall books in every room. I was entranced.

The conversation was broad and broad-minded and I listened in fascination. They talked about mysticism and magic as if they were the most normal things in the world, as mundane as coffee and cake. I had grown up with magic, but had never heard it discussed in an intellectual way like this. Unlike most other adults, they treated me as an equal and included me in their conversations.

Aldo put a magical pendant round my neck and warned me to keep it on, as it would protect me from unwelcome influences. Then he turned to my mother:

'Bruna, she will be a very famous psychic one day. She has the sight in a special way. Don't worry about her, she is protected and always will be protected.' Lucy sprang into my mind and he gazed directly at me, nodding slightly and raising an eyebrow as if he knew all about her. All the way down the mountain I wondered about that look. I had wanted to talk to him about Lucy; she had been on my mind so much.

Over the years I had become so used to Lucy that, crazy as it may sound, I had clean forgotten that she and I were twins. She had just become this voice, this reassuring presence, this other part of me. As I grew older and more aware of the spiritual world and how it worked, I suppose I thought of her as a spirit guide, a wise presence who looked after me and gave me guidance, who told me things, who kept me safe. But here in Italy there was a big – and final – shift in our relationship.

I loved the ice-cream in Italy: it was like nothing on earth. This was before England had anything remotely exotic and the taste of pistachio ice-cream blew my mind. I used to hang out at a little *gelateria* licking an ice-cream, and then playing pinball with Lucy. I would set up a two-player game. I would take my turn and then she would take over and play. She always won. I was glad she was here as she hadn't been around much since my suicide

attempt and the glue-sniffing. I had missed her. Then, as
we were in the middle of a game, she suddenly shouted in
my head.

– You had a twin who died at birth.
– What?
– You had a twin. She died when you were born.
– Don't be silly. You're just saying that 'cause I used to
like Elvis and he had a twin that died at birth.
– No. You had a twin. That twin was me.

I reeled. What on earth was going on? I always trusted
Lucy, but this was just too much to take. Was I going mad?
Was Lucy real or was I making her up? I was near to tears,
in severe shock. How could I have had a twin and not
known? It was totally impossible. I sat down, my head
spinning. Lucy was perfectly silent, as if waiting for me to
take it in. When the panic cleared so did my thoughts. I
listened to my heart and then, all of a sudden, it made
perfect sense. Of course she was my twin. How could I
ever have forgotten?

– I'm sorry, Lucy.
– Don't be. It's all right. But now it's time.
– For what?
– To tell her.
– She'll freak. She won't believe me.
– Trust me.

I looked up. Mum must have come in while I was playing. She was perched on a bar stool, smoking a cigarette. I walked over to her.

'What do you want to drink, Michèle? Let's go to the square and have a drink.'

We walked out together, Lucy's words ringing in my ears. I barely knew where I was walking.

She bought me a Coke and I looked round the square. It was a wide, open space, bordered by gracious tall, white marble buildings. At one end was a big clock tower; its clock staring down at us with its blue and gold face. There was a large ornate fountain in the middle and all the cafés and restaurants had put out tables and chairs round the edges, with large umbrellas to keep the fierce sun away. We took our drinks and sat down at one of the tables. Not many people were about and the air seemed still and peaceful. We didn't talk, we just sat sipping our drinks, enjoying a rare moment of quiet peace between us. Then, I couldn't help myself, the words just tumbled out of my mouth in between the Coke and ice cubes.

'I had a twin who died at birth, didn't I?'

Mum went white as chalk. She stared at me blankly, as if she had misheard me.

'What did you say?'

'I had a twin who died when I was born.'

'Don't be silly. Who told you that?'

'I just know.'

'*Porco dio*. How did you know that? Nobody knew about

her. Only two people knew and both of them are dead. Your father and Joan. How did you know that, Michèle? I need to know.'

She had come out in a cold sweat, pearls of perspiration forming a fine film all over her ghostly white face. I stared at her, suddenly feeling anxious – she looked so horrified.

'No. Michèle. You must tell me. Who told you this?'

'She told me. My twin. She's been talking to me for as long as I can remember. She looks after me.'

Something lifted and my mother breathed a sigh of relief. When she realised that it was something supernatural that had given me the knowledge, she seemed to relax a bit. She took the fact that my dead sister had been talking to me for my entire life completely in her stride. This made sense to her; this was something she understood.

'What was her name going to be?' I asked.

'Luciana Rosa. We would have called her Lucy, I expect.'

So there it was – the final proof.

'What happened to her?'

'I never saw her, but your father did. He said she was perfect except for a hole in her back. She had slightly fairer hair than you. She was perfect – but dead. I blame the accident. I fell down the stairs when I was *pregna*.'

Tears welled up in my mother's eyes. She looked at me long and hard then put another cigarette to her lips.

'I don't want to talk about it ever again, Michèle. It is just too painful. All those years wanting a baby, then losing one. And you both nearly died. You were dark blue when you were born. I thought you were going to be a black baby, but the doctor he told me it was because you had no oxygen. Maybe that's why I have all this trouble with you. Maybe I wanted a child too much. Maybe the other one would have been a good girl. Different, eh?'

That felt like being stabbed in the heart. Maybe Mum would have rather Lucy had lived, and I had died. Mum stood up and shook out her skirt and stabbed her cigarette in the large white ashtray. She patted me absent-mindedly on the shoulder and walked, slightly unsteadily, back across the square. I sat, thinking about everything she had said. To think I should have had a real living sister, a twin. To think I needn't have gone through all the misery on my own but could have had her with me, physically with me, all those years. It just wasn't fair.

— Lucy. Are you there?
— Yes, but I have to go now. You had to know the truth. It will be important. It is who you are. It is the answer. I won't be able to speak to you any more but you will be fine now. Many wonderful things are going to happen to you, but you have to look after yourself. Promise me?

The meaning of her words sank in. She was leaving? I couldn't bear it.

— You can't leave! Not now, not now I know who you are. I always wanted a sister. I always felt as if I should have

a sister. Lucy, I'm sorry I forgot who you were. Please don't leave.

– Michèle, my dearest love, I have to go. You will understand one day. But you will always be protected. Don't forget you know what I have taught you – you know how to create your future. Don't forget and don't ever stop believing in magic – it is all around you.

With that she was gone. She left me in Italy.

16

Two Lives That Shine As One

Why had Lucy left me? I simply couldn't work it out. Was it something to do with her telling me we were twins? That didn't make sense. All I could think was that she had told me things she wasn't supposed to tell – about my future. She had broken some spiritual law. Later on I wondered if maybe it was time for her to come back into incarnation – that maybe somewhere there was a baby who held Lucy's soul. But the bottom line is that I still don't know. Not yet.

Back home in London, I fell straight back into my old pattern. I was spending increasingly more and more time in an Evostik stupor. Occasionally I would go back to my old alcohol/Mogadon mix for a bit of variety, but really I spent far more time unconscious than I did conscious. Life had become a blur. I can only really remember it by reading my diary from the time. It doesn't make for pleasant reading. Sometimes there are gaps of days, even weeks and months:

13 May: Have taken a lot of glue this week. Nearly got charged for breaking the peace for smashing milk bottles in the kitchen. Spent four hours at Acton police station.

20 May: Had a fight with Russell. All I seem to do is take glue.

2 June: Kirsten [a friend] has threatened to kill me. I've just got to carry on. Lucy, help me! I know you can see the future, what does it hold?

3 June: I'm going to start learning from my mistakes.

5 June: Got drunk, took lots of pills.

8 June: been off my head on Valium and Moggys and glue and drink lately. Lay down on a patch of grass in the middle of the motorway and wondered what it would be like to be buried. I still have such love and faith in people, even when they do such awful things to me.

11 June: Nick tried to beat me up. Took some Moggys off my mother.

14 June: Kirsten beat me up badly – she kicked me in the face with Doc Martens on. I feel really ill.

22 June: Went to *Shocking Pink* meeting but haven't slept for 24 hours and feel awful.

Then there's a gap – no diaries kept until November. Maybe I didn't write one or maybe I threw it away – I really don't remember. But nothing much had changed – or so it seemed.

26 November: Didn't do much except sniffed.
29 November: Dyed my blonde streak bright pink. Had
my nose pierced. Sniffed. Mum did the tarot for me.

Now that is a day I do remember very clearly. Mum was
downstairs and had just finished doing a reading for
someone. I heard the door click shut as the client left, and
Mum's footsteps padding out into the hall. She called up
the stairs:

'Come down here, darling. I'll give you a reading.'

My mother's readings always came true even if I didn't
like them. She hadn't done one for a while (the last few
had been awful) so I hauled myself off the bed and
wandered downstairs. She was sitting in the dining room
at the wobbly old dinner table (a donation from one of
the wealthy women she cleaned for). She nodded at the
chair across from her and I slouched into it. I watched her
hands as she shuffled the pack, worn soft and scuffed with
age and use. She shuffled longer than usual, an intense
look on her face. Finally she seemed satisfied and placed
them down in front of me with a firm nod:

'Cut the pack.'

I cut the cards into three piles as I had been taught as
a child, and had done so many times before. This was a
little ritual between us, a way of getting close, a connection.
She wanted to make sure I was all right, that I was safe,
to see what was going to happen to me. Some mothers
have a physical eye on their kids, keeping them home, not

letting them out of their sight. Mine kept a cosmic eye on me.

She was brutally honest. Many mothers would have said what they wanted the cards to say, nudging the truth aside in favour of the ideal message. But Mum always told the truth, even if it irritated her or she didn't approve. She was always proved right. Sometimes she would read the cards and then, without warning, lean over and give me a clip round the ear.

'Hey, what's that for?' I'd yelp. 'I haven't done anything.'

'Eh, maybe not yet – but you will!' And she'd give me another, just for luck. She knew when I was going to step out of line even before I did. Given that, I still wonder why she didn't have a clue about the abuse. She sure as hell knew about everything else. But then psychics don't know everything – we can have blind spots and this was clearly one of hers.

She bent over the cards, then ran her hands through her hair and pointed to the spread.

'Right then. The Queen of Cups, and the Ace of Pentacles. I see a very rich woman here. She has fair hair. She's coming into your life and there will be love for a while. She will make you happy, then she will go away.'

'A rich woman? Yeah right! What do you mean "she will go away after making me happy", that's not good, is it? Rich woman? I can't see that happening.'

'I tell you, Michèle. I see a rich woman. She will come and help you.'

'Chance would be a fine thing.' I pushed back my chair

and, with a shrug, went out hunting for some more glue. I didn't think another word about it.

19 December: Had really bad pains in my heart, due to too much sniffing.

22 December: The world is so unfair – it's not in the right order. The glue sniffing is doing me in. It could kill me, so why am I wasting my life when others haven't even got the choice to eat properly? I feel guilty, very guilty.

A month later, on 24 January 1982 (I've never forgotten the date), I decided to go out. There weren't many clubs in the area, but once a month there was a gay night at a grubby pub in Acton town. I had been there once before and remembered it consisting of one big cavernous space, smelling of stale beer and cigarettes. A long bar slid down one side of the room and there had been about two or three gay men dressed in clone gear perched on stools drinking lager and lime. I don't think there could have been a more unappealing place.

But hope springs eternal and when Debbie, someone I used to know from school, suggested we meet there for a drink, I agreed. After all, I had nothing better to do.

I walked into the club in my best black bondage trousers, my hair spiked up with soap and with a bright scarlet streak through it. I was fifteen but I could pass for much older – nobody ever queried me about my age.

I saw Debbie sitting at a table. I grabbed a pint from the bar and joined her. Gloomily we surveyed the scene. There were a few more people than last time, but it was hardly buzzing.

'Bloody rubbish here. Remind me why we came?' I said, sipping my beer.

She shrugged and lit a cigarette. I looked up and over the rim of my pint glass, squinting to try to make out the blurry figure by the cigarette machine. I rubbed my eyes. Heck, I'd only had one beer and already I was seeing things.

'Wow, weird. She looks just like Olivia Newton-John from *Grease*!'

'You what?' Debbie said.

I leaped from my seat and headed towards the cigarette machine where the Olivia look-alike was struggling with the machine.

'Can I help you with that?' I asked. It was a bit of a gamble as I'd never used a cigarette machine in my life. Despite all my other vices, I never smoked.

'Sure, that would be great.' She had a strong Australian accent.

I gave the machine a big thump and out popped her cigarettes. I was amazed, but tried to look nonchalant – as if I did this trick all the time.

'Where are you from?' I asked, then held up one finger to stop her replying. 'But before you do, let me tell you this for free – wherever you came from, you've landed in the wrong place. This is the armpit of the Universe.'

She gave me a broad grin. Her teeth were perfect, gleaming white, and her eyes were sparkling blue – they beamed right into mine and I had the strangest feeling that I had known her all my life.

'I'm on holiday from Sydney, Australia.' She looked round the club with a rueful grin. 'Yes, it is a bit different,' she giggled.

'I'm Michèle,' I said, holding out my hand.

'No way! My name's Michelle as well!'

We exchanged looks for a fraction of a second too long, taking each other in, and I felt an electric charge run down the back of my neck as if someone were walking over my grave. Then I gave a little shrug. 'Clearly it's Fate. Come over and join us. Let me buy you a drink.'

Two lone men jigged around on the dance-floor to the song 'YMCA' as we made our way back to our table. We couldn't stop talking. Debbie got the picture and said she was off, waving a brief goodbye and giving me a wink.

I learned that Michelle had had some troubles of her own. She was a fair bit older than me – twenty – and used to take drugs. Her father was quite wealthy and she had lived a pampered but lonely life. She'd had fabulous holidays and mixed with all sorts of celebrities, but had generally felt ignored. Poor little rich girl. When she was thirteen, she'd been seduced by an older man on a cruise ship and had got into drugs. We had a lot in common. She thrilled me with tales of Australia and how wonderful it was there. I was transfixed.

When she went to the loo, I bounded up to the DJ and asked him to play a song for us – to Michelle from Michèle. The song was the love theme from *A Star is Born* by Barbra Streisand – 'Love, soft as an easy chair . . . .'

Two lives that shine as one? If only.

We danced and the lousy surroundings faded away. We could have been on a beach in Australia, watching the sun come down. We could have been anywhere. It was magical and, as the night drew to a close, Michelle smiled widely and said: 'Why don't you come back to my hotel in Kensington? It's behind Harrods. I want to talk to you some more.'

We hailed a black cab and headed off to her hotel.

'Wait here while I see if the coast is clear,' she whispered, and then sneaked me up the stairs to her hotel room. We talked all night. It turned out that Michelle had had a cyst of hair and bone that the doctors thought was a part of what should have been her twin. It was like she had been carrying her twin inside her. I found myself telling her all about Lucy. She was the first person with whom I had felt I could talk about it.

It was bizarre. It felt like we were kindred spirits. We were both called 'Michèle' (me with one L, her with two). We had both had a strange twin experience. We had both had problems with our families. Her father had threatened to have her locked up in an asylum if she continued to say she was gay. She worked in Sydney but was away on holiday, hoping to get her head straight – in more ways than one.

It clearly wasn't working. She had just come back from a skiing trip and was simply passing through London.

Finally, in the very early hours of the morning, as dawn broke over Kensington, we went to bed and lay there, wrapped in each other's arms, lost in each other's eyes, kissing gently.

I felt as if I had stepped into a dream. I didn't always call Mum to say where I was but, the next morning, I felt compelled. She had just come in after her night work.

'Mum, guess what? I've met the person you saw in the cards and I am bringing her home later to meet you!' I said excitedly.

'OK darling. I told you it would happen, no?'

We'd had no sleep, but Michelle was full-on in love with life.

'Come on! There is so much I want to see in London,' she said. 'I want to go to the Tate Gallery and Portobello Road Market for starters.'

She dragged me around art galleries and talked to me about all the paintings. She loved Joan Miró and cubism and I was inspired by her knowledge of all the artists. By the time we got to Mum's, I was exhausted. I was a bit nervous as we walked into the hall, hand in hand, but I needn't have worried. She and Mum got on like a house on fire.

'Come here, darling . . . give me your hand.' Mum grabbed Michelle's hand and started to read her palm before she had even taken her jacket off. She waved me off and I wandered happily upstairs. The day before, Michelle had read me the riot act. She had bought me some brown hair dye and told me to dye my hair to a normal colour and get a job. Above all, she made me promise I'd *never* take glue again. So, while Mum was reading her palm and doing her cards, I went and dyed my hair. I don't know what my mother told her, but when I came down she was white as a sheet.

'What's up?'

Mum stood behind Michelle. 'Leave her, Michèle. It's private, eh?'

Then she looked up and noticed my hair. She gave a broad smile.

'Go on, girls. Go have fun. Live for the moment.'

I smiled back.

The day passed in a haze of happiness. I have never experienced so much unconditional love. Michelle listened to me, *really* listened. She held me and hugged me. She accepted every part of me – for someone with my background it was almost too much to take.

That night we went out to a club and danced some more, and talked some more, and for the first time ever it felt like the world was spinning in time with me, rather than pressing against me all the way. It was totally heady and almost unsettling. I wasn't used to this kind of gentle, accepting, pure love.

The next day and night were the same, locked in deep conversation with her loving me all the way. We laughed, we connected, we bonded deep as deep can be. I had never in my entire existence felt loved like that, with real understanding. It healed something deep. When I think of it now, it was as if she was channelling pure love. I always refer to her as the angel who dropped into my life and turned it around.

But the next day she had to leave. As I went with her to the airport she said firmly:

'Now, no freaking out, Michèle. I'm going to come back and in six months' time we'll be living together and we're going to have a fabulous life!'

'It might not work out.'

She nodded. 'It might not,' she agreed. 'But, hey, even if we don't work out as lovers, we will be best friends, always.' She gently touched my face. 'Now. No more glue, no more nonsense, it's time to really grow up.'

Michelle took hold of my little notebook and wrote down her work address and phone number in Australia, along with a note on the time differences. I nodded and smiled. Then I pulled a small box out of my pocket and gave it to her. It was a silver charm of a cat. As her flight came up on the board, I was as good as gold. We held each other and kissed. I said 'See you soon.' And off she went.

I never sniffed glue again and I determined to succeed. I even got a job in the Wimpy to impress her – no matter that it wasn't strictly legal as I was under-age. I was totally determined to transform and, for the next three months, I really did clean up my act. I ate properly,

I went to work, and I wrote letters to her all the time. She wrote back and sent photos. I would call her at work when I could – I didn't dare phone at home as her father didn't approve of me in any way, shape or form.

But I felt I had to make an exception on her twenty-first birthday. I knew there was a chance that her father might answer the phone, but surely he couldn't make a fuss, not today of all days. Sure enough, he picked up the phone.

'Hi. Is Michelle there please?'

There was a long pause. For a moment I thought I'd got the wrong number.

'Er, hi? I wanted to talk to Michelle. Is she there?'

'No. I'm sorry. She's been in a car accident and she's in hospital right now.'

I felt a sledge-hammer whack me in the stomach.

'Oh my God,' I stammered. 'I'm so sorry. Is she hurt? She is going to be all right, yes?'

The voice seemed cold and distant. 'We don't know yet. I'm sorry but I have to go.'

The phone went dead.

I was devastated. I wanted to phone every hour, but I made myself wait until the next day. I spent the whole night on my knees praying, praying that she would be all right, praying with my whole heart. My diary smacks of desperation:

If she dies, I don't know what I'll do. I would take her place in hospital if I could, I really would.

With my heart in my mouth I dialled the number again. The same voice answered.

'Hi, it's Michèle again. I just wanted to know how Michelle is.'

Again, that awful pause. I felt an awful sickness spreading through me. Something was wrong, horribly wrong. Finally he replied.

'I'm sorry. She died last night.'

I hung up the phone in shock. Michelle dead? She had been so vibrant, so alive, it just wasn't possible. She had filled me with all that positive energy, we had planned a future together. And now, bang, she was gone? How could it be that the angel that had saved me was now no longer here?

This was what I wrote in my diary:

I love her. I can't believe it's her. I think I'll write and they will say it was a mistake. How can they bury her in the ground? I would take her place – she was worth that much. Why her? Why her? We had our whole lives ahead of us. My first real love and the first woman to know me, really know me, and she dies. I still think she's going to knock on the door. Death can't be the end. Her spirit must live on – it was too strong to die. I miss her so much.

I was too numb to cry. So I wrote a letter to her father saying how amazing she was, how she had saved me, and had given me so much in the time I had known her. He never replied.

17

Went Rushin' Down that Freeway

It took me a long time to get over Michelle dying, and for a while I was in a state of total shock. It all seemed so capricious somehow, unfair. You meet a person and think they will be part of your life for ever – and then all of a sudden they're gone. Maybe, I wondered, she really had been an angel – sent purely to put me back on track with my life. Without Lucy, I sure as hell needed someone.

But time heals and I was young. Towards the end of my fifteenth year, life took a surprising turn for the better. It was spring and I met a woman called Faye. She was in her early twenties, with beautiful auburn hair – she looked just like David Bowie. She was a teacher and incredibly kind and inspirational. I fell in love with her, with her intellect and her maturity. Amazingly, she seemed to like me in return. I felt guilty about finding love after Michelle's death and my diary at the time is full of anguish about whether I was betraying Michelle by being with Faye. I spent hours talking to her, and she didn't seem to mind a bit. We talked about spirituality and she talked to me about drama and poetry. She encouraged my creativity and my desire for learning. I still craved intellectual stimulation. I wanted to learn about everything. I also wanted to try to understand what made it go so wrong. I instinctively knew we are all one and that it is easier to love than hate. So why was life so cruel? Why were people so cruel? Why was I still so out of control? Since Michelle's death I had slowly found myself sliding back into my old bad habits. I gave up my job at the Wimpy. I was back on Mogadon – though I kept my promise to her about the glue. I was also drinking far too much.

Poor Faye. She found me hard going a lot of the time. Also, my mother was behaving very strangely concerning her:

'Why you hang out with her? It's disgusting. If she don't leave you alone I'll call her school – I'll tell them they have a dirty woman working for them! I'll call the papers! I'll tell them what going on. Disgusting!'

I found this totally strange as she had never stopped me doing anything before. She had positively thrown me at Michelle. She had never been judgmental. Crazy, yes. Judgmental and bigoted, no. Why she suddenly objected to Faye (who was such a positive influence), I really didn't know. I was terrified that mum would drive Faye away from me – and she did. Faye met someone else, someone older and less mucked up, and I was devastated when she left. No longer able to spend most of my time at her place,

I found myself sitting back in my room at home with Mum and Russell screaming at each other downstairs. Nick was descending into despair – nobody seemed to have any idea how to help him.

I had to get away from the house; it was driving me crazy.

Then one night I bumped into a woman I vaguely knew called Danni at a disco.

'Hey, Michèle,' she said, leaning against the bar, shouting over the thumping bass-line. 'You don't know anyone who wants to move into a squat with me?'

'What?'

'I've found this dead cool house in Brixton. It's been deserted for over seven years. It's on a road with other squats and it's really fab. But I need someone to move in with. You know anyone?'

'Me! I will! I love Brixton! When shall we move? I'm sixteen in a few months so no one can stop me.'

'Cool. Let's move in at the weekend then.' We punched fists and it was settled. Just like that.

I'd grown to like Brixton the year before when I used to go to an illegal drinking club. The club was in the basement of a house and it was called Pearl's (after its owner, Pearl – a large black woman in her fifties). She would take the money at the door and the place wouldn't close until the sun came up. Then, when we were finally chucked out, we would reluctantly leave and trek down Coldharbour Lane to buy fried dumplings for breakfast.

We'd puff ourselves up and look tough as we walked past the drug addicts and other night characters. I loved it. It felt real, it felt funky, it felt alive. Unlike the suburbs where I'd grown up, Brixton was edgy and uber-urban. It was teeming with squats, with people like me who were into politics, feminism, alternative spirituality and music. It was, above all, young.

Nursery Road was a quiet street behind the back of Marks & Spencer. It was a row of two-up, two-down terraced houses with cute little front gardens. The council had left several houses empty for years and they had fallen into disrepair. A railway bridge ran over the end of the short street and the back of the road was blocked off, though if you went through the narrow alley you'd find a small traditional pub. The rundown houses had been taken over by squatters, mainly students just out of university, although there was a gaggle of slightly older middle-class hardworking people who would move in and do them up. Eventually the council gave up on the houses and turned them over to the squatters – a co-operative was formed.

Inevitably there was a scene when I told Mum. She was horrified at the idea of me living in a squat; of me living with older women; of me leaving home, leaving her. She took it as a huge rejection. She had given up all ideas of me continuing with my schooling. She had even given up all ideas of me becoming a 'nice' girl who would dress properly, work hard, have decent friends. She realised I was never going to be a dutiful Italian daughter and marry a respectable man and give her scores of cute grandchildren. But she hadn't counted on me upping and leaving her, with Nick slumped in his room and Russell even more psychotic than ever. She even told me she thought Russell wanted to kill her, that he wanted her dead so he could have the house. But none of it worked. I was leaving home and it was the happiest day of my life.

As soon as I walked down the alley and into the road I felt a huge sense of coming home. It was an oasis in battle-scarred Brixton and had a comforting traditional feel. Danni had sourced a house that was very different to the others – it used to belong to an old lady who had died many years before, obviously without any family to bequeath it to. It was like walking onto the *Marie Celeste*. There were tins of food seven years out of date; piles of old-lady clothes; half-filled bottles of sickly lavender scent; endless drawers of thick tights and big pants – all with a faint but distinctive smell of wee overlaid with mildew. Water was dripping through the ceiling, droplets nudging their way down the electric light fitting. There were holes in the damp-stained ceilings and roof, large enough to see the clouds passing overhead.

The walls were turquoise with swathes of mould. It was rotten with damp and felt strange – the old lady's presence filled the house from top to bottom. I sensed her immediately, but she didn't seem to mind that we were there; in fact, it was almost as if she liked the company. The place was a death-trap really as everything was falling apart.

I spent the first night alone as Danni was off at work. I was terrified, but excited. I lay in the cold damp room by the broken front window unable to sleep, listening to the drip drip drip of the water coming through the hole in the roof and hitting the old enamel milk-pan I'd put under the drip. I couldn't help but think about burglars or rapists as there was such a large hole in the front window-pane. But by the time I woke up the next morning, I knew I was safe. The little house was quiet and calm and I felt an unusual sense of comfort. I was totally sure that the old lady was looking after me. I was safe from men. I was safe from harm. I was totally over the moon.

Danni had a motorbike and she was always taking speed. I myself was no angel of course, what with the glue, the Moggys and the Valium. Yes, I'd taken the odd upper or downer, including speed, but they'd never really done it for me. Drugs weren't really my thing – certainly not after Lucy had warned me off them at the children's home and after Michelle had read me the riot act regarding the glue.

Not long after we moved in, Danni taught me to ride her motorbike. When I say 'taught', it was more that she bunged me on it, showed me how to put it into gear, how to accelerate and brake – and then pushed me off up the road. I wobbled violently (and had a moment of panic when I thought the bike might topple and fall on top of me – it was big and very heavy), but I managed to get the hang of it. Of course I never took a test, never had a licence.

I realised pretty quickly that Danni had taught me for a reason. She would pack me off on the bike to pick up her drugs. She figured that, as I was a minor, nothing much would happen to me if I was caught. Ever eager to please, off I went, weaving my way down the road and then stalling horribly on Acre Lane. The gods must have protected me as firstly I couldn't really ride a motorbike, and second I had no clue how dangerous it was to get her drugs. But it all went OK – nobody stopped me, nothing hit me, and I got the drugs and obediently brought them back.

Danni was pleased and gave me a line of speed for picking it up for her. She was very charming and I liked to think of her as my big sister. I looked at the line. I used glue to get 'out of it', to dodge the pain of life. I'd taken speed before but couldn't really understand why anyone would want to make life more real than it already was. But I wanted to be accepted, wanted to be seen as one of the gang. I bent over the table and snorted it up. It felt different to the tablets I'd taken before. There was a flash in my head, a blinding surge of energy, and it felt as if someone had cranked my brain up about six gears. I felt smarter, brighter, more alive somehow.

It was to become a destructive habit. It kept me awake all night, which got me over the fear of being in this strange house alone. But it also stopped me eating again, and within three months I had became a drawn white ghost as my eating disorder returned.

The big plus side of Nursery Road was that it was the

first place I felt true happiness. At last I had a proper family, a family that cared about me, that looked out for me – or that was how it felt. There were four houses down the road, all occupied with squatters. There was a real sense of community and everyone would help one another and listen to one another's problems. There was always someone to talk to and people always wanted to check how you were, to find out if you were OK. I had never had this before and it felt incredible. It was everything that my former home life hadn't been. I didn't give home a single thought – except to be profoundly grateful that I had escaped in one piece. Everyone was exploring all aspects of life as fiercely and greedily as they could. They were trying to create utopia and, while these things rarely last, it was a miracle to experience. It was 1982 and anything went.

There was Pink Sarah who had dyed her hair neon pink and had just finished law school. There was Sarah Thomas who was half French and very posh. There was Racine Ripple who was a voluptuous mixed-race actress and a true inspiration to me. She was big and beautiful and had a very powerful character – she later appeared in the film *Scrubbers* with Pat from *EastEnders*. Funnily enough, she didn't initially take to me. She used to call me a 'spoilt brat' and give me withering looks if I entered the room. She was Queen Bee, and I bowed to her superior wisdom and made the effort to buck up my ideas and get myself together.

To my intense joy, I became very popular due to my tarot readings. At long last, 'psychic' was in. It was a pleasant surprise for me as I had learned, over the years, to be wary of talking about my gift. I was fed up of being considered a freak. But now everyone was trying to learn the tarot; everyone had crystal balls and everyone pored over the I Ching. It was quite funny really. I took my gift totally for granted; it was just the way it was. For as long as I could remember I was able to look at people, talk to them, and then know exactly what their life comprised and what was holding them back. I could go into intricate detail about it, and it always stunned people.

Being away from home had, as always, done wonders for my relationship with Mum and she had started taking me to psychic fairs. I can clearly remember the first time I had a table of my own to do readings. I was still only fifteen. The first client sat down and I laid the cards on the table. I turned them over and looked at the woman sitting across the table.

'I know this is going to sound very odd, but I see that you are married to a very possessive man. So possessive that he goes as far as having you followed. You are thinking of leaving him.'

She went white. 'Yes, yes, yes. He is on his third private detective. I'm at my wits' end with it all.'

Details like that came easily to me, but I didn't feel totally confident with giving professional readings. Mum wanted me to do more fairs, but I needed to prove it to myself before I would go on. So I did readings for my fellow squatters and their friends in Nursery Road. I would often end up with a queue of people wanting readings. I never charged them anything; I was just happy to help in any way I could. I started to get quite a reputation and, when my predictions came true (which they always did), people would come racing back – often very swiftly as I was very accurate with short-term predictions.

It led me to reassess my gift, to take it a bit more seriously maybe. I started to research spirituality in earnest and read every book I could get my hands on. I still felt that there was a piece of the puzzle that we were missing; that there was something that could make the world a better place if only I could find it. I began to feel that it was more likely to lie in the world of spirit than in that of politics (though that still remained a passion).

My mum and I continued to have a tempestuous relationship, even though we were living apart. It was love and aggression all the time. I never fully trusted her – how could I? But there was one incident I still regret and that still hurts my heart when I think about it even today. It was my sixteenth birthday and I was so relieved finally to be an adult (as only a child can be!) that I had been out partying all night and slept in late. I heard a knock at the door and could hear my mum shouting.

'Michèle . . . happy birthday, darling! I've come to say "happy birthday."' I peered through the crack in the door and saw her piercing eagle eyes through the letterbox. I hid, not wanting to see her. I was an adult now. I was free. But I didn't realise then just how cruel I was being.

My poor mother had got the train all the way from Hanger Lane to bring me a birthday cake and I wouldn't open the door. She knocked on all the neighbours' doors, searching for me, crying all the way. She came back a few times, calling forlornly through the letterbox, but I couldn't move. Eventually, she turned and walked up the road, her head low, her shoulders shuddering. I knew she'd be sobbing all the way home and that my selfish rebellion would cut her to the quick. If I had a time machine, that would be the single thing in my whole life that I would change. I would open the door, tell her I loved her, invite her in and be kind and gracious. Hindsight.

Tamsin came to the street from Australia and I was drawn to her as she reminded me of Michelle. She was ten years older than me and a vegetarian. We were from different worlds but we got on really well. It was just as well as, about this time, Danni ran off with all my money, leaving me pretty destitute. There hadn't been any rows or anything and I didn't even particularly bear her any ill-will – obviously she had had her reasons. But it didn't fit with the fundamental integrity of the street. With Danni gone, I didn't want to stay in the house on my own. It had been good to me, but I was getting sick of not having decent plumbing and safe power and having a ceiling full of holes. So I moved into the house where Tamsin lived. It seemed like a palace – it was much bigger and had decent electrics; you weren't terrified of electrocuting yourself every time you turned on a light.

My new room was amazing. Pink Sarah used to live there and had painted the floorboards bubblegum pink. I had a black cricket net over the ceiling and there was a perfect little fireplace, and even my own en-suite bathroom – luxury by anyone's standards.

One day I received an invitation to go to Colchester to see a drummer and her friend. I had never left London on my own and saw it as a huge adventure. I got the train and headed to Colchester, eager for a great night. When I arrived the drummer handed me a tab of acid. I was reluctant to take it, but didn't want to appear rude. I had had it once before and had at first had this incredible feeling of being totally at one with the world. But pretty soon I'd felt that the earth hated being encased in concrete, which had freaked me out.

I looked at the little red microdot and popped it in my mouth, not wanting to seem uncool. For the next hour, nothing happened but we were preparing to go to a disco.

'Hey, Mich, has that kicked in yet? I can see colours all around your head!'

'No, not seeing anything at all. Maybe that was a dud, give me another one.'

Not the brightest thing I had ever done. She handed me another tab, this time a little square with a smiling face on it.

I popped it in my mouth and we headed out the door. As soon as we got to the club I started to feel strange. I went to the toilet, with the music blaring and shapes forming all along the dingy corridor to the loo. I looked in the mirror and my face was totally grotesque and distorted. I felt a flow of what can only be described as poison flood through my veins. It looked like the veins in my neck were standing out and I became filled with sheer unadulterated terror. I stumbled out of the toilet.

'You've got to take me to the hospital now! I'm dying . . . I've been poisoned,' I cried.

'We can't do that, man. We'd get done. Ride it out, OK?'

'No, seriously, I ain't messing about. I NEED to go to the hospital! I think I might drop dead.'

They started to whisper to themselves. I could hear their words – sometimes from what sounded like miles away, sometimes as if they were yelling in my ear:

'Maybe we could lock her in a room in the flat?'

'Nah, that's no good. If she does die, we'd get left with a dead body on our hands. How we gonna explain that?'

They were terrified and also very annoyed as they could not think of a constructive way to get rid of me.

'Just take me to the station then, I'll get home somehow.'

I was terrified. The club felt as if it were pumped full of negativity and I couldn't bear to be there a moment longer. They looked at each other and nodded. So they drove me to the station and nearly threw me out the car, driving off so fast their wheels spun.

Feeling as if I was dying, pulsating with what felt like mercury or lead in my veins, I tried to get a grip of the situation. All I really wanted to do was drag myself into a corner and die. I simply wasn't sure I was going to make it. Then a voice boomed in my head:

Do you want to die a junkie on this station? Enough now, Michèle! We cannot protect you for ever if you are intent on destruction.

I didn't recognise the voice but I heard its message loud and clear. And I knew it had a point, a good point. I had a purpose. There was something I needed to do with my life and throwing it away on drugs was no way to pursue it. I made a promise there and then that I wouldn't take drugs again. I remembered hearing that sugar can help bring you down from acid, and so I stumbled to the little kiosk and bought some barley fruits. I sucked as if my life depended on it – as it felt it did. I knew that if I got through this, it was the last chance saloon. I had to stop taking drugs for any reason and make something of my life. I sucked those sweets and visualised myself coming through. I focused on feeling safe. I knew I was protected and I knew that this was a great big slap from the Universe and a wake-up call. I didn't want to die, aged sixteen, on a train platform in Colchester. That was not my destiny. Somehow (I have no idea how) I got on a train and then the underground and eventually arrived back in the sanctuary of Nursery Road. I must have been protected.

I kept my promise and stopped all drugs. The only price I had to pay was putting on five stone in five months as I had destroyed my metabolism in the process. No longer taking speed and finally eating was a shock to the system. It was also the start of my spiritual journey.

18

Life in the Fast Lane

Tamsin, the Australian, was working as a motorbike courier at the time, and one day she announced that she'd buy me a bike of my own so I could become a courier too. I loved biking and had always wanted a bike, even after my scary experience with Danni's, so I jumped at the offer. It also made good sense work-wise. While I was having a great time in the squat, money was tight, to put it mildly. I was finding it difficult, if not nigh-on impossible, to get a job at this stage as I had a one-foot high pink Mohican which – understandably – made would-be employers a little nervous.

But, with a motorcycle helmet on, nobody could be put off by my appearance. Of course, getting a motorcycle helmet on in the first place was no mean feat, but I'd cross that bridge when I came to it.

Frankly, it all sounded too good to be true and I decided not to hold my breath. But Tamsin kept her promise and one day I opened the door to see a Honda 125 parked on the kerb. It wasn't a huge bike, but it certainly had enough poke to nip around pretty speedily – it could easily do 70 m.p.h. which, given I'd never had lessons, was quite fast enough for me to get into trouble.

My childhood terror of death was still with me and I often wrote in my diary that I was scared that biking would be the death of me. But it didn't stop me riding it, not for one moment. I loved the freedom it gave me, the curious feeling of silence that came from the roar of the engine blanking out all other sound, the ability to escape and go anywhere. The problem was I would often slip into a world of my own. It wasn't just on the bike either – I would wander along the street in a total daze, my mind off else-where, thinking about life, the future, how my life might end up.

Late one night I got into a fight down Nursery Road. I don't remember how it started – some jibe about me being lousy as a courier possibly. But it escalated, the way such things do, and my part in it wasn't entirely honourable either. I lost my temper, told home truths, went too far. The next thing I knew I was getting a well-deserved smack. Then it turned nasty and while one person grabbed my hands behind my back, the other one punched my face over and over again. I couldn't believe what was happening, but what was even more unbelievable and upsetting was that, in between punches, I watched a friend walk by, crossing over to the other side of the road, and speeding up her step. Eventually, after what seemed like a lifetime, my attackers got bored and left me on the pavement, blood pouring down my face. A few final desultory kicks and they were gone.

My first thought was to get away – anywhere and quick – and my bike was the answer. I wiped the blood out of my eyes and clambered painfully on to it. I just drove, not really knowing where I was going, and was almost surprised to find myself heading for Hanger Lane. How funny that, when the chips are down, you find yourself going home, no matter how dysfunctional that home might be. I got there at about 2 a.m., climbed stiffly off the bike, and banged on the door to wake up my poor mother.

One look at my broken face and she was instantly awake and in full fury mode. Not at me, but at my attackers.

'What's happened to you, Michèle? I'll kill whoever did this to you! What are you doing on that flickin' bike as well? It's no good, you're going to get yourself killed!'

'Yeah, yeah. It's nothing, Mum. Let's talk tomorrow. I'm so tired, I've got to sleep.'

I limped up to my old room and crashed out on the bed. I felt very uneasy being there and wasn't really sure why I had come. But some part of me knew that my mother was always loyal to me and would fight my battles. Russell was still there, and still violently unstable. It wasn't a great refuge. But it was familiar and Mum was a Taurus who remained there for me in the ways that she could. I knew that if she were to see anyone hurt me, she would fight to the death.

I lay in my old bed, smelling the old familiar smells,

feeling the old uneasy feelings that being 'home' brought. I looked at the gouges in the door, reliving scenes from the past. I didn't sleep well and woke up at 9.30 a.m. with a jolt, remembering that I had to get back to Brixton by ten to go to a job interview. I staggered out of bed, not even washing my face and walked out the door, stiff and sore.

'Where are you going? You come back and we talk, eh?'

'Can't, Mum. Sorry. Got to get to a job interview.' Knowing that would please her, I shouted a cursory goodbye and revved the engine, roaring off down the road and on to the A40. I pulled the throttle all the way and opened up the engine, pulling straight into the fast lane. I was keeping one eye on the road, but my thoughts were mainly preoccupied with the events of the night before. I kept running it through my head, over and over again.

For some totally inexplicable reason I didn't use the indicator; I stuck out my hand while changing lanes at top speed. As I did so, the bike hit the central reservation in between the two sides of the fast-flowing A40. Time suddenly slowed right down and, to this day, I can remember the sensations and images that flew by, burned into my brain, of being on the central reservation with the bike totally and completely out of control. My last thought was that it looked like a film and not real, as if I were outside of myself. Then, by some pure miracle (and I truly believe that was what it was), the bike suddenly veered to the left. Witnesses said I was dragged several hundred metres up the road.

I heard someone say, 'Take his helmet off.' I murmured, 'I'm not a boy: I'm a girl,' and promptly passed out.

Looking back, I cannot believe I survived that experience. If the bike had tipped one inch the other way and into the oncoming traffic, it would have been instant death. Yet again I had been protected.

A few hours later, two policemen knocked on my mother's door to inform her of the news. When she saw them through the glass in the door, she was convinced I was dead. She fainted clean away in the hall.

When I came out of hospital she took me home for a while, but we both knew it wouldn't last for long. Before a week was out, I limped back to Nursery Road, battered and bruised.

Although I loved living in the squat, it wasn't always a calm or safe haven and Brixton wasn't always an easy place in which to live. At seventeen, I wasn't an easy person to live with either – I still drove people mad. It was no picnic being me either: I often drove *myself* mad. Although I wasn't taking drugs any more and I was eating properly, I was still drinking too much and still living far too close to the edge. I was struggling with my rebel nature all the way. While I dressed to look as tough as possible, it was all to hide my huge vulnerability. I was plagued with anger and anxiety. I wanted to make a success of my life, but I didn't know where to begin.

Lucy had left me with some inspiring hints about my future and I think it was these promises of better times to come that really kept me going. In particular she had given me four key pieces of information, to which I clung like a drowning person clutching on to a piece of wood floating by:

One: that I would be all right.
Two: that I would make a success of my life.
Three: that I should never worry about money.
Four: that I could create my future just by asking for it.

The last key I practised from time to time, with some truly astonishing results. I didn't call it cosmic ordering then – the term simply wasn't used – but that was what it was, without any shadow of a doubt. The knack, which had started way back with my Chopper, took a little longer then than it does now (when I can summon most things pretty swiftly). But what I wanted, I could always summon eventually (even if it wasn't exactly what I needed). A classic case was the Orient Express.

The railway tracks ran down past the end of Nursery Road and every Friday the Orient Express, in all its quintessential romantic glory, would chug slowly, grandly, over the old railway bridge. The locals would gaze up at this timeless train, carrying the rich folk off on their wildly expensive, wildly romantic breaks. I would gaze too, looking on in wonder at this beautiful historic train, sweeping through the harsh poverty of South London. I was mesmerised and used to just stand stock still, staring up at it, gazing at the passengers who either stared back or, more often, gazed at one another, lost in their own romance.

'I will be on that one day,' I would stubbornly say to myself. 'I will be on that train and I will go past this place and this will all be but a dream.' In my heart I knew it to be true.

But that cosmic order was a long time coming – though come it did. Others manifested themselves more quickly. Sometimes I wasn't remotely surprised when my wishes came true, and sometimes it was a total surprise when Fate answered my desires. One afternoon I was out shopping in Brixton. Well, I suppose you could call it 'shopping', but really all we did was to collect any spare veg that had been left over when Brixton Market closed. Often you'd find spare potatoes, and cabbages were discarded merely for having the odd bruise or rather battered outer leaves. I had never eaten much in the way of vegetables (other than mushy peas with fish and chips) before coming to Nursery Road, but it was amazing what the vegetarians in the house could do with an old cabbage and some cheese sauce.

As I was heading back to the squat, weighed down with unwanted produce, I noticed the woman in front of me had dropped a cucumber out of her trolley. At the risk of dropping my own haul, I scooped it up and ran after her.

'Excuse me, I think you dropped this,' I said. As the woman turned round, she stared at me with a pair of shockingly familiar china- blue eyes. It was Brenda, from the children's home.

'Brenda? I don't believe it. What are you doing here?' I said.

My heart skipped a beat as I had prayed and begged to bump into her one more time, but hadn't really believed it would ever happen. I knew I had unfinished business with her; I knew I had been unfair to her and I desperately wanted to set things straight.

She was equally surprised. 'Michèle! I am *so* glad to see you! I often wondered and worried about what happened to you. Do you live here?'

'Yes, I live in a squat just over the road. Would you like to come back for a cup of tea?' I said, shoving the rather squashed cucumber back into her trolley. She came back to the squat and we sat and chatted. Brenda confessed that she had often thought about me – I think she had also cosmically ordered our meeting.

She also confessed that she had been very worried about me. Reading between the lines, I think she felt I wouldn't make it, that I would end up dead without a shadow of a doubt.

Brenda seemed genuinely pleased to see me, genuinely relieved that I was still alive. She didn't stop long and was also clearly shaken by the unusual coincidence.

My spiritual journey was continuing apace. I was doing more psychic fairs now, and gaining a reputation for myself for being precise and accurate in my readings. I was still reading furiously and going to all kinds of meetings and groups. I related intensely to the archetype of the wise-woman, the magician and the healer combined into the Goddess. She plugged me back into my lineage, into the magical ancestry I had inherited from my mother's family. But it wasn't the whole truth for me. I needed to do my own thing somehow, rather than be subsumed by any one group. So, while I loved the Goddess, I never committed myself to any particular path.

However, I was still plagued by fear after Michelle's death and had panic attacks and a general obsession with death. Everyone I had ever loved seemed to have died: Lucy, my dad, and then Michelle. I thought about the way she died, in a car crash, and remembered the prediction of the horrible Satanist, Connie, who had promised I would die in a car accident when I was thirty-eight. That prediction, funnily enough, had saved my life when I was younger. Whenever I had thought about ending my life, I always held back because I felt it wasn't my time to die. But now I couldn't get it out of my head. It came back to haunt me over and over again and made me avoid getting in cars whenever possible (I have only quite recently learned to drive).

We tend to believe the reality we receive. It doesn't make it necessarily true but our clever brains absorb the reality with which we are presented. This is why it is so important to be aware of what you believe, for what you believe you create. Mind you, maybe that's why I had a charmed life and survived so many near death experiences? I had decided that my reality would last to at least the age of thirty-eight, so I never had any ordinary fears – until, of course, I reached the age of thirty-seven!

The bike crash wrote off my bike and so, when I was seventeen, in 1983, I started work in a nightclub down the back of an alley, underneath the famous club called Heaven. This place, however, was called Zombies – a fitting description for those of us who frequented it (myself included). We mostly slept all day and partied all night, looking – as a consequence – pale and drawn. I had the dual role of bouncer and glass collector and I took my new role very seriously. I was good at my job, superlative actually, because – being a psychic – I had a useful skill that gave me the edge. Just like my mother, I could always see trouble brewing, well before even its instigators really realised what was going on. I could slide in and make the peace before even a ripple broke on the surface of the atmosphere.

The club had the most intriguing manager – a remarkable woman called Caroline. She worked for Virgin and was much posher than the average club person. She was always smartly dressed and bore an uncanny resemblance to Annie Lennox. I was slightly in awe of her as she seemed out of my league, way out of my world – I assumed she was stuck up and would never even deign to talk to me. But, one night at the end of my shift, I passed Caroline as she was cashing up on the front desk. To my huge surprise she started to chat to me in her friendly lilting Welsh accent. She was so warm and also hysterically funny: within minutes we were laughing like old friends, our voices rising higher and higher, our laughter getting more and more wild. How had I ever thought she would be stuck up?

'You're so funny, Michèle. What's your star sign?'

'I'm an Aries.'

'Really? So am I! When's your birthday?' I sensed what was coming next.

'16 April.'

'No! That's my birthday too! Wow, we are astrological twins. Aries are the best; I love other Aries!'

Right there and then, I had the strongest sense that Caroline was going to be incredibly important to me, tied into my fate in some way. She had the kind of goodness and warmth I had always admired and needed in my life. She saw straight through the tough girl image, the mile-high Mohican: she saw the real me underneath it all. I swear that she was another angel sent to shove me in the right direction.

It didn't take long before the Mohican disappeared and I toned down my image. I wanted to succeed like Caroline; she became my role model and my inspiration. Caroline also worked at a famous club called The Venue where acts like Chaka Khan (one of my heroines) played. Caroline was into astrology and the psychic stuff and she asked me to give her a reading. She was so blown away by it that she vowed to get me work as a psychic in one of her clubs. Before long I was the resident psychic at the ritzy Roof Gardens in Kensington, somewhere I never thought I would ever set foot.

I also had no idea that an event that was going to change my entire life was just around the corner.

19

Do You Hear the Crystal Cry?

Caroline rang me up one day, brimming with excitement. She was talking so fast, I could barely keep up.

'Michèle, you won't believe this but I've had the most profound weekend of my life. I've been on this crystal healing and past-life workshop and it blew me away. I went through loads of past lives and, of course, you were in some of them. There was one where you were a big hairy Greek actor and I was a shepherd girl. You took my virginity and broke my heart. It was all very intense. We cleared our chakras and opened our hearts. It was incredible. You absolutely have to go to this workshop!'

'I was *what*? A big hairy Greek actor? I was a man? You were a shepherdess?' I was desperately trying to keep up.

'Yes, but it was incredible . . .' And on she went.

Caroline was always animated, but this time she seemed perfectly ecstatic, high as a kite. I was intrigued by what she was saying but also slightly cynical. All you seemed to read at that time was about people who 'went back' and discovered they were Napoleon or Cleopatra or Anne Boleyn . . . nobody ever seemed to be an ordinary peasant or housewife or road sweeper. But shepherd girls and hairy actors seemed a bit more reasonable, so I was certainly open to the idea.

In fact, I had always been fascinated by past lives and had had several flashbacks and vivid memories, including one very strong one about Venice and the Rialto Bridge. Although my mother did not practise regression, ours was a household in which past lives were certainly never dismissed.

The workshop was being run by a woman named Tara who used to be the astrologer for the *Daily Star*. She had had an epiphany predicting floods and severe weather changes, but everyone thought she was totally mad. As it happens, of course, she wasn't mad, just twenty years early in breaking the news.

The only drawback of the workshop was that it was expensive – hundreds of pounds, which was a heck of a lot of money then – and I only had about 15p in my pocket. Undaunted, I asked the cosmos to help and fixed my mind on attending the workshop.

A few days later the thought popped into my head quite clearly: 'Ask your mother.' So I decided to bite the bullet. Things had got a bit mad in the squat and I had, reluctantly, realised my time in Brixton was over. Without any other options, I had gone back home. I had made it clear to Mum that this was strictly a temporary measure.

'Mum, can you lend me some money to go on this crystal workshop that Caroline went on?'

She sucked her teeth and frowned, the lines furrowing her brow.

'It sounds like a cult. They'll hypnotise you and I would have to kidnap you back. I don't like the sound of these people.'

In every atom of my being I knew I had to attend that workshop. I cajoled, charmed and begged my mother until she finally relented.

'OK, I'll give you the money. But you be careful, Michèle, that they don't hypnotise you!'

My mum was always generous with money, if not with her time or compassion. I was in! The weeks before the course seemed to last for ever but, eventually, I found myself walking to the smart Kensington hotel where the workshop was being held. I was unbelievably nervous. I was only seventeen, horribly shy, and I felt sure I was not going to fit in. But I took a deep breath, approached the front desk, and picked up the tag with my name on it. I was really there. I walked cautiously into the hall and took a seat near the back, so I could watch unobserved and get my bearings. I looked around. There was a table full of beautiful crystals, quietly glinting like hidden treasure. In the background lulling New Age music was tinkling; a lilting tune of pan pipes against the sound of running water.

Tara made her entrance, accompanied by her partner, Orion. Tara was an older woman: quite buxom and still attractive, with a definite strong presence. Orion looked a little like an alien – he was tall and good-looking, but very pale and with an air of not entirely being all there.

I muttered to myself that, if this were a con, I would expose them to the *News of the World*. There was a crackle of excitement in the air. This kind of workshop was relatively unusual at that time – crystals and chakras weren't being discussed in national newspapers then; it was all still considered rather weird and bizarre.

Tara welcomed us in a resonant compelling voice. She was a strong woman not dissimilar to my mother, sort of solid and powerful.

She introduced us to the crystals which, on first inspection, looked like bits of glass to me. I couldn't see how they were going to change my life. She then asked us each to choose a crystal from the vast array on a long table covered in a white cloth. I simply grabbed the first one that came to hand and studied it. Yep, it looked like a piece of glass to me.

'Hold the crystal in your right hand,' she crooned. 'Breathe in peace and tranquillity, breathe out any stress or tension. As you breathe in, breathe in peace and tranquillity; as you breathe out, release all your stress and tension . . .'

I could feel the crystal in my hand heating up as if it were a radiator. I followed the breathing.

'Now I want you to enter the crystal. Let go, and sit inside your crystal,' Tara said softly.

Without any time for scepticism, I was suddenly zapped into the crystal. It was quite extraordinary. I couldn't quite believe what was happening, but it felt wonderful. With my consciousness inside the crystal, I felt immediately, totally and powerfully protected. I didn't want to leave; I wanted to stay in that safe warm place of power and tranquillity for ever. But Tara's voice broke in and, firmly yet gently, instructed us to leave our crystal and bring our consciousness back to normal waking reality. As I stamped my feet on the ground to bring myself totally back, I realised that all my scepticism had vanished. I was hugely impressed and could feel that all around me shimmered a powerful protection.

We broke for a short while and I sat down, quietly drinking water and assimilating the shift that was going on inside me. My intuition had been right all along – this was definitely the step I needed to take.

Tara then took us through a ceremony designed to open up our heart chakra, the vortex of energy that spins around our physical hearts. 'Only love matters,' she said, in that deep soothing voice, 'Unconditional love is always the answer.'

When I heard these words it was as if my whole life suddenly made perfect sense. I knew that, in essence, I had always known this and that it was a deep and profound truth. Something within me stirred, shook itself out, and woke up. I found myself uplifted, as if a huge and heavy burden had been lifted off my back, off my heart. Love.

Unconditional love. It made sense of everything. People may react with fear but, in essence, they are really pure love. We are separated from the whole and yet really we are all just one. I knew that love permeated everything even if we are often blind to it. Love was the question and love was the answer. People cling to romantic love because they know it is the most precious substance on earth. What we sometimes don't understand is that love is around us all the time. We *are* love. It is only our fear that creates all our shadows and negative patterns.

The next step was to start to clear our chakras by the use of voice and visualisation, the power of sound and colour. Initially I felt incredibly self-conscious. Visualising the colours was fine, but making noises from deep within me felt weird and a little uncomfortable at first. But as I let go, a huge, nearly overwhelming, wave of energy surged through me. As we progressed through the chakras, I felt deep and nearly unbearable pains from my past come up for inspection and then dislodge, splintering off and dissolving. It was indescribable.

It was an intense and highly emotional experience. It was the first time I had ever really faced what had happened in my early life, and it shook me to the core. I couldn't eat a thing at lunchtime – I was too churned up. In the afternoon we went on to our first past-life regression. I lay on the floor and a line of crystals was placed down the centre of my body, each crystal corresponding in colour and resonance to the various chakras.

Walking into a past life was as easy as falling off a log. I followed the instructions and walked down a long stair- case, going down, down, deeper and deeper all the time. At the bottom of the stairs was a door – it seemed incredibly real, and the easiest thing in the world to lean forward and push it open. Once inside the door, I was in the world of the past, *my* past.

It had the strangest quality of being both here and there. We were shown how to direct the experience, to discover who we were, where we were, and what lessons that life had to teach us. At the end of each regression we would touch in to find out how that person, that form of 'I', had died. Although I had been sceptical at first, I found it impos- sible to hold on to that feeling. The detail was extraordinary and there was an emotional truth to the experience.

In the first 'life' I saw, I was a little boy and a woman was strangling me. She was my stepmother in that life, but I recognised her immediately as my birth mother in the here and now. I could feel myself being lifted off the floor and being throttled – it was so real that I came back quickly, shocked and choking.

After that the lives came thick and fast. My mother was in every single life I recalled, every single one. Our rela- tionship was always tempestuous, always dangerous. She was variously my wife, my stepmother, my husband, my sister, my brother. Closer than close, but always threatening too. There was not one life in which we had peace. My deaths were all violent too – in one I clearly remember being shackled up in a cave and starving painfully, horribly, to death.

On reflection, this kind of extreme workshop can be dangerous, too much opening too soon. Some of the people must have had their minds blown to bits. Ten past lives in one day, plus chakra clearing, plus looking at the Akashic Records (a sort of spiritual reference library); plus meeting your spirit guide; plus opening the heart. It could have been way too much, way too soon. But, for me, it was exhilarating and I felt myself go through several levels of opening and awareness shifts.

That night I went home, wide-eyed and full of excitement. Unusually, Mum was in, sitting in the kitchen as I walked through the door. I was thrilled to see her: I was bursting with all the new information, all the fresh awareness, and I had to share it. I started burbling at Mum.

'Wow, it was amazing, Mum! The answer and the question is love. We must all show unconditional love for each other! We are all one! It's incredible – I can see it all now!'

My mother looked at me, quite horrified.

'I told you they were a cult. This is terrible. You mustn't go back tomorrow.'

'No, Mum, it's fantastic. We are all love, don't you get it? If we all loved each other and remembered the truth, the whole world would be healed.'

'I don't like it, Michèle. You are dabbling in things you shouldn't. You are doing too much, too soon. Your spirit is not ready.'

I thought this was a bit rich coming from a woman who regularly talked to the dead, performed spells, and put curses on people.

'But it's all positive, Mum. It's all about love.'

My mother snorted. 'Sounds like the sixties again, eh?'

The message was clear as day to me and I gave a dramatic sigh. My mother obviously wasn't as highly evolved a being as I was – or so I thought in my youthful arrogance.

Interestingly, the idea of sharing past lives (and violent ones) with my mother did not make me feel remotely hostile towards her. In fact, quite the opposite. It gave me a huge feeling of empathy for her. I had had tough lives but so had she. We had shared some terrible experiences, time and time again. The workshop, without a shadow of a doubt, was the start of my healing. It taught me that anger and recrimination were not the way forward. In order to be free of the past, you had to understand it, forgive it, and let it go.

When I went back the next day, we underwent still more regressions, delving into yet more past lives. In our past lives gender is flexible – we can be men or women, which can feel weird at first. I discovered the interesting fact that, when I was a man in my past lives, I was very weak (especially in love) and that when I was a woman I was too powerful and fiercely independent. I had also died early in all my lives, and I felt this was a very powerful message warning me that, unless I transformed myself, this would be my fate in this life as well. This life, I realised, had the potential to be a real turning point for me. My mother wasn't the only fellow traveller through the ages. Caroline and I shared many lives, which confirmed that we were linked karmically. In one life, I was a man and was madly in love with her – but she ended up stabbing me to death. In another she was my brother and we were having a fight in a lake and I was accidentally drowned.

I discovered, to my surprise, that karma does not work in quite the way that I had thought. I always imagined that, if you did bad things in one life, you would be directly punished for those deeds in the next life. But it seems not. When we die the only judge we have is ourselves. We see our life played out in a hologram of knowledge that our earth souls cannot understand. We see all at once how each word and each action affected the lives of the people around us. How a moment of kindness can change a life and a sharp word can affect someone for ever. Words and actions are far more powerful than we realise. It's the pebble-in-the-lake effect – even the tiniest pebble thrown into water will create ripples right across the lake. We don't need to be punished because, when we have viewed the consequences of our actions on all the souls we have met, we have remorse enough. I believe there is no external judge. We must face ourselves.

When we got to the time for meeting our spirit guides I was nearly bubbling over with excitement. I felt quite sure I would find Lucy. Who else could it be? I had missed her so much and the anticipation was both thrilling and terrifying.

The meditation/visualisation was a powerful technique that took me to a private garden. I waited there, listening to birdsong and smelling freshly mown grass, a waterfall bubbling nearby. I kept looking around for Lucy, and listening for her voice. But when my guide finally came it wasn't Lucy at all, but a Tibetan monk. He told me his name was Yannish and I realised grudgingly that he was exactly what I needed at this stage in my life. He was very calm, very quiet and inordinately kind. He suggested that I should tune into him every day for the next few months as the immediate future was going to be a huge turning point for me. He said I would have some vivid dreams and not to worry. He smiled at me kindly and then he was gone.

I found the whole experience peaceful, but oddly disturbing. It felt as if something important was going to happen and something fundamentally vital was going to change; that my life would never be the same again. Above all, I started recognising patterns. Over and over, the same patterns were repeating themselves in my lives, throughout history. I knew that, if I wanted, I could choose to change the pattern. I couldn't rewrite history or change the past, but I could most certainly change the present and the future, the life I had right now and the lives I had to come.

So many of my past lives had been lived in danger and ended violently. I knew I had to step away from danger and become more aware of my life.

As I walked out of the hotel at the end of the weekend,

the course had left me, on the one hand, totally loved up and far too open. On the other, it had instilled in me a solid awareness of the dangers I had been in. I was by no means totally healed but I had been patched up, put back together, and my eyes had been opened to where I was going in life. I knew I had to share the message that love is all there is, and that unconditional love is the answer and the question. We are a unique shard of God separated from the whole. But in order truly to transform myself I had to bring my splintered self back together. It was going to be a huge task, but I was quite certain I would be helped.

Sure enough, Yannish appeared every day to coach me on how to change and transform. He taught me always to seek the best in people and to keep creating my future, always checking and examining what I really wanted or, rather, what I really needed. I had vivid dreams of tsunamis and earthquakes: something deep was shifting.

In the course of the weekend, Tara had made some freaky predictions, one of which was that Glastonbury was one of the few safe places in the world and that we should all consider moving there. I felt her predictions were pretty extreme and I wasn't that keen to leap in and move to Glastonbury. It seemed too over the top and, ironically enough (given Mum's warning), a bit cultish.

I knew I would have to move eventually, though. Living with Mum and Russell was never a long-term option. The question was where? In one particularly vivid dream, the Post Office Tower in London was blown up and falling down, and I couldn't escape it. The dream was so vivid it stuck in my mind.

Little did I know that within the year I would be moving to Euston and that, for the next fifteen years, I would see that tower every single day of my life.

20

The Mother and Child Reunion

During the months that followed the workshop I meditated every day and gradually became much clearer about what I wanted for my future. I felt quite certain that I wanted to work with crystals. I also knew that somehow I had to use my psychic gift, but I couldn't see exactly how that was going to happen. Yannish, however, was very relaxed and calm about it all. He said I shouldn't worry; that the path would become clear – and quite swiftly too.

Meditation was a powerful experience for me. It gave me a lodestone, something to ground me and keep me balanced. It was not an instant solution and I had to work at it incredibly hard. I still had that terribly self-destructive streak. It was waning, virtually by the day, but it had not abated totally. I was in a strange space with twin sensations of total elation and utter pain. The awareness of my past hit me again and again and I no longer saw it as totally normal, as something to dismiss or accept. Instead I realised, all too clearly, the dangers I had been in and the damage that had been done to me. I had survived this far and it was a miracle that I had. This was a turning point and, if I wanted to live beyond that, I had to make large changes in my life. It was time to figure out what I was going to do, where and how I was going to live. It was a crossroads, I knew that – but I had no idea just how seismic the changes were going to be.

One morning, while I was meditating in my room, I had an incredible shock. Yannish told me I was going to get pregnant. He was quite adamant that I would have a baby, a son, and that this child was meant to be and that we had chosen each other. Mother and son. Although I had come to trust Yannish totally, I baulked at this. Surely it could not be right. Surely this wasn't in any way my path in life? I didn't even have relationships with men, so this had to be impossible? But Yannish was adamant. I was going to be a mother – and soon.

While I am prepared to be ruthlessly frank and open about the vast majority of my life and experiences, there are just a few things that need to remain sacred. So, out of respect for my son and his privacy, let us just say his conception did happen suddenly and unexpectedly one month later. It was a total surprise – to put it mildly. The chance of my being pregnant after one sexual experience was remote and incredible. I suppose you could say it was a miracle – though very much a modern-day one. I can say, categorically, that – however curious the beginning and begetting – it was the best thing that has ever happened to me.

I had a sense that I was pregnant almost immediately and took a test, but it came back negative. A short while after that, Mum said she had to go to Switzerland to see a client who lived in the mountains. She asked if I'd like to go with her and, always eager for new experiences, I said yes without any hesitation. I was feeling very strange and unsettled, so I thought it might do me good to get away from London.

I can't remember much about the trip except that Switzerland was stunningly beautiful and the woman we stayed with only ate plums! My mother had the habit of drawing the most eccentric people to her like moths to a flame. I think I was in a daze though. I couldn't quite believe what was happening to me. I certainly didn't consider myself mother material in any shape or form.

I couldn't stay in Switzerland. I needed to get home, to work out what was happening to me, so I took the train back from Switzerland on my own. It felt so strange, watching the beautiful countryside flash by, knowing I was returning to London and all its problems and to a new life – one I had never anticipated. Sure enough, I had my first bout of morning sickness on the train. I went to the doctor, who confirmed it – I was definitely pregnant. Yannish very nearly did an 'I told you so' – which seemed pretty out of character for a Tibetan monk. He then told me that he was leaving as my guide. I don't know why – he didn't say. Once again I felt hurt and abandoned. First Lucy, now Yannish. Why didn't my guides stay the course?

When Mum came home from Switzerland, she knew immediately something was different.

'I need to talk to you, Mum,' I said, nervously. I had no idea how she would take my news. 'I'll make a cup of tea, maybe.'

She stared at me and pointed to the settee in the lounge. 'Sit. Tell me. What is it? What has happened to you? Something is different.'

There was no point in beating about the bush.

'I'm pregnant.'

Her eyes widened.

'You're what? You're *pregna*? How did you become pregna? How did this happen? It was that easy for you, eh? You don't even like men and you become *pregna*?'

She was furious. How unfair it must have seemed to her that she had tried and tried, prayed and prayed for a baby for all those years, and I should fall pregnant after one brief encounter.

I didn't say anything. What could I say? I was as confused and muddled as she was. I watched her warily, ready to leap up and run if her anger and puzzlement turned dangerous. I may have been uncertain about being a mother, but I had no doubt whatsoever that I would do anything to protect this little being I was carrying.

Emotions flickered across her face so fast it was dizzying. Her eyes flashed and her hands plucked distractedly at her skirt. Then, amazingly, beautifully, the anger and annoyance turned. I think it dawned on her that she would be a grandmother, that this was another baby sent by God for her to adore. Maybe this time it would work out, not through her but through me, her daughter. Her face lit up and I realised I had been holding my breath. I let it out in a large sigh.

'It's a miracle. A grandchild. My grandchild.' My mother gazed into the air, a rapt expression on her face. Then her forehead furrowed and she glared at me.

'You are keeping the baby, aren't you? You get rid of that baby and I get rid of you. You get rid of that baby and you never come near me again, you hear me Michèle?'

I held up my hands to stop her.

'Of course I'm not going to get rid of the baby. Why would I ever do that?'

She relaxed. Smiled all over her face.

'Eh, you sit down. I'll go make the tea. You need to rest, look after your baby. Look after my grandson.'

Grand*son*? Oh yes, Mum hadn't lost the knack.

Living at Mum's house was never easy, but living there while I was pregnant was positively dangerous. She was still married to Russell, who was, by now, a living nightmare. What really concerned me was that, despite her delight at my pregnancy, Mum was going through a particularly hard time and seemed to be on the verge of some sort of breakdown. Her life had always been hell, but in the past she had coped somehow. She was a powerful woman, a tremendously strong person, but everyone has a cracking point and maybe the past was catching up with her too? Maybe it was a time of reckoning for all of us.

One day when I was about three months pregnant I was sitting reading a magazine in the lounge. I heard the door open and instantly felt something wasn't right. At first I thought it might be Nick, stumbling in, either drunk or possibly hurt (he was often attacked by racist thugs). But no, the tread wasn't right. It was Mum but something was very wrong. I went out into the hallway and saw her staggering into the kitchen.

'Mum. Are you OK? What happened?'

She slumped on to a chair, her head in her hands. I could hear strangled sobs.

'Mum, what on earth is the matter? Is it Russell?'

She shook her head.

I couldn't get her to speak. She seemed to be in some great trauma. I reached out to her with my mind, but was repulsed by a monumental feeling of anguish and horror. I made tea but she wouldn't touch it. Then I poured her a glass of brandy and held it to her lips.

'Mum, drink this. Please.'

She took a sip and choked slightly. But it seemed to bring her out of her almost mesmerised state.

'Michèle.' Her voice was barely a whisper.

'Yes, Mum. What is it?' I was getting frightened now.

'Michèle . . . how do I say this? Did Russell ever . . . touch you? You know, *dirty* touching?'

I was stunned.

'What?'

'Michèle. It's important. I was talking to a neighbour and she said she heard you screaming all the time. She thought that Russell was abusing you or raping you when I was at work.'

Mum looked down at her hands. I noticed they were shaking. 'She also said . . .'

'Yes?'

'She said she thought you had been abused for years, since you were a child, by other people. Tell me this isn't true, Michèle. Please, for the love of God, tell me she's lying.'

I was shell-shocked. Someone had actually noticed. They never had before. But why hadn't the neighbour said anything before now? I wasn't bitter – I was just hugely puzzled.

In fact, I laughed. Partly from the irony of it; partly because it was a way of reacting to the shock.

'Why are you laughing?'

'I'm sorry, Mum. It's not that it's funny, but just that she got it wrong.'

A look of hope flashed across her face. 'I knew it. I knew it was a lie. That *cattiva*. Why did she lie like that? I'll kill her.'

I had to tell her then. That no, for all that Russell was psychotic and dangerous, he had never touched me sexually. But that plenty of other people had. She stared at me blankly as I told her what I remembered. At that time, I couldn't remember everything by any means. I had blanked out a lot of the incidences of abuse, particularly the early ones. But I remembered enough to make Mum turn pale. Her hands were shaking so much she couldn't even light a cigarette. I had to do it for her.

'Can we talk about it, Mum?'

She shook her head. She could barely speak. I made her drink the brandy and we sat there, in silence, for about half an hour. I could hear the clock tick – it sounded so loud – and I thought about what had happened.

It tipped her over the edge. In her funny way she had always wanted me to be safe – ironic, I know, given her own attempts on my life. But I think she dismissed all that as just part of our everyday drama. Suddenly, without any warning, she got to her feet, stumbled past me, and ran to one of our other neighbour's – a friend. I ran after her but she pushed me back.

Several hours later she came back, crawling on her hands and knees, drunk and wailing.

'I didn't know you were hurt,' she sobbed. 'I didn't know anyone had hurt you. I wouldn't let anyone hurt you. Not hurt like they hurt me.'

'Like they hurt you?' I was puzzled.

She was hysterical; she could barely hear me. I somehow managed to get her to sit down and, between sobs, she told me how her father had raped her when she was only a little girl.

'I didn't know this was happening to you. I had no idea. I would never let it happen, not to you,' she said.

I was stunned, and could barely take in what I was hearing. Part of me felt enormous compassion for my mother, realising consciously for the first time that this was an evil pattern that had been handed down the line of our family. But, on the other, I was pregnant. I was in the most vulnerable place in the world and this was all just too much. I couldn't handle it emotionally at all. My mother had just heard that I'd been abused through my childhood and, instead of talking about it with me, she got blind drunk and talked about her own experience. Then she must have realised that she had been pretty violent too. Her sobs grew louder.

'Darling. I never meant to hurt you. You know that, eh? Not ever. Things have been a little mad sometimes, eh? But I would never hurt you. I love you.'

She had just assumed all the madness was normal and that I would be safe. But the accusations of abuse obviously triggered something deep in Mum. It hit a powerful and painful chord.

I didn't know what to think myself. It was all too much to take in. I wanted to talk about it with her; I wanted to tell her everything that I remembered. It wasn't that I wanted her to feel bad, but I would have loved to have been able to express some of the huge hurt and pain. But I could see that she wasn't in any state to hear my story.

'Are you all right, Mum?'

She looked at me, her eyes bloodshot, her hair tussled and wild. She nodded shakily and gestured upstairs to the bathroom. I helped her up the stairs and she stumbled into the bathroom, pulling the door shut behind her. I sat down heavily on my bed and sank my head in my hands. Would the drama never end? I tried reading a book, but my attention wasn't there. I was listening out, waiting to hear a thump as she passed out on the floor, or a fresh attack of sobbing. But it was all quiet. Ominously quiet. I didn't need to be psychic to realise something wasn't right. My mother didn't do quiet. I padded back to the bathroom and gently opened the door. Mum was sitting on the floor, her back against the bath, shovelling paracetamol down her throat.

'Mum! What the hell are you doing? Stop it!'

She stared dully at me, her face black with mascara, suddenly looking old and dispirited. Her hand slumped by her side and I snatched the bottle. More than half were gone. I raced to the phone and dialled 999.

The ambulance seemed to take for ever. I managed to get her downstairs but then just kept pacing up and down the hall, looking out the door every two minutes. I couldn't be in the same room as her. I felt the greatest compassion for her, yet also I couldn't help feeling totally abandoned by her. Once again she wasn't there to listen to how I felt, or to deal with what happened. I was shocked at how cold and hurt I felt. But I was pregnant (and still in shock about it): I wanted and needed stability from her, not yet another drama.

Eventually the ambulance arrived and took her to

hospital to have her stomach pumped. Of course I couldn't help but think back to the time when it was me lying on the bed, having the doctors quizzing me on my life. I kept trying, over and over, to connect with the unconditional love I knew I should feel. But the hurt had given way to fury. I was just so incredibly angry. How could she do this to me when I was pregnant? How could she not worry about *me*? How could she not think about protecting *me*? Why was it always about *her*; *her* drama, *her* pain? Who was ever going to listen to me? However, as I sat in the stark waiting room, one thing became crystal clear in my mind. I had to look after myself. I knew, without a shadow of a doubt, that I had to get out of the mad house. All the instability was rocking me just when I needed to think straight and focus on the time to come. I was nineteen, pregnant, and I was thinking of making myself homeless.

By luck, I met a woman called Julie in a club and, in the easygoing spirit of the times, she said I could stay at her flat in Euston. It was far from ideal as there were five people squashed into a two-bedroom flat along with three cats. The bath was in the kitchen – when you wanted to cook you simply put a work surface over it. The litter trays were there too. Frankly it was a hygiene nightmare, and a psychic nightmare too as the people living there were far from stable. Sometimes I wondered if I had jumped from the frying pan into the fire. It seemed I had – as after about three months, when I was six months pregnant, one of my flatmates had a psychotic episode and tried to kick and stab me in the stomach. I ran as fast as I was able to from the flat and found myself on the streets, quite literally with nowhere to go.

I wandered around, trying to break into empty council properties, desperately trying to squeeze my big pregnant belly through the windows.

It was insanity, but where else could I go at such short notice? My mother's house was absolutely not an option. Since her suicide attempt we had barely spoken. I tried once to bring it up, but she turned her head to the wall and ignored the question entirely. Clearly, it was not up for discussion. I didn't really feel ready to go there either. Being pregnant has a curious effect on your mind – it's as if Nature cleverly protects you from painful thoughts. My mind would glaze over when I thought about the abuse, about Mum. I had other priorities – I needed to keep myself and my baby safe and Mum's house wasn't safe for either of us. I'd rather sleep rough than go back there. Finally I managed to get into a dilapidated flat and spent an uneasy night on the floor, praying for guidance, praying I'd be safe and that no one else would crawl through the gap that night.

Morning dawned and I was OK. A few desperate phone calls and my old network kicked in again. Julie's sister was moving out of a squat and she offered her place to me and Julie (who was also desperate to move out of the flat). It sounded great in principle except for one thing – there was a guy still living there. Julie and I could have the bedroom to share but, if he wanted to go to the bathroom or kitchen, he had to walk through our room.

Beggars can't be choosers and we moved in. It was actually quite a nice flat, off Gray's Inn Road. It had stripped wooden floors and looked out over a courtyard. The council wanted to pull down the building so the flats were all empty. The thing I liked most of all about that flat was that someone had painted a five-foot-high mural of The Hermit from the tarot on the wall of our room. I found it very fitting, as The Hermit is the symbol of solitary reflection. If it comes up in a tarot spread it indicates going within in order to discover the next stage of the journey.

We settled in as best we could. The guy already living there was a recluse so he avoided us as much as possible – except when he needed to walk through our bedroom in the middle of the night to go to the bathroom!

In fact, the flat was pretty crowded once again as there were also two manic border collies, Bessie and Jasper, and two cats.

I was in denial about my pregnancy in some way. I ignored it as far as I could, and also found myself meditating less. I was, without realising it, doing what all pregnant women do, which is to go within, to withdraw, to take my focus away from the outside world. Equally, the focus is so much on the body that the profoundly spiritual often withdraws too. It's as if spirit knows that a mother-to-be has one big important job to do – to prepare for the coming of her child. Nothing else is important, everything else has to wait. When you're building a new human being, meditation often gets pushed aside.

I wondered how on earth I'd get out of this mayhem. I asked the universe to provide me and my unborn child with a home. I prayed for a way forward. I was still obsessed with reading and travelling forward on my path. I may not have been meditating so much, but I hadn't abandoned the spiritual path one little bit. I had taken up crystal healing and was still doing the occasional reading with Mum. We were back on speaking terms, but I did not want her to be too near me at the time. Even though the squat was pretty tough, I would never have gone back home. Instead, I spent hours curled up on the bed, reading (Carl Jung in particular) and loving the knowledge that was opening up to me.

I read about archetypes (universal forms and patterns that exist in our psyches) and of course I was intrigued, in particular, with the concept of the Mother archetype. Sadly, my mother rarely embodied the 'Good Mother' archetype; all too often she segued into the 'Witch', the negative mother, the raging, angry, spell-casting crone (in its most literal form). As I stood on the brink of motherhood myself, I thought long and deep about how I would be a mother, what kind of mother I might become. Could I throw off my evil inheritance and be a 'Good Mother' for my child? Or would I repeat all Mum's mistakes? As I drew near to giving birth, Mum tried to build bridges. She promised she would end her relationship with Russell; she said she wanted to be a good grandmother to my baby. But could I ever repair our relationship? She was such a strong personality: I was terrified that she would subsume me; that she would take over my life when I had a child of my own. I was so confused, so troubled by it all. I was standing on a threshold, about to leave childhood behind once and for all. Was I ready?

21

Baby, I Love You

Mum insisted on coming to hospital with me for the birth and I was surprised to find that I was actually glad to have her with me. Maybe, when it comes down to it, you need your mother at such times, no matter how she has been, whether good mother, the consuming witch or, as in my case, a confusing mix of the two.

It was a difficult birth. My baby seemed to be just like me – unsure that he wanted to be here. Together we went through forty-eight hours of labour and, like Mum before me, I ended up having surgery. Once again I found myself in the operating theatre for an emergency caesarean – although this time it was my baby hanging back, not me and Lucy. This time it was me on the operating table in place of my mother. The doctors had told me I would not wake up during the procedure but, the moment they pulled my baby out, I came round. The midwife placed him in my arms and there he was – Julien Marco – all wrinkled and with a mass of black hair. He looked just like a little Tibetan monk, totally peaceful, totally at peace with himself. The thought flashed through my mind – he's Yannish reincarnated. So maybe that was why my guide had departed? But whether he was or wasn't, I knew we had a special journey to share and the bond was instant. A tiny part of me was almost scared to love him, in case he died. Like Lucy did. Like I nearly did.

I was so exhausted after the birth I barely knew how to get from one day to the next. The panic attacks were now coming on full and fast. I had terrible post-natal depression and was freaking out all the time. Is it surprising? I was a young mum for whom the role of mother was perplexing and terrifying. After all, my direct experience of a mother was as a screaming, slashing harridan. I knew that wasn't right, but I had nothing to guide me, no sense of what was normal.

Going back to the flat on Gray's Inn Road with my son was like taking a huge epic journey. I hunkered down and tried to come to terms with this huge rush of new feelings, the sheer fear of not knowing how best to care for this tiny imperious little being. The first time I left the flat after Julien was born I went to a café. It was like an acid flashback – everything went bright, too bright, voices were too loud and colours were too vivid and swirling. I felt sick and lurched home. I crawled under the duvet, shaking like a leaf. I was convinced that any moment I was going to drop dead without any warning. On reflection it was probably a form of post-traumatic stress syndrome, but nobody bought into that then.

I used all the spiritual skills I could muster to pull me through. The crystals helped me a lot and I spent hours working out which crystals alleviated which symptoms. I had yet to discover the greatest method of healing of all, which is simply to ask for help. It works every time. However, maybe even if I'd realised this fundamental truth then, I wouldn't have used it. It's a funny thing but sometimes, even when you have the knowledge, you don't follow it when it's most needed. We humans are contrary creatures.

Despite all this, having Julien was my greatest blessing. I was over the moon with him. I gazed at this precious package and handled him as if he were fragile glass. I was terrified he would break: he was so small and so perfect. With his perfect hands and toes, I thought he was the most beautiful child on the planet. So, really I was just like every other mother after all! I made a solemn vow always to protect him in all the ways I had not been protected. I felt that he was my redemption.

I wasn't the only person to be over the moon about Julien. Right from the moment of his birth there was an instant deep link between Mum and Julien. Right there, in the operating theatre, she gazed at him and it was love at first sight.

My own feelings were complex. I loved that she loved Julien but, if I'm very honest, I also felt horribly jealous. She had never really been a good mother to me, but I had certainly had her attention – for good or bad. But now, all that attention was focused firmly on Julien and I felt left out. I battled with those feelings as I knew, deep in my heart, that it was better this way. She couldn't give me what I needed as a mother, but I could still love her as a human being. She couldn't be a good mother, but maybe she could be a good grandmother.

He was a Taurus, just like her – two little stubborn bulls. I could see her transform in some way before my very eyes. It was as if, just by being alive, he started a healing process in her. After his birth she became, in many ways, a different woman. She found the strength to get rid of Russell once and for all. She was, without any doubt, always the perfect grandparent. Right from the start, she looked after Julien for me – we shared him. Curiously, I never once felt any danger for him with her.

There was just one incident that soured it. After Julien's birth, I had been unable to stop thinking about the abuse. Once the memories had started I couldn't stop them. They threatened to overwhelm me and often I thought I was going mad. I finally realised I needed to talk about this with someone. Mum seemed to want to blank it out, but I couldn't. I found a therapist and we started talking. I don't think she could believe the extent of my abuse – she hadn't had anything like this to deal with before and, in retrospect, she didn't have the experience or the sensitivity to handle it. She thought, rather predictably, that my father had abused me when I had been very young.

That evening I went to collect Julien, determined to ask

Mum about it. I was standing in her study with Julien in my arms. She was just outside in the hallway.

'Mum. I know you don't like talking about the abuse stuff, but I need to know. Do you think it's possible that Dad hurt me when I was a baby?'

Her face contorted. I caught the madness in her eyes and swiftly, with an unconscious reaction, slammed the door shut on her. She went berserk. I stood, with my back against the door, trying to soothe Julien. First she yelled and screamed, then she raced off. No. This couldn't be happening. Not again. Not with Julien here. I heard her feet thumping down the hallway, her voice rising with fury.

'How dare you! How dare you say things like that about your father! He was a good man. *Cattiva! Disgraziata!* I kill you!'

A huge thud made the door slam into my back. She was crashing at the door with a hammer.

'Get out here, *cattiva*! Come out. Your father never touched you. He NEVER touched you. You hear me?'

She smashed a hole through the panel and peered at me, still screeching furiously.

'Mum! Please. Calm down. I've got Julien here.' At that point he started crying. I think I was so tense, so terrified, I had been holding him too tightly. He felt the tension in my body.

It was as if someone had waved a magic wand.

'Oh my God.' She started crying. 'I'm sorry. So sorry.

Please, Michèle, come out. It's OK now, I promise. I'm so sorry.'

I could barely breathe. I opened the door and she stood there, arms hanging by her side, the hammer dropped to the floor. I stepped over it and we walked, stunned, to the lounge and sat down. Mum couldn't take her eyes off Julien's face. She was shocked to the core.

'I forgot he was there. I didn't realise . . .'

I looked warily at her. I wasn't sure I dared bring up the abuse again. Yet I had to know.

'Mum . . .'

She stared at me, dragging her eyes from Julien's face to mine.

'Michèle, it was not your father, never your father. But I think I was blind. There was a man . . .'

She told me about Duncan, about how she had found him masturbating over me in my cot. I was shocked. Thoughts crashed through my head; memories came flooding back. Why had I been left with him? What else wasn't she telling me? I could sense that if I questioned Mum further, it was likely that neither of us would be able to cope with what might emerge. Julien was my top priority. For now, it had to be enough. But a wave of relief swept over me. My father had not hurt me. The circle of mistrust did not stretch to include him. I could keep my memories, my happy memories, of him intact. I had always felt that, if he had not died, maybe he would have finally realised what was happening to me. Maybe he would have been the one to save me. If he hadn't died, Mum would never have become so mad. There would at least have been some boundaries, some sense of protection. That thought was a lifeline. Someone in my life had not hurt me. My father had not seen or stopped my early abuse, but he had never hurt me. He was not an abuser.

I stopped seeing that therapist, but I continued my quest. I tried rebirthing, where you can go back to birth, and even before birth, and discovered how my relationship with Lucy had begun (which was incredibly healing and soothing). I still missed her so much. I did wonder if she had been reincarnated, if she had a life elsewhere now as a small child. Would I know her if I saw her? I was quite sure I'd know her anywhere. I also tried the metamorphic technique, a wonderful form of healing that also helped me uncover layers of my abusive childhood in a safe way.

The incident with Mum and the hammer did not stop me leaving Julien with her. If anything, it had proved to me that her love for him would not let him be harmed with her. Her issues were all with me, not my gorgeous son. She might be a mad, bad mother, but as a grandmother she was all good and kind and loving. Anyhow, I felt he was much safer with her than with me in my flat.

The flat felt too transient; it wasn't in any way a safe space. The block had junkies and ex-prisoners living there and, although there was a lot of creativity and spontaneity around, there was also an air of violence. Once you become a mother, you start to see the world so differently. One day there was a violent knocking at the door. It was the man from the flat next door, who had just been released from prison. He had put a package down on the stairs and someone had stolen it. He assumed it was someone from our flat and was screaming and yelling at the top of his voice. I had Julien in my arms and was terrified: it was like a horrible reprise of my episode with Mum. I was just about to double bolt the door when he gave it an almighty kick which sent me reeling into the bookcase and nearly knocked Julien out of my arms. When he came in he was so enraged he didn't even notice that I had a newborn baby in my arms. He screamed in my face and went to grab me by the throat when all of a sudden something stopped him and he looked down at Julien. Without saying anything more, his hand dropped from my throat, he turned around, then left. I knew once again we had both been protected. I called the police and made the decision there and then to go to the council to get rehomed.

The waiting list for a council flat in those days was about three years. But I focused firmly on being offered a new home and sent out my wish. Whether it was the cosmic ordering or simply because our situation was so extreme, it wasn't long before a letter arrived saying that a council flat was available for me, Julie and Julien. I was overjoyed. It was a divine blessing.

On the day we were due to move out and into the new flat, I bumped into the neighbour on the stairs. He looked haggard and grey, yet underneath it he was still a handsome

man with short cropped hair and dark staring eyes. Behind
the scowl I sensed a softness that had got lost somewhere
along the way. He had been arrested for violence in the
miners' strike and had been left by a girlfriend who was
pregnant. As I walked past him I was shaking violently,
but I made myself look him in the eye and smile.He glanced
at me, but his eyes couldn't hold mine and, as he spoke,
he kept them fixed firmly on the floor.

'I'm sorry for the other day.'

I nodded; I barely trusted myself to say anything in
return.

He raised his eyes to mine. 'Do you want to come in
and have a coffee?'

The logical part of my brain told me this was probably
not the wisest move I would ever make. But the psychic
side of me felt that somehow it was important.

'Yes, I'd love to.'

His flat was ridiculously tidy with endless bookshelves
overflowing with books in neat rows.

'I have something I want to give you for the baby,' he
said, reaching up to one of the shelves. 'My dad used to
read this to me every night and I thought you might like
it.'

He started to read aloud, softly and melodically. It was
the Rudyard Kipling poem 'If'. It brought tears to my eyes
and I hugged him and thanked him as I left. I could see
the relief on his face. He had not meant to hurt me, but
was caught up in his own pain and was still lost in a feral

place which was a shadow of prison. I read 'If' to my son every night and he always had it framed on his wall.

Our new home was in Somerstown, a notoriously rough area, but the flat itself was nice. It was on the ground floor (handy for a pushchair) and it had been newly done up with two quite spacious bedrooms. We moved in straight away and furnished it partly from bits and pieces from skips. Julie was an astonishing artist who could whip things up out of next to nothing: we had a hairdresser's row of PVC seats painted like a zebra and junk turned into tables. It was definitely very cool, but we couldn't afford carpets and the floors were concrete – hardly ideal for a tiny baby. I also couldn't afford a proper cot so Julien slept in a carrycot which had to be balanced on a mattress on the floor. Writing this and thinking back, I am amazed that I thought this was normal.

I started work almost immediately, helping disabled people in a housing scheme. Mum would look after Julien on the three days I worked.

My mother was totally transformed, a different woman altogether. She really was the most amazing grandmother. She cooed softly to Julien and sang to him in Italian. She was possessive and protective. It was as if his birth created a huge healing within her. She was still tempestuous with me from time to time, but never again in front of Julien. We were getting on so much better. She helped me get a cot and bought us our first second-hand electric oven. Things were finally coming together. I was still fighting my demons, still battling with panic attacks and (if I'm honest) still suffering from depression. But I was continuing to deal with my early life, still having regression, still processing the awful things that had happened to me. Above all, I wanted to succeed – not for myself so much as for my son. I wanted to create a stable, safe environment for him. I was adamant that he would not live surrounded by the danger and chaos that had permeated my own childhood. I made sure he brought his friends home, that our home was a refuge and a fun place for him. The place was always full of children and I loved it that way. He had the most amazing birthdays and Christmases, however little money I had.

Julien was my salvation in so many ways.

However, it was a tough job keeping our home safe in Somerstown. It was an edgy place and a particularly dodgy area in which to walk around at night. If I walked home late, I would always be looking around me, with all my senses on full beam. One night Julien was staying with my mum and I was in bed, just dozing off to sleep. I was suddenly hauled back to full awakening, my heart pounding, by awful screaming. There was nothing remotely unusual about hearing screaming, but there was something about the pitch of this that made me sit up and listen. It seemed to be coming from almost directly outside my window. I cautiously pulled back the curtains and peered out. In the middle of the road, right outside the flat, there was a woman screaming and slashing her arms with a piece of glass. She was howling and wailing and bleeding quite profusely. Once again, I found my head and my heart battling and the heart won out. It wasn't the brightest idea, but I grabbed my clothes and rushed outside.

'Are you all right? Come on, calm down. Give me the glass,' I said, tiptoeing towards her as she continued to scream and cry and slash. 'Come on. I'll take you into my flat and call you an ambulance.' I was sending her unconditional love all the time I was talking, visualising her being OK, calming down. She looked up at me, her face covered in black streaks of dirt and mascara.

I remembered my own pain in the past and felt total compassion. Any thought of my own safety vanished in a second. She dropped the glass and I scooped her up and took her inside. She lay weeping on my kitchen floor and I was uncertain of what to do as she seemed too drunk or out of it to communicate. So I waited a little, allowing her weeping to subside.

'He stole everything, that bastard,' she finally panted, blood flowing on to the yellow concrete floor.

I wrapped her arms in a towel and went to call the ambulance. When I came back into the kitchen she had managed to find a carving knife in the drawer and was aiming it at her stomach in an alarming fashion.

My mood changed. Rather than being frightened, I started getting annoyed. Clearly the softly, softly approach wasn't working.

'OK, don't take the piss,' I said. 'I invited you in here

and now you go through my drawers and snatch a carving knife? Give it to me now, please.' I sounded like a schoolmistress rounding on a naughty pupil.

She looked up at me with big pained eyes, all blurry with drink or drugs, and a moment of lucidity seemed to flash through her.

'I'm sorry. You have been very kind,' she said, dropping the knife. I grabbed it and put it out of reach. At that moment the police and an ambulance arrived.

'Hello, Sarah,' they said, seeming to know her quite well. She was a local prostitute and they seemed to think I was also on the game. I suppose their reasoning was that nobody else would be stupid enough to open the door and let someone in under those circumstances. I felt guilty, even though I hadn't done anything. As they took her away, they gave me a lecture about never doing something like that again. I was amazed by their attitude. I was also stunned that nobody else would have helped. How can people watch someone in danger and pain and leave them there, possibly to die? Several things like this happened in Euston but, touch wood, I was always protected.

A clear example was when I met my brother Nick again. I hadn't seen him for many years as he had moved away from home, and I still had a very real fear that he would harm me. I always loved my brother and I know, deep in my heart, that really he loved me too. But he had been through his own tough times and I felt it best if I kept out of the way. He seemed to feel the same way as our paths never crossed, despite the fact that we both regularly saw Mum.

One day I was standing in the front of my flat when he walked by. He had been looking for me, much to my surprise:

'Hello, Michèle.'

'Hi, Nick. How are you?'

It was a silly question. He looked terrible.

He ignored the question. 'I'm playing guitar over the road. I wondered if you wanted to come and listen?'

My heart instantly went out to him. 'Yeah, of course I will.'

I was horrified to see the pub he was playing in as it was a particularly dodgy one down a dark alley near the flat. It frequently had its windows shot out or chairs thrown through them. When we went into the dark smoky bar several rough-looking blokes gave us the once over. I sensed immediately that the colour of my brother's skin was not going down too well. But fortunately the rest of the band was there and nobody said anything. We sat down by the bar and ordered a drink. One of Nick's friends started to play pool. When one of the locals turned and asked Nick if he was with the band, he said something weird (I forget exactly what). It was clearly very much the wrong thing to say and, the next thing I knew, five men jumped on him. I didn't think twice – I launched in and tried to pull them off him. One man jumped on the table and, reaching down, grabbed my hair, pulling my face towards him while his fist drew back ready to punch me square in the face.

I reacted quite instinctively by looking him straight in the eye. Time suddenly slowed right down and I found myself thinking back to when I had been looking through the door at Dennis with his axe. The same thing that had happened all those many years ago, happened again. I felt a huge surge of love rush through me.

'Please don't hit me,' I said quietly. He looked at me for a split second and then just let his fist drop. He let go of me and went to join the men who were kicking my brother. I dived in between them and shielded Nick's body with mine.

'Please don't hurt him. Please don't hurt my brother. He's my brother; leave him alone.' I was crying the words over and over. Somehow I managed to drag Nick away, to get him out of there. The strange thing was that, even though I was right in the middle of the fight, I did not get a single bruise or injury from that experience. I knew that I was protected from that particular family karma. It was no longer a part of my energy. I dragged my brother out of the grotty pub and helped him limp back to my flat. I had no choice. He had broken ribs and had to be admitted to hospital.

The experience shook me and made me realise once again the chaos that always seemed to follow my family. I felt great compassion and sadness for my brother but he continued to spiral into hell.

I visited him when he was in hospital and we talked about the past.

I had got through my upbringing somehow, but Nick hadn't. It had consumed him. Our relationship had always been one of love/hate. We had loathed each other and been jealous of each other, yet we had also been through the most awful of times together and had often fought battles for each other. It was a mixed-up, muddled-up relationship and no amount of therapy ever really sorted it out for me. I think I had always hoped that, when we got older and wiser, we would be able to sit down and talk and have some kind of healing, some kind of deep reconciliation. But, by the time we were adults, I couldn't reach Nick. Maybe I should have tried harder, but I had my own problems, my own demons. The kind of evil that people like Connie and all those other abusers perpetrate can linger on for decades, even lifetimes.

Looking back, it was a crazy time. I had a young baby; I was working three days a week at the housing scheme, and I also decided I needed to do voluntary work. I have always had this very strong belief that I had to 'give something back'. Don't get me wrong – I was no saint. I still had a furiously fiery temper. I was still screwed up. I was still suffering panic attacks. But I was healing. Julien was – happily – a sunny, easy baby, the perfect baby really. Everyone loved him and there was always someone more than willing to babysit – they just loved being around him and his energy. So I started to train with a counselling helpline and did shifts for that when I could.

As if all that weren't enough, I was still doing my readings and past-life work. My mother was always sending over her clients for a second opinion. I never thought about charging for this and I loved doing it – it was as natural as shelling peas for me; I would look at someone and know them as if they were a friend. It wasn't spooky or unreal: it just *was*.

One of those clients was a woman who was going to change my entire life.

22

All the Way from America

I loved being a mother and I adored having Julien in my
life. But at twenty-three I was still very young and I did
think wistfully about other experiences, about other places.
In particular I thought a lot about America and I wondered
if I would ever go there. I had always been intrigued by it
and really wanted to see for myself what it was like. So,
rather half-heartedly, I put out a wish.

'OK. If the magic still works . . . Let me see America.'

Being a single parent in the bleakest of financial situations I knew that only magic could possibly get me there.
Funnily enough, what happened next was a big turning
point in my understanding on all things magical.

One day my mother sent a client of hers, called Christine,
to see me. Christine was a musician and a business woman,
a canny entrepreneur who sold vintage fashion and also
dabbled in property development. She would do up
houses and sell them on for a neat profit. She was
American. When I gave her the reading she was blown

away by the detail I went into about her complex business situation.

'You're good,' she said, with that typical American twang. 'Far too good to be wasting your gift in this dump. I like you and I'm going to help you when I can. You've really got something, girl.'

I smiled, but didn't pay it that much attention.

I continued to give her readings and one day she asked me to advise her on her next trip to the States. I saw that someone was going to let her down and warned her that she should expect upheaval around the trip. The very next day her PA announced she was pregnant and would not be going to America.

'Michèle, you are amazing! You were spot-on. Lauren pulled out and I am screwed. Look, I need someone to come to the States with me. I can't do it on my own as I have to carry loads of really expensive jewellery.'

She paused and looked me straight in the eye with a grin. 'Have you got a passport?'

Did she mean what I thought she meant?

'What, *me*? Come with you to the States?' I was amazed.

She nodded. 'I'm doing LA and New York. I'm staying at the Sunset Marquis. You will love it, I promise. Look, what's to lose? It's all free. Though obviously I'd want you to give me readings.'

My mind was in a spin. Going to America? In four days' time? What about Julien? But, in my heart, I knew I couldn't turn this down. Julien was three now, a happy bubbly toddler. He loved my mum to pieces and was as happy with her as he was with me. It would be a wrench, but I just knew this was Fate prodding me very hard.

'OK. I mean, yes. Yes! Of course I will.'

'Good. It'll be a blast. Now then, no disrespect, but we gotta change your image. Let's go shopping and get you some fitting outfits.'

'Sure. But let me call Mum first.'

As I suspected, Mum jumped at the chance to monopolise Julien for a while. The next thing I knew I was on a plane to LA with Christine, wearing very smart clothes and dripping with antique jewellery. It was like a dream – a dream I had conjured out of nothing. From that moment on, I truly understood the power and reality of cosmic ordering. In fact, Christine seemed to know it as well.

We arrived in LA and I was blown away by it. The accents, the smells, the shops. Twelve-lane highways packed with limos and sports cars. The bustle of the city; the crashing waves and the vast stretches of sand. The beautiful people and the depraved. It was like stepping right into the telly. Christine had rented a red Corvette and she drove us to the Sunset Marquis. Last time I had been to a flash hotel in flash clothes it had been as a presumed prostitute. This time I was here as the psychic and side-kick to a smart businesswoman. The contrast could not have been greater.

Christine was a genius and was gorgeous. She was older than she ever told anyone but could get away with it as she looked about twenty-two. She was half native American and had a deeply tanned dancer's body. She looked like a dolly bird and people always underestimated her intellect (often to her advantage). She was dead smart, sharp as anything and way ahead of her time. She would read books on quantum physics like other people read chicklit. She also had the longest life-line I had ever seen: I used to joke with her that she would find the fountain of eternal youth – or maybe she already had.

The Sunset Marquis was a small but deeply hip hotel in the West Hollywood hills. It was *the* place to stay in LA – or so Christine said. I was pretty green, totally naïve when it came to things like pop stars and fashion. Being a rebel, I was still wedded to the punk ethos of slashed jeans and safety pins.

When we walked into the lobby the first person we saw was Bruce Springsteen. I had actually never heard of him, but Christine was over like a shot, chatting and batting her eyelids. We saw him a lot as he was staying there with his brand-new girlfriend Patti (who's now his wife). They were madly in love and seemed to be a permanent fixture in the bar, spending hour upon hour kissing, wrapped around each other like two drowning children. He seemed very down-to-earth, a nice guy. But I felt sure he was, like Christine, another person who hid a keen intellect beneath a simple, 'good ol' boy' routine. It was quite odd. But he was charming and kind, and I liked him a lot. Funnily enough, in retrospect, I was far more star-struck at seeing Dave Stewart of Eurythmics.

The place was dripping with film and pop stars. Eddie Murphy was wandering about, and you couldn't miss the watch encrusted in diamonds that flashed ostentatiously from his wrist. It all started to feel very unreal and a long way from my council flat in Euston. Here I was in the bright lights of LA, while at home I would have to charge the electric key and sometimes we didn't have any electricity at all. Julien was never allowed to go to the door in case it was the bailiffs or someone coming to cut something off.

As I sat in the Jacuzzi in the hotel, sipping champagne by the pool area, I couldn't help but blink. This was really far out.

If you wanted to go anywhere there was a free stretch limo waiting outside to whizz you there. All you paid was the tip. I felt totally out of place and found myself observing it all, almost from outside my body. During the day, I helped Christine drag her jewellery around. At night she was seeing a talented young singer and mixing with various producers, and I tagged along. I liked LA but it felt very superficial and totally unreal. I couldn't get used to people saying 'Have a nice day' yet not appearing to mean it in any way whatsoever. It was all lost in translation.

After a week in LA we flew to New York. When the plane landed and we headed to a rank of the famous yellow cabs, it felt even more surreal. As we were driving over a bridge I had the only out-and-out vision I have ever had. I was gazing at the Manhattan skyline, looking over at two huge skyscrapers, wondering how many storeys there were and then, whoosh, all of a sudden I saw them in graphic 3-D, on fire and collapsing. I was absolutely terrified. I tugged on Christine's sleeve.

'Oh my God, Christine. I just saw something totally weird.' I told her my vision. 'I don't think I like it here.'

Christine nodded, thoughtfully: she didn't remotely dismiss what I was saying.

'Well, Nostrodamus reckons New York is going to get it sometime. Perhaps you're picking up on that?'

For years I told everyone this story and in fact, just before 9/11, I was talking to a therapist (I was still shifting the panic attacks all those years later) and said in passing to her: 'You know what? Seventeen years ago I went to New York and I "saw" all these tall buildings exploding. It terrified me. But, hey, it never happened so I am not going to live in fear any more about terrible things happening.'

But the very next day it did happen and she was gobsmacked. But nowhere near as gobsmacked as I was. Funnily enough, after that I never had a panic attack again. It was as if I had been waiting for that tragic event all my life.

I decided as soon as we got to Christine's swanky New York apartment that I wanted to go home. I felt terrible about letting her down, but I just had to get out of there. I felt unsafe and it felt so far away from nature – there was no green anywhere to be seen. I know that must sound funny as I was a Londoner, living in a huge city anyway, but London is a much greener place than New York. This really was an alien environment for me. Christine was not at all happy, but reluctantly accepted that I was adamant.

On the plane a man got talking to me. He seemed very friendly and he put me at ease by saying he worked with blind people and was off to a conference. He was all smiles and gold teeth, his hands covered with large turquoise rings, and a huge cowboy hat perched on his head. Now I may be psychic, but I'm not always a great judge of character when it comes to people connected with me. I'm much better at it now, but back then I would make far too many mistakes. I think it's because I see past the mundane – possibly unpleasant – stuff and straight into the light we all have within. I see people's potential, the best that can be. Sadly, that doesn't always reflect how they actually *are* right here and now.

He started to talk about blindness and how it affects people. It was really interesting and he seemed genuinely nice, so I didn't bat an eye when he put his flight blanket over both of us during the conversation. He gently took my hand in his, which made me feel slightly uneasy, but there was something about him that plugged me straight back into my childhood experiences. I hadn't been touched inappropriately by a man for many years now but it was as if I were suddenly ten years old again, the abused obedient part of my personality splitting off and acting in a way my adult self would never do. The attendant came around at that moment and I saw her notice it, which was a bit embarrassing. Then the man took off his stetson and started to rest his head on my shoulder as if to go to sleep. This seemed very odd behaviour, but I really didn't know what to do. This was the first time in my life I had flown alone, but I was pretty sure this wasn't standard flying etiquette. The ironic thing was that he was sitting next to a work colleague who was taking it all in his stride. My mind was racing, but I was in the window seat and so, basically, trapped. Perhaps if I pretended to go to sleep he would leave me alone?

The next thing I know his hand was groping inside my shirt and he was roughly squeezing my nipple. I froze, like a rabbit in headlights. Then the most curious thing happened. One part of me went into my usual abuse mode, in which I thought, 'OK, here we go again – just get it over with'. But the other part was absolutely furious. This was a first for me as, like most people who have been serially abused, I would usually go into a form of splitting in which you detach from the reality of the situation and allow it to happen. It's a survival mechanism, but at a price – it breaks a part of your spirit each and every time. I paused, almost giving him the benefit of the doubt, hoping he'd come to his senses, but instead he got rougher and started to head for my trousers. All the time, his eyes were closed, feigning innocent sleep; his headphones on as if he were listening to music. I don't know where I got the courage, but I suddenly pulled the headphones back and hissed loudly in his ear: 'Men like you have ruined my life but I've had enough now!'

I got up abruptly from my seat, pushed past him and his colleague and stalked off to find the stewardess.

'That guy just touched me. Can you move me please?' It was the first time in my life I had addressed the fact that someone was trespassing on my boundaries. I couldn't believe he worked with blind people – it was horrific.

The stewardess looked at me sideways. 'I thought you were with him. You were holding his hand.'

I saw how it looked and blushed bright red with humiliation. She went off and had a word with him but, of course, he denied everything. I sat at the back of the plane and could feel him sending me daggers. On the one hand, I felt totally ashamed and freaked out, but on the other I was just so glad that, for once, I had stopped the pattern. It seems that there are some people who can spot the vulnerable or abused and, no matter how strong you are, they sense they can be inappropriate with you.

He didn't give up easily. When the plane taxied to a stop and we started gathering our things, there he was – lingering around, beckoning me over. I got off the plane and ran hell for leather to the baggage check-out. If I could only get out of the baggage hall fast, I'd lose him. He'd said he was getting a connecting flight, so I'd be safe. All went well, and I was so relieved to be home I didn't even notice or care about the fact that my flat was so poor and tiny. I was safe.

I dumped my bags and raced over to Mum's. The moment Julien saw me his face broke into a huge smile. I dropped down on to my knees and held out my arms.

'Mummy!' He raced over as fast as his little legs would carry him and flung himself into my arms. I clutched hold of him, breathing in his clean toddler smell, feeling the force of his chubby arms around my neck. I never wanted to let him go.

'My darling, darling boy.'

I gave him the baseball cap and the toys I'd brought him and he sat in my lap playing happily. I felt like my heart would break with love for him. How could anyone abuse an innocent child? I couldn't get my head round it at all.

America had been an amazing experience. It had given me a glimpse of another way of life. Lucy's words came back to me and I knew that this wasn't going to be my only brush with famous people. But I also realised that it was an unreal way to live. If I were ever to be famous, I swore to myself that I would keep my feet firmly on the ground. I would never lose track of who I was and where I came from.

One day, not long after the America trip, Christine popped around to my rundown flat. She looked around and gave a deep sigh.

'Something's got to happen here. You can't live like this.'

I smiled and said I was just fine.

'No, you're not. Right, Michèle, I'm going to get you an office anywhere you like in London, rent free, for a year – just by asking.'

'What? How is that possible?'

She tapped her nose. 'Watch and learn, watch and learn!

Anything is possible. It's just that people don't bother asking most of the time.'

Now I already believed in cosmic ordering – after all, I'd had a Chopper, a motorbike and an all-expenses paid trip to America to show for my own attempts. But this was as if Christine were giving me the missing piece of the puzzle.

I shrugged and smiled. 'OK. I would like a place in Covent Garden please.'

Christine dragged me out of the flat, barely giving me time to grab my jacket. She flagged down a passing cab.

'Covent Garden, please,' she said, dragging on one of her Dunhill cigarettes.

We jumped out of the cab near Neal's Yard and hadn't even walked down two streets before we stumbled across a courtyard with a sign that read 'The American Centre'. Could this be Fate?

Inside a small courtyard just off of Endell Street there was a new development – six brand-spanking-new shops of different sizes with a café in the middle.

Christine hunted down the owner. 'Hi there. Can you help us? Are these retail units for rent?'

'Hello,' said a small balding Asian man with intense smoky-blue eyes. He gave Christine the once over. Men loved her and she had his full attention in a nano-second.

'How much are the units? My friend here is one of the best psychics in London. She would be a huge draw for this place. She'd bring a vast amount of traffic to your centre.'

I shifted uncomfortably, as he eyed me curiously.

'£300 a month,' he said with a smile.

I gasped. There was no way on earth I could afford that.

Christine wasn't remotely fazed. She looked as if she was thinking about it, and then cocked her head to one side and drew in a breath, as if she were about to offer him the biggest favour of his life.

'Look, this is a new place. You're just starting out and you've got no rentals and no customer traffic. How about we do you a favour? We'll try it out for six months and give you 25 per cent of any profit. What do you reckon?'

He eyed her for a few seconds then, to my utter shock and delight, stuck out his hand.

'It's a deal.'

So just like that, I was in possession of a prime-site crystal shop; a place where I could run workshops, give free healing and do readings. 'Michèle's of Covent Garden' was born out of a big cosmic order and a heck of a lot of audacity. I was stunned but Christine didn't even bat an eyelid.

'Now,' she said, 'we need to talk about how to get you your stock.'

The magic was only just beginning.

23

Shiny Happy People

At last it seemed as though my life was starting to make sense. It felt as if I was finally getting on track. My relationship with Mum was so much improved as to be unrecognisable. Without Russell, she was less stressed, and Julien continued to mellow her. Fortunately, she didn't take up with any more deeply unsuitable men and we rubbed along OK. It was never going to be a totally harmonious relationship but, compared to how it had been in the past, it was positively blissful. My son continued to ground me, to keep me centred and focused. OK, so I wasn't the most conventional of mothers, but he was surrounded by love. We didn't have much money, but it didn't remotely matter: the things we loved to do didn't require cash. We spent hours in the park, feeding the ducks, looking at the trees, watching birds and insects. Nature was a common love for both of us.

I also felt I had discovered my life work. Since the workshop, so much had come together. I was finding my own spirituality, taking the best from Mum's psychic tradition, but also discovering my own path, my own passions. Crystals were key. I felt that they were beacons of unconditional love that can help draw in the divine; magic wands of positivity that can enhance our wishes and heal our souls. There I was with a practically free retail unit in the heart of Covent Garden. It was the living embodiment of all I believed: I had asked and it had come.

But there was just one problem: it was empty. I needed a plan, and again I just asked and, as if by magic, all the right characters walked through the door. First there was the graphic artist who designed my leaflets and gave me incredible support and bagloads of helpful advice. Then there was the journalist who wrote a rave review about me in the press. My mother was infinitely proud of what I was achieving and she gave me money towards stocking the shop with crystals. I also received loans (some large, some tiny) from friends. I could not have asked for more help and positivity. I was never very good with money though – I had a perhaps naïve, yet powerful, conviction that life would deliver all that I needed as and when I needed it. My job was simply to do all that I could to heal and help people.

When the crystals were displayed, the shelves full, the shop looked amazing. People would come in and immediately fall in love with one of them.

'Oh, I love that! Isn't it gorgeous?' And then they would look at the price tag and their shoulders would slump. 'Oh no, I can't afford that much.' I could see their need; see that the crystal was speaking with them; that it belonged to that person. I couldn't help myself:

'Take it. It's yours. With love.'

Then they would flee the shop, clutching their crystal, before I could change my mind or come to my senses. They looked at me as if I were mad. They needn't have hurried: I wasn't going to change my mind. I was always quite sure that my generosity would be repaid. Maybe, in retrospect, it was a little foolish and I certainly didn't think enough about the people whose generosity and love had given me the means to fill the shop. However, of course, like magic it all worked out even though I gave three-quarters of my stock away. To this day, I feel that my current success comes more than partly from my earlier generosity. Generate random acts of kindness whenever you possibly can – they will always be returned.

Life in Covent Garden was never boring; quite the opposite. So many fascinating people walked through the doors. My days were filled with people wanting to know if their relationships would work out; if they would find happiness or success. There would be celebrities walking in, fresh off the stage in the West End. People who were battling with unrequited love, broken relationships; those who were struggling with their sexuality or trying to overcome fears. There was even a woman who wanted to know where and when her beloved parrot was going to be reborn.

At this stage, I felt very uncomfortable taking money

from needy people and would often give readings for free. I'd even give out my home phone number, which led to my being called at all hours of the day and night. I didn't mind: I was totally lost in the work of healing. So lost, in fact, that I forgot to look after myself and stopped my own healing. It wasn't long before I was on the path to total burn-out.

Then I met a man whose slogan was: 'Teach the world to smile like a child'. He couldn't believe what I was doing to myself.

'Michèle, listen to me. People will never really take what you say seriously unless you charge them. They won't value what you say. They won't listen.'

'No. You're wrong. You should give freely if you have a gift like mine. It has to be there for everyone – whether or not they can afford it.'

He shook his head and explained about the energy involved in giving money. I fought him long and hard on this as I really didn't want to believe it to be true. But now, after long years of experience, I can say without a shadow of a doubt that he was right. Just like then you get a free lipstick from a magazine – you might chuck it in the back of your drawer and forget about it. You didn't pay for it, so you don't value it. But if you buy yourself an expensive Chanel lipstick, for example, it has value. You prize it, you use it, and it gives you a buzz when you put it on.

I still do free readings sometimes, but nowadays I have much more balance. In the days of the American Centre, though, it was not unknown for me to give a reading to someone, see they had no money, and march them out to the ATM to give them a handful of notes – money I really couldn't afford to give away. Many times, though, I was delighted when their ship came in and I would find an envelope stuffed through the door with a note of thanks and the money repaid – usually just when I most needed it myself!

My personal life was still a mess. I met women and had relationships, but they just didn't last. The problem was that my psychic abilities made me hypersensitive. It was no fun having relationships as I could feel every thought and mood shift in my partner. It made it impossible for them – and draining and hurtful for me. I was still very damaged from my early abuse. While I now recognised it had happened, and had started on the work of clearing it, there was simply too much to release in one go. As a child I had learned mistrust, I was incredibly wary of my emotions. Abuse is a horrible virus that infects every area of your life – it prevents you from letting go, from trusting. I freely admit that I drank far too much, but only late at night when Julien was asleep, in an attempt to shut down my memories, and my psychic powers. It was the only way I could get to sleep at night.

I didn't have my boundaries in place at that time, so I felt everyone's problems far too acutely. I simply couldn't leave them at the door. I would worry all the time about people who had come for help, long after they had left the

Centre. I would also carry out free spiritual healing for people who had cancer and other serious illnesses. I didn't realise I was taking on too much. I felt so strongly that I had to do all that I could to eradicate the pain of others. I was young and had not, at that time, realised the important lesson that sometimes pain is a journey; that instant solutions are not always available and should not always be sought. This is a hard lesson for many people to learn but I can honestly say that the most serious pain I have had in life has always led to a breakthrough. It is a gift, but one you can only understand later on with the benefit of hindsight.

Although life was hard in many ways, this was a productive time. My incredible good fortune continued to bring me the right people at the right time. Sometimes it felt as if all I had to do was click my fingers and they'd appear. Go after your dream. It was a constant theme at that time, and there were always constant reminders to keep me on track and angels that would turn up just when I needed help. I truly believe that, if you have unconditional love for others even in your darkest hour, the universe will mirror it back to you.

Throughout all this I was juggling my work with being a single parent. Julien was always a very sensitive and spiritual child, but also quite introverted and intense. We had an incredibly strong bond right from the word go. My mother continued to be a wonderful grandparent and helped me enormously, but I was keenly aware that, while he had strong women around him (me, my mother and my many women friends), he desperately needed a male role model to balance all the female energy. Like all boys, he needed a strong male influence. Luckily I had a very good friend called John, who was incredibly intelligent, kind and grounded. He got on with Julien from the start and I was thrilled to see their relationship develop – gradually, he became like a father figure to him. John would take Julien to school when I had to work early, and would pick him up when I had to work late. He has been in Julien's life since he was three years old and has supported us throughout. He really was a godsend (in the original, literal sense of the word). We became a rather unconventional family unit (I never had a physical relationship with John, only a very close emotional one). He gave me invaluable unconditional support and the huge comfort of knowing that Julien was in safe hands with a loving, solid father figure. He was a very grounding influence for both of us and John and Julien are still just as close to this day.

For some reason the American Centre never really worked. Wedged between a sauna and a café, it had a hidden energy – so that most people just seemed to miss it, to pass by without even noticing it. I wasn't particularly worried because I felt that, whatever happened, this was the beginning of my journey. I was on the first step of my predestined path. All the incredible cases of synchronicity in the past had brought me to this point and now it was time for the magic that had saved and nurtured me all my life to be used to help others. I felt a passionate and crystal-clear calling that now was the time to start sharing my knowledge, all I had learned, about the key to life. I had to tell people that, if only we know how to ask, all the magic and help in the world is available for us.

Over time, the Centre went from bad to worse. A dodgy modelling agency started up downstairs and the energy was awful. Then they decided to shift away from modelling and instead to set up a psychic agency. I knew the time had come to leave. Once again, I simply put out the request – I need new premises. Out of the blue, I got a call from a property owner who had an office in Neal Street to let. This was also in Covent Garden, with interesting shops all around. It was within my price range so I went to look at it and fell in love. It was a tiny space, high up in an attic, with just enough room for a table and chair. I loved it! I painted it lavender and set to work. Funnily enough, I only went in when I felt like it and wasn't motivated by money. I always felt it would be there for me.

I was still occasionally working at the Roof Gardens in Kensington, and one day I met a man there who was blown away with my reading. I do not ever talk about clients unless, of course, the reading was done in the public domain on camera, but I have asked permission from this client to tell you one of the most amazing past-life experiences I have witnessed.

During his reading, I saw that he had a real love relationship – a strong spiritual bond. I told him everything that was happening, business-wise, and he was astounded. The following week he set up an appointment for his lover. The minute I met her, I was blown away. She had a timeless beauty and a powerful energy that was quite unique. She was elegant, well-spoken and full of humour and intellect. I became their regular psychic and they took me under their wing and supported me in my journey. They accepted me unconditionally even though I was a working-class kid: they never judged me. They would often take me out to dinner in smart restaurants. I was unaccustomed to such kindness and it touched my heart.

One day they asked me to give them a past-life regression, something that (following the workshop) I used to do a lot. I went to their house in Chelsea and started the session. What is extraordinary, and has always stayed with me, is that although I conducted their regressions quite separately and without the other being present, they both saw exactly the same thing. They went back to the Middle Ages and, in that life, they were from very different social backgrounds. They fell in love but could not be together, and one of them was arrested and sent to a tower to be imprisoned in a small room. All they could do was to write yearning love letters, year after year. They were stunned and quite shaken when they discovered that they had shared such a tragic life. The detail had been quite remarkable, and there was no doubt in either of their minds (or mine) that this was a genuine recall. Also, it seemed that this theme had not finished; there were still lessons to be learned.

I did try to warn them of this, but they were so entranced by their romantic link that the warning went unheeded. Anyway, many years later the lady in question was arrested and imprisoned in a foreign country for, shall we say, an error of judgement? She spent two years in jail and the only communication she had with her lover was by letter. She spent the whole time writing and reading letters of longing and yearning. When she was released the experience had brought them much closer. I was astounded that events had turned out quite so strangely, that their past had been replicated in such an obvious way. But then again, lives do have a habit of repeating themselves. Fortunately, she is happy and at peace with herself now and still as gorgeous and lovely as ever.

People often ask me how come people are always something special in their past lives? How come there are so many ex-Napoleons or Queen Elizabeths wandering around? All I can say is that all the past lives I have taken people to have been astounding for their ordinariness. Often they were very tragic, and past lives do give a humbling insight into how tough life was in the past; how much suffering we have undergone well before we were born this time round. I remember someone who had a life as a potato farmer with TB in a small damp cottage in Ireland. Then there was the woman who in her past life was a lonely man who worked in the city and went home alone every night until the loneliness became too much and he finally hanged himself. There were all sorts of tragic and mundane existences that needed to be released.

Sometimes our past lives lurk like shadows and, if this is the case, it's well worth exploring them and releasing the trapped energy that presses on you in this life. On the whole, I do not tend to use past-life regression so much now as I feel we must focus on grasping the magic of each moment rather than reflecting on, or poring over, the past. We only have *now* in which to create something magnificent.

I had experienced so many strange and wonderful things in my life that very little surprised or shook me. Yet one day something really odd and inexplicable happened. I had a client coming back for a second reading. In the first reading I had (probably foolishly) revealed that I had seen he was an arms dealer. It was a hot summer's day and I was wearing linen trousers and a light shirt. I had a large bunch of keys in my pocket and had just been out to lunch with another client. She was an agent to a well-known pop star, an ebullient American who always made me laugh. We had a fabulous time over lunch, laughing so much that my face actually hurt. I'd lost track of time and had only five minutes to get back to the office for my appointment. As I kissed her goodbye, I went to get the keys out of my pocket. To my horror, I couldn't find them. We turned and went back to the coffee shop and searched it from top to bottom. She even went through my pockets for me in case I had missed something, but no, the keys were nowhere to be found. We spent half an hour carefully retracing our steps, certain I must have dropped them accidentally on the way there or back. By this time I had totally missed the client. Suddenly we heard a jangle as I walked forwards. I stopped, put my hand in my pocket, and pulled out the keys. We were both totally gobsmacked. Those keys had not been there moments before. We both saw it – it was simply not possible for them to be gone and come back like that. I have no idea what it means other than the fact I was not meant to do the reading for that particular client. We were both shocked and, to be honest, quite freaked out by it. But I am sure there was a good reason for that to have occurred. Inexplicable perhaps, but further proof that life has more dimensions than we can see.

Another time I came back from a holiday in Greece and found that a crowd of reporters and photographers were staked outside my building with cameras. I pushed my way through and climbed the stairs. The walls in my office were paper-thin and it wasn't long before I realised what was going on in the office next door. The Maxwell brothers had come there to work and try to recreate their empire just after their father, Robert Maxwell, had died and before their court case. They had a big chunky-framed picture of their dad that took over a complete wall. One of them would poke his head around my door and say 'Good morning' in a very charming manner. It felt very surreal to be giving readings while the Maxwells were wheeling and dealing next door in loud voices.

Neal Street was full of magic, weirdness and extraordinary memories. If I were to write down all my experiences there, it would take ten volumes.

There was one encounter that stayed with me for a long time. I was in the café at the Covent Garden General Store one day and noticed a woman with long dark curly hair and startling blue eyes. I felt an incredibly strong connection with her; I was certain that we had some shared destiny, but I wasn't sure how or when.

'Hello,' I said, smiling at her.

She turned around and gave me the most beautiful smile in the world. 'Hi.'

'Sorry,' I began, 'but I just had to say that you have the most amazing energy. You're gorgeous!'

Her smile went even broader, if that were possible.

'Thank you.' She blushed.

At that point a group of people – obviously her friends – came in and swooped her away. As she went, she looked back over her shoulder and our eyes locked.

What an amazing person, I thought. I will meet her again one day.

24

I Ain't Afraid of no Ghost!

I was like two people at that time. One side of me was strong and in control, working non-stop to help people, trying to save the world one person at a time. That side of me was also the 'good Mum', creating a cocoon of normality for my son. But the other side of me was still in self-destructive mode. Once Julien was in bed, asleep, I would start drinking, trying to blank out the memories that threatened to subsume me every time I stopped the busyness and frenzy of working life. The full horror of my childhood was slamming into me and I realised that it was literally a miracle that I was alive and functioning at all. In my mind there was little doubt that I had been protected – otherwise how had I survived? Many people think it's strange but I have always had a total trust in the universe. I have always been an optimist: I totally and utterly believe in happy endings.

Julien and I were still in that little council flat in Euston with the British Library extension being built nearby. The work went on for years and we lived with a background soundtrack of drilling and the thundering of cement mixers. It was hardly a peaceful environment, but it was safe and it was home. Julie had moved out by now: it was just the two of us.

There was not one single defining moment when I turned the corner away from the madness. There were many moments. Having Julien started the healing and transformed my relationship with my mother. The crystal workshop marked a profound shift, not only setting me off on my own deep healing journey, but also showing me how I could help other people – my life's work. Going to America widened my horizons, and Christine taught me that there were no limits; that I could achieve anything I wanted. Getting my shop was a summation of all of that – a clear sign of my inner shift. But there was one more part of my life that needed to change in order to bring about balance. I needed to flex my intellect.

So, as if my life were not busy and crazy enough, I decided to resume my education. By pure serendipity I heard about a new degree called 'Independent Study', a little like a miniature PhD. That's it, I thought, great! My fascination with social and sexual politics was as strong as it had ever been and I was still baffled at how unfair and unbalanced our society was. I wanted to discover how we as a race had got ourselves into such a mess. So I decided that I would study women's changing sexual and religious roles, from prehistory to the modern day. Little did I know how revealing it would be and how it would heal me in quite a profound way.

Doing a degree felt incredibly important to me. I knew I had to balance my intuitive abilities with intellectual work as I was horribly out of balance. I would know things with an innate inner conviction and could argue passionately, but I was unable to articulate my convictions clearly and logically. I was all emotion and no reason. Too much Venus, not enough Mercury.

When I was accepted to do the degree at the University of East London, I knew that, even though the degree was incredibly flexible, timing would still be tricky. Here I would be doing a full-time degree, yet still working enough to keep the office open in Neal Street and, of course, being a mother too. It was going to be a fine juggling act, but I was determined. I marshalled the troops (Mum, John, other friends) and between us we figured out a way to make it work – just. There was absolutely no room for error.

When I arrived for my first day it was to find that the entire timetable had been changed around. I was caught between a sense of impending doom and total fury. I had just planned out my life to the last second in order to be able to accommodate the original timetable. What on earth were they thinking of? How was I supposed to balance everything if the ground kept shifting underneath me? I stormed into the Dean's office and gave him a stern piece of my mind, complaining vociferously that single parents simply didn't have a chance if colleges were going to behave like this. I must have scared him half to death: when I met my personal tutor, Ericka, for the first time she confessed that she had downed a stiff vodka before our meeting! She had happened to go into the Dean's office after my tornado of a departure and had found him shaking, warning her about the hellcat she was going to have to supervise.

But Ericka was a powerful woman in her own right and we became firm friends from the word go. Fortunately, she found my cheek amusing. I was a bit bemused when she told me about the Dean and her own pre-meeting fears of me. I still didn't have a clue as to quite what a strong character I was. I simply didn't realise how I related emotionally to other people – how intense I was, how like my mother I was in that regard.

None of it really mattered, though, as once I got into the work, I was transported to a new world. I had become fascinated by the early Goddess religion in which the earth was respected and people related in totally different ways to one another. I wanted to see not only how society had changed, but *why* it had changed. While my main area of study was anthropology, I also studied social science and philosophy.

I fell in love with my subject and couldn't stop reading, writing, digesting, debating. The degree transformed me in several unexpected ways. It helped me rein in my ferocious wild spirit and gave me the power to express myself in a different way. But, most of all, it enlightened me and helped to heal some of my sexual wounds.

I was fascinated to discover that, not only had an earlier egalitarian society existed, but it had existed for many thousands of years. This early civilisation was in Sumer (now modern Iraq) and it was a highly sophisticated society with a complex system of law and education. The Sumerians were believed to have invented astronomy and writing, and also brewed the first alcohol. Even more intriguingly, these inventions were all attributed to women. It is also where one of the most powerful early divinities can be found: Inanna, Goddess of Heaven and Earth. Like the Egyptian gods, Inanna was also believed to have been an earthly ruler, a queen. She was the archetypal modern woman – juggling the roles of ruler, partner, mother, friend, homemaker and law-maker. She governed wisely and well, yet was also a highly sensual Goddess – and the descriptions of her relationship with her husband, Dumuzi, are worthy of a Hollywood bonkbuster. She was the divine Goddess of sexual expression. The priestesses of Inanna lived in temples and were highly regarded members of the community. They were thought to be the embodiment of the Goddess. Sex was considered a sacred act, a sacrament and every woman became the embodiment of the Goddess when she made love. There was no distinction between the genders: all people were considered equal. Women also had comparative sexual autonomy at this stage.

That sexuality was originally a sacred act made complete and total sense to me – but seeing it written down in black and white, espoused by professors, was a bit of an epiphany.

I felt there was something about sex that took it out of the purely physical sphere. But now it all became clear: sex was an act of divinity in which making love was to become the Goddess. Sex was a sacred act and something that could express spirituality. This revelation healed something very deep within me.

However, all good things come to an end and gradually, over time, invading tribes created a need for a stronger Hero God. Enter the Babylonian Gilgamesh and a new phase in the history of our planet. A gradual separation between nature and humanity appeared; however, the Goddess was never really forgotten and she appears throughout all developing religions. In fact, for many thousands of years a Goddess was represented in all faiths and a sense of balance with nature was considered an essential element of religion. At the time I was astounded that this wasn't widely known and it gave me a sense of waking up to knowledge. The balance between male and female, between people and the earth, wasn't just some pie-in-the-sky idea of mine.

I would now consider myself multi-faith. I believe that all religions have a seed of truth in them and we have to find our own individual way to express our spirituality. Our interpretation of the world is unique; our experience of life is unique – that is the very beauty of life. We all see things differently. If we could be aware that we are both part of the whole and yet beautifully our own, I know for a fact that peace would be much nearer.

I struggled to balance all my different roles in life as I was determined to complete the degree. It was releasing so much and teaching me so much. I was supported throughout and had many messages (both earthly and from spirit) to continue. But it was tough and, right up to the last minute, I thought I would fail, that I would fall at the last hurdle. But I didn't. I completed it and gained my degree in 1994.

I also changed my surname. My studies in anthropology had taught me the importance and power of names. I felt I needed to change my name in order to cut free from the past and set myself up for a new phase in my life. I needed a name that signified who I was, in my deepest soul. I wanted a name that defined me. At the time I knew someone called Paul Knight and his surname rang out to me. Knight. Yes. I had always seen myself as a knight, riding on my charger, questing to find answers and to save the innocent. From that point on I became Michèle Knight. It's a good name.

I was never one to rest on my laurels and, rather than resting and regrouping, I decided that now was the time I needed to get across the truths I'd learned in a bigger way. I had already started running workshops – teaching groups of individuals – but I needed to get the message out to even more people. I decided that the next obvious step for me was to get into the media. It didn't once cross my mind that I couldn't do it. I had no training, no contacts, but that didn't remotely put me off. I put out my order and, within a short while, there I was on a Channel 4 programme called *Takeover TV* in which I explained the journey from prehistoric times to the Goddess religion in a three-minute segment. It was incredibly exciting and I was over the moon at being able to express different views to a wider audience. I remembered that Lucy had hinted that this would, and should, be the right direction for me, so I asked for more help to continue on this path. I was curious to know if Lucy had been right and if I really could move into television with ease, so I sent out a cosmic order to get more media work.

Three days later I received a call from a TV company asking if I would agree to be filmed giving readings to the members of a few 'boy bands' who were playing at a festival. I was blithely unaware of the whole boy band phenomenon – I'd never heard of Worlds Apart and Bad Boys Inc, who were headlining. It was a wildly superficial situation and I was tempted to say no. But I had cosmically ordered it, so I thought I'd better go along with it and see where it led.

It was a pretty insane experience. I hadn't counted on the level of hysteria with the young female fans, and during the concert one girl got crushed at the front and was pulled up on stage out of the mêlée. I took care of her backstage and, as I was comforting her, she started talking to me about her life. It all came tumbling out: how her father was beating her up and telling her she was totally worthless. She sobbed and I held her in my arms and gave her healing. I told her I understood, possibly more than most people could, and I think I was able to make a difference. I gave her support and advice and told her where she could go to get more help. The following week she rang me and thanked me and told me she had got help. It was as if a light had been turned on. I knew that I would always be sent where I was needed and that this path was the right one. Yes, it had been a superficial situation, but I had been able to do good. Everything you do, however small, can be a turning point for someone else.

I was doing too much however. I hadn't had any kind of break or holiday for more than three years and I was feeling totally burnt out, both physically and emotionally. I asked for help or a sign, and almost immediately bumped into someone who felt like another of my guardian angels. She lived down the road and her name was Wendy. She was half Tobagoan and half English. She even looked like an angel: 5' 10" with perfect coffee-coloured skin, a mop of curly hair and a smile that simply brimmed over with unconditional love and kindness. We bumped into each other by chance and spent two days and nights solidly talking, sitting cross-legged on my threadbare carpet. Her mother had been tragically killed in a car accident when she was young, but nothing had dampened Wendy's joy of life and love of other people. She would often just pitch up at my door in the morning with freshly baked croissants. Or she would pop a lovely and loving note through the letterbox full of inspiration or photos that she had taken. Wendy loved life, loved people, and had that special avatar vibe. She was, I have no doubt, sent to heal me. She wanted nothing from me – simply to fill me with the inspiration I had forgotten. One day she brought round some photos of her childhood in Tobago – pictures of her playing happily on the most perfect beach.

'Oh, it's absolutely gorgeous. What an idyllic place.'

'Michèle, you have to go to Tobago. It will heal your soul, I promise.'

I laughed. 'Wendy, I'd love to but how on earth could I? I'm totally skint. I'm up to my neck in student loans. I have to work and I have to look after Julien.'

'Just ask,' she shrugged. 'I'm sure you will get there if it's meant to be.'

Although Wendy didn't know about spirituality in particular, she was naturally aware of the magic of life.

I put in my order there and then, and within a very short space of time my best friend, Caroline Day, called me up, excitement buzzing in her voice.

'Michèle! I'm up to win a competition to go to Egypt. Send me some good vibes and I promise I'll take you with me, all expenses paid!'

'That's great. But I ordered Tobago. Can you swap it?' I said, knowing I was being very cheeky.

'The Caribbean? That would be top! I don't know, but I can find out. For now, just send me the vibes to win.'

I sensed that something important was happening here. When I was doing my degree, I had put out the wish that I wanted to go to Egypt, but nothing had happened. But right now I knew Tobago was the place. My friend rang me back the next day.

'Pack your bags! They changed it. We're going on an all-expenses paid trip to Tobago!'

My first thought was about Julien, but Mum and John stepped in immediately and insisted I went. Julien himself very seriously told me that I needed a holiday and that he would be fine. So, within one month of putting in my request, there I was sunning myself on the white sands of Tobago where Wendy had played as a child. If I had any doubts about cosmic ordering, this was the final confirmation. Tracey was right – Tobago was exactly what I needed. I allowed myself to rest and relax very deeply, and could feel my batteries recharging by the day. The people, as well as the weather, were warm and soothing. I felt very loved by the Universe and ready for the next challenge.

After returning from Tobago, things carried on as usual but there was definitely a shift, movement, something in the air. Very soon little media jobs were springing up all over the place. My ultimate aim was that one day I should gain enough success that I could open a grief centre where people could go (free of charge) to recover from relationship breakdowns and bereavement. It would be a safe space in nature to heal the broken-hearted and to empower people. This is still my long-term goal and, like everything else, I am quite sure it will happen when the time is right and when I am ready. To get into this position, I needed to build my profile.

In 1997 Channel 5 was launched and I was asked to take part in a new show, to be called *Housebusters*, a sort of psychic *Changing Rooms*. I was over the moon. It felt totally right, as if my destiny were unfolding in front of me. Lucy had been spot-on – everything was going to work out well. I was going to be on prime-time television doing what I loved most – helping people with my gift.

Housebusters felt powerful and different from the word go. The idea behind the show (which was initially fronted by Russell Grant) was that three psychic experts would be taken to a home that was causing difficulties for its owners. We would each individually diagnose the problem without meeting the inhabitants or being given any clues by the producers. We couldn't even discuss it with one another – the experts were all kept strictly apart. The expert whom the owners felt was most accurate would then be asked to sort out the problem. It was a great idea and a wonderful challenge.

I was taken to a house in south London in a block of flats and asked to explore one particular flat and work out what the problem was. The moment I walked in, I felt a bad vibe about the place. It was heavy, uncomfortable, brooding. A shiver ran down my spine and I could tell that the film crew could sense something too as they looked uncomfortable and there was none of the usual banter. I knew instantly that the woman who lived there was not sleeping. The bedroom was the focus for the problems – although, to be honest, the whole flat was pretty horrible.

I felt quite sure that violence had occurred there in the past as it had a very negative energy. Standing in one corner of the front room, I couldn't shake off the feeling that someone was watching me. The energy was cold and malevolent: I had goose-pimples all down my arms. It reminded me all too clearly of the times I had been haunted in my room as a child. I also had a very clear conviction that the owner had a block in her relationships. But, on a brighter note, I felt that her cat was very protective, a good influence.

I didn't meet the other experts and had no idea what they had said. But the owner of the flat had been impressed with me and I was chosen to sort out the problem and give the flat a psychic makeover. When I met her, the owner confirmed exactly what I had said – she couldn't sleep and her relationships were disastrous or non-existent. She also revealed that someone in the building had been murdered.

When I asked about her cat, she smiled broadly and said that yes, indeed, her cat had always been a soothing, protective presence and had even once saved her from a fire.

I didn't like the presence in the flat but, thanks to my unorthodox upbringing, I knew exactly how to deal with it. I smudged the house (wafting burning sage into every corner to push out negative energy – it's an ancient native American space-clearing technique which is very powerful). I also placed protective crystals over the windows. I moved things around in the bedroom and, after two days of hard work, calm was restored. In fact, she slept like a log and even started dating. She was over the moon and so were the show's producers. It was a clear display of the supernatural and how psychic solutions can solve very real problems.

However, some months later she rang to say the problems had started again and what could she do? I was puzzled as the cleansing had been thorough and the energy had felt quite clean when I left. Then a thought occurred to me.

'You haven't moved anything new into the bedroom?' I asked.

She paused and I just knew she was going to say yes.

'Well, someone brought me back this incredible voodoo doll from a trip. I put it in my bedroom.'

'OK, that's it. Get it out of there. In fact, get rid of it altogether.'

Fortunately she followed my advice, got rid of the doll, and started sleeping again. Funnily enough, many people don't pay enough attention to their bedrooms. I found that a huge number of the problems I encountered on *Housebusters* were bedroom-related. A bedroom is a sanctuary for the soul. It's the place where your spirit replenishes and it is essential to treat that room as a sacred space. You must give it priority above all else. If your bedroom is OK, in good shape, it will give you added strength. It's never a good idea to have a computer or television in a bedroom, and equally it should be kept clean, clutter-free and attractive and welcoming. Make it a boudoir of love – especially if you're single.

In this job you are always learning and can never afford

to let yourself become complacent. One of the other houses I visited in the first series of *Housebusters* had, quite incredibly, been built opposite a nuclear power station. When I stepped through the door I felt an intense frenetic energy that increased tenfold when I walked into the lounge. I had a very strong impression that this was a place where a woman always had to be doing things. One of the rooms was packed to the gills with stuffed animals: foxes, stags' heads, badgers, all sorts. I was horrified. It wasn't just the wrong energy for that house, but the wrong energy for *any* house. What intrigued me most was that the house was in the direct path of an ancient burial ground with a passage grave. Perhaps the owners were drawn to all things dead and stuffed because of this? When I was picked as the expert to correct the house I had a slight cough and cold, but it was nothing much and I continued quite happily.

It turned out that, once again, I was right. The lady owner could never relax; she always had to be doing things and every one of her kids had moved out as the place was too frenetic. I set to work changing the colour scheme and protecting the windows from the energy of the passage grave. I also buried the dead animals in a big hole in the front garden. It all looked overly dramatic, on screen, but it certainly was necessary. Needless to say, it also made great television.

But that night, as I made my way back home, everything went from bad to worse. The train broke down, and I had to walk with big bags in the pouring rain. I stopped to help someone who had trouble walking, so I had to walk in the rain twice. By the time I got home I was feeling very ill and had the start of a serious chest infection. I felt that the sudden onset of it wasn't right and perhaps it was something to do with the house. I realised with horror that while I had sealed the energy off from the house, I hadn't made any appeasing offering at the passage grave. I had obviously angered whatever energy was there. Now this energy was pretty angry in the first place, but I had just made it possibly ten times more furious. The only good bit of news was that the clearing of the house had worked and the woman was at last able to relax and could even fall asleep in the lounge. Over the next few weeks, all her kids moved back home.

It took me a few weeks to get over the infection. I lit a candle to appease anything I had angered and my illness finally passed. It is essential always to pay attention and not get caught up in the ego in situations like this. I had made the basic mistake of being caught up in the whole drama of television and, as a consequence, had forgotten a very elementary part of psychic lore. It was a clear lesson to me that we are all just channels for a higher power. Individual glory is meaningless – each of us is simply a unique part of the whole.

The show gave me a huge boost in my confidence. I had never really doubted my gift – it had been part of my life for too long – but seeing how impressed other people were by my accuracy gave me a huge lift. My self-esteem soared.

As a huge bonus, Julien (who was about eleven now) loved the show and was very proud of me, as was my mother. She would ask me loads of questions about the people whose houses I saw. She wanted to help, and we would often argue about the way I handled the problems. Being Mum, she could never just quietly agree with anything. As I became more popular, the producers really 'bigged me up': I would roar up to the house in question in full motorbike leathers, on a huge bike. Quite an entrance.

Housebusters was the start of something big for me and it took me by surprise. Radio and television offers came in thick and fast. Also, I started receiving sacks and sacks of letters from people needing help: people having problems with their family; those suffering grief, illness, terrible pain. I wrote back to each person personally and did a number of free sessions, but once more I was taking on too much and pretty soon the old pattern started repeating itself. I was getting burnt out again as I found it very difficult to let go of people's pain. I felt hugely frustrated that I could not do more. Suddenly, all at once, I had a clear and sudden conviction that I had to get out of London.

25

Total Eclipse of the Heart

The eclipse in 1999 brought huge changes for lots of people – and I was no exception. London had become an impossible place for me to live; it seemed like everyone wanted a piece of me. Try as I might to keep my boundaries intact, I was doing too much. More and more people were asking for help and my home was like a refugee camp for the lost and lonely. Julien was thirteen now and he too was finding London harsh. He craved the country. Every Sunday we would have a ritual of going to Regent's Park to feed the ducks. It was good, but it wasn't enough. Somerstown was a tough place to be a child and a dangerous place to be a teenager. It was not unknown for children as young as eleven to be hooked on drugs. Now it was getting rougher and rougher.

I was beginning to feel as if I couldn't breathe. The climate was changing and London was starting to have tropical muggy weather.

My intuition was telling me very clearly that it was time

to make another major change in my life. The curious thing was that, since Yannish, I had not had any named guides. To my intense sorrow, Lucy had never returned and, since Yannish departed, no one had come to fill the vacuum. I missed Lucy so much. The more I had uncovered in regression and rebirthing about my twin, the more I felt the loss of her. I often found myself thinking what it would have been like to have gone through life with her, my sister, my twin. Would she have followed my path or been totally different? Would she have been psychic? What would she have been like as a thirty-something? Would she have had a smart professional career? Would she have married? Would she have had children? I wondered what any children she might have had would have been like, and had moments of huge regret for the nieces and nephews I wouldn't ever know; the cousins Julien missed. Would we, together, have found a way to stop the abuse?

Although I missed Lucy horribly as a sister, I didn't really need her any more as a guide. My psychic ability was now so finely tuned that I was able to just 'know' what was needed. And what I knew at that point was that it was time to leave London for good.

Not for the first time in my life I decided to pray and truly ask for help. If you ask for help, you always receive it one way or the other. The old adage that is woven into all religions, 'Seek and ye shall find', has always proved true for me.

From the time of the chakra workshop I had it fixed in

my head that the West Country was a safe and good place to live. While Glastonbury itself seemed too weird and unsettled in its energy, I fell in love with the area further west – where the Somerset Levels give way to rolling hills, dense woodland mingled with rich farmland. The air is clean, the energy bright and welcoming. This would be my home. I put out the cosmic order and waited. It didn't take long to materialise.

Marie was yet another angel brought into my life to further me on my path. She lived in a Hansel and Gretel cottage in the middle of nowhere, deep in the heart of Somerset. Some people you are just *meant* to know – they teach you vital lessons. I moved from London to live with her without a second glance.

Here, surrounded by nature, I could heal. It would also be a place of safety for my son. I can still remember the moment we arrived. We got out of the car and just stood, breathing in the pure clean air. Then Julien looked at me, grinned, and ran off to explore. It was as if a weight had been lifted from his shoulders. Julien adored Marie – they had an instant bond. Together we visited several boarding schools and found one that was perfect. Julien could board during the week and come home at weekends.

Julien changed overnight into a far happier, more relaxed boy. We would take our three dogs for long, long walks. There were two Scotties, Razzy and Rachel (both larger than life), and Misty, a large Alsatian. We walked through the woods laughing and filming home movies. One of the most beautiful qualities Julien has brought into my life is laughter. He is an excellent mimic and does a whole host of *South Park* characters that always have me in stitches. He had grown into a sensitive boy, but he also had a tough exterior.

Like me, he has the gift. He could be in a room and tell instantly if someone was upset, even if they were smiling and laughing on the outside. He'd go up and ask what was wrong. But, like most young people, he was more interested in music and in being an MC (he's brilliant at it).

I felt, more than ever, that having Julien saved my life in many ways. He allowed me to focus on the positive. He is, without any doubt whatsoever, the best thing that has ever happened to me. Every Saturday night in our new home, we would have a curry and watch a film together in front of a log fire. It was heaven. It felt like having a proper family for the first time in my life and it gave me the space to deal with my inner demons.

The contrast could not have been more different. I went from surviving in the very heart of one of the world's great cities to living in a cottage in the middle of nowhere. Instead of being woken by the sound of drunks shouting or windows smashing, I would be woken by the shrill scream of a fox or the soft to-and-fro hooting of the tawny owls. Instead of smelling exhaust fumes and the sickly smell of rubbish, I filled my lungs with clean, clear air tinged with the resiny scent of distant pines, with the heady perfume of blossom. I looked on this as a time to withdraw from the world a bit. The tarot card that had been painted on my room in Euston gave the clue. The Hermit. I went deep inside myself and, for a while, became just that – a hermit. It was a time of deep healing – just being in nature, surrounded by the green, was a balm to the soul.

But I wasn't allowed my peace for very long. *House-busters* was just the start of my television career. Before long, other producers tracked me down and badgered me to appear. I was torn. In many ways, I just wanted to with-draw from the world entirely, but in another way I knew this wasn't the time for me to turn my back on the media. If I wanted to achieve my long-term aims, I would have to return to London from time to time. I would have to appear on television. I would have to continue to immerse myself in the celebrity culture that pervades our society.

People always ask me about my celebrity clients and I always say the same thing. I never, ever discuss private readings with anyone other than the client. I have given readings for countless very famous people, for hordes of household names, but you will never hear a word about their private lives from me. The only readings I will ever discuss are those that were given in the public domain (either on television, radio or on stage), so they are already 'out there' if you like. I would never ever break a private confidence.

One public reading was with Tara Palmer-Tomkinson. She had just come out of a very bad patch and it was just before she went on *I'm a Celebrity, Get Me Out of Here*.

She was going to be dropped into the jungle with a load of other celebrities – including another client of mine, Rhona Cameron. Tara and I sat down and I instantly liked her – she was open and not remotely arrogant or difficult.

I tuned into her family dynamics and talked about her early life and her relationship with her parents. It was all very intense and, in a way, I got a bit alarmed as too much explosive stuff was coming out and I wasn't comfortable with it being on camera. I realised that my ability could make people very open, perhaps *too* open, for something that was to be shown on mainstream TV. As the reading progressed, I talked to her about what I was picking up about *I'm a Celeb*. I said she would do very well, that the programme would turn her life around, and that she would get other work from it. She was terrified of going, but I reassured her that it would all be fine providing she didn't flirt with someone unsuitable as that would cause problems!

As we talked about the past, she revealed that she used to have a ghost that followed her and that, if she left the house, people would hear something running down the stairs behind her and the door slamming. This kind of thing is quite common in people that have had addictions. Alcohol and drugs weaken the aura and spirits can easily become attached. You have to wonder why alcoholic spirits are called 'spirits'. So many indigenous cultures have been destroyed by alcohol and had their spirituality robbed by it. Alcohol takes you away, not only from yourself, but also from a deeper connection to the whole. Being dropped into the jungle was probably a real life-saver for Tara as she got plugged back into nature and the earth. I knew she would be all right, and that this was something big for her. I was totally delighted when it all happened just the way I had seen it.

The next person I read for was a stunning young man with big brown enquiring eyes and a very strange wild haircut. He was just filming a series for PLAYUK and his name was Russell Brand. I bonded with him immediately – he was so warm and open. He had just got the boot from MTV and had come out of a relationship in Spain. He was like a beautiful toddler, all open-hearted and warm. I knew instantly, without a shadow of a doubt, that he would become very well-known and that he had that special magic that produces celebrity. It was a very intense reading that talked about his demons and the past. I saw that he was almost too open – in a way he wanted to heal the world, but was not sure how to go about it.

He talked about his relationship with his parents and his passion to do something with his life. I knew that things would turn around for him, but not instantly: his forth-coming project was risky, but it was also a big rebirth for him. I think it delighted yet terrified him to be given a show where he had a free rein to do what he pleased. We talked about how cathartic one episode was, where he boxed with his father. There was nothing at all fake about Russell Brand – he was a shining light and a sweetheart. I, like many others, had no doubt he would be the Next Big Thing once he sorted his head out. Interestingly enough, at the time of doing the reading, he was involved with my old friend Christine, the American.

More public readings came with a bizarre show called *Mystic Challenge*. During the show celebrity guests would sit in front of a series of psychics, heavily disguised in a cloak. They would be totally covered up and would not say a single word. My task was to do a reading and see what came up – live on air.

This didn't faze me – I don't remotely need to see anyone's face to do a reading. So I sat back, quite relaxed, next to the heavily cloaked guest and the information started coming out in a complete torrent. I immediately got the word 'camaraderie' and knew that this man (I knew instantly it was a man) lived around horses. I picked up that he had had problems at school with his education and that he was very romantic and more sensitive than people realised. I also saw that there had been a scandal around a relationship and a sudden death. When I delved in more, I touched the energy of someone who was, I felt, nice but perhaps lost. I saw that he was writing a book, and also that he was in a relationship with someone who wanted more but that he was not ready because of the past.

At this point I was allowed to look at his hands. I saw someone who was very uptight and had taken a beating from an emotional storm. He had something very formal about his energy and I immediately knew psychically that this could only be one person: James Hewitt, the ex-lover of Princess Diana.

After the break, it was revealed that it was, indeed, James Hewitt. He looked a bit pale as so much of the information I had intuited was correct and not even public knowledge. For instance, he had had dyslexia at school. We chatted when the show ended and he told me how amazed he was as he hadn't believed in psychic stuff. I also picked up a specific message from a certain someone that was short yet sweet, and it seemed to put his mind at rest. I feel there are many things we don't know about the relationship James had and I am sure he really isn't a bad person. Over the past few years I have bumped into him several times and found him utterly charming and beautifully polite and considerate, if still a little lost.

Another of the mystery guests was the 'New Age messenger' David Icke. I picked up that he was surrounded by water where he lived; that he had been in a big public smear campaign; and that he was a true visionary even though many people thought he was mad or eccentric. Many of David's predictions from years ago have come true. Even if some people feel he is far off the bat, he is definitely tapped into some ability to know the future. He is also a very kind man but, in a way, not of this world. I found the whole experience quite intense.

This kind of very public work was tough on me. I felt so cocooned in my beautiful valley that I had to drag myself up to London and I dreaded leaving my refuge. Living in the country was giving me another opportunity to heal and I found myself once more delving back into the past. When someone has undergone continual and sustained abuse, it is often quite impossible to heal it all in one go: it's just too much. You have to work slowly. It's like peeling an onion – you take off one layer and there is always another and another and another. So my healing was an ongoing process, a long and painful journey. I would work on it for a time and then come up against a brick wall, as if my psyche were warning me that I'd gone deep enough for the time being. So I would stop, go back to normality and wait, trusting that the time would come for further work.

Over the years I tried almost everything out there, both psychological and spiritual. I saw a raft of psychotherapists – some good, some not so good. I tried standard psycho-analysis and also psychosynthesis. I used hypnotherapy to help me retrieve lost memories. Homeopathy and acupuncture helped – to a degree. I also continued in my spiritual quest, hoping that more metaphysical techniques could help to bring me peace. I sat in sweat lodges and underwent shamanic purification ceremonies. It was all helpful, but there was no single 'Aha!' moment.

Abuse is insidious. It pervades all of your being and it never ends. Yes, the actual abuse may finish, but the effects never do. It shatters your spirit and you have to piece that spirit together piece by tiny piece. In fact, the more you uncover, the tougher it gets. You have to be endlessly patient, infinitely loving and forgiving of yourself. No matter what you do, the sad truth is that the scar will always be there. Just as an alcoholic can never say that he or she is 'cured', but instead 'recovering', a victim of abuse can never say it is finished, only that he or she has reached a level of understanding. It goes on and on.

One major impact was on my relationship with Julien. It made me paranoid for his safety, overly protective perhaps. I was only really truly happy when he was with me, at home, where I could see him and protect him.

The more I learned about abuse, the more I realised I was just one in a long line. Abuse is hereditary, it goes through families like an evil virus. My mother had been abused, and so had her mother before her. Doubtless this evil had shuddered back through the generations. Understanding this gave me a huge empathy with my mother. Her breakdown all those years before and her suicide attempt had convinced me that she had been totally unaware of what had gone on. I didn't blame her for putting me in such danger – she had her own misery. Our relationship continued to be interesting and challenging: moving away from London was the best possible thing I could have done. We needed the distance it gave us. Talking on the phone and short visits were fine – we got on pretty well. I was, without a doubt, far calmer and rational. As the years passed, she too had become more mellow. But she was also becoming unwell.

One day I got a call from the hospital saying they thought my mother was dying. I got there as fast as I could, praying my hardest all the time that she would be all right. When I got there she was coming round. She looked at me, smiled, and said: 'Darling, you called me back. I was walking through a tunnel into a beautiful garden and many people were there. I was walking along a long, long corridor and I was so tired and suddenly I heard your voice saying: "Mum, come back here. Where do you think you are going? Come back now!" So I came back and here you are!'

It was the first of many near-death experiences for my mother, although I did not realise this at the time. Each time she would be brought back by the doctors who were stunned by her tenacity to live – she was legendary in the hospital. Inevitably, once she perked up a bit, she would start giving readings to the doctors, nurses and patients.

My mother took life and death in her stride and she wasn't going to die until she was good and ready, so she fought it tooth and nail. There was my powerful mother hooked up to oxygen 24/7 with only *The Golden Girls* and *Jerry Springer* for company. Whenever I visited her she used to drive me mad with marathon sessions of *Jerry Springer* where she would join in with the audience, shouting at the television.

'That bastard, you leave him! He slept with your mother!'

She kept telling me she wanted to meet Jerry and give him a kiss. This must have been lodged in my unconscious as one day, out of the blue, I received a call from a production company who wanted me to audition as Jerry Springer's side-kick for his new celebrity chat show on ITV. Now normally I would have run like the wind in the opposite direction – it wasn't my thing and felt very superficial. However, when I rang my mum and told her, she was adamant I should go.

'You've got to meet Mr Springer for me and give him a kiss.'

I met some interesting guests on the show. Glenda Jackson was utterly genuine and charming – very kind and compassionate. The other guests were Martine McCutcheon, Tom Jones and Robbie Coltrane. Tom Jones sat next to me, and he has energy unlike anything I have experienced. It felt as if he had been kept in a different era. He had this incredibly intense masculine energy – so very strong. You can tell he is still at home with his roots, and all I can say is that he is the most *male* male I have ever come across. He sang 'Sex Bomb' two feet away from me and it was an incredible experience. He is a true legend. He was friendly but detached and I felt that, remarkably, he was one of those artists who are still slightly nervous before they perform (like, in my experience, all great performers are).

At the after-show party, I brought Julien along to meet the guests and Martine was very sweet to him. What I noticed about her were her strong hands. She is someone who will always get where she wants to go; she has great personal power. Before I left I said goodbye to Jerry and gave him the message from my mother. Then I leant forwards and gave him the kiss from her. He looked me in the eye and said: 'You were great. See you in the series.'

Yet, as I looked into his eyes, I knew it was the last time

we would see one another. Sure enough, the series format changed and I didn't return.

But it didn't matter in the least. My mother was cock-ahoop and it gave her a new lease of life. On the negative side, it did lead her into even more compulsive viewing of the *Jerry Springer Show* – which I am sure was not a good thing!

26

The Wind Beneath My Wings

My mother would come down to the West Country to visit three times a year. It was always an arduous trip for her as she had now developed serious COPD (chronic obstructive pulmonary disease). She needed an oxygen tank as well as a wheelchair.

We would sit by the open fire, I would get out my tape recorder, and she would talk for hours about the past. She told me the story of her life and it helped me to understand her on a deeper level.

The massacre in Filetto had affected her very deeply – she talked often about the war and how the priest's lack of compassion had made her lose her faith in the Catholic Church. She talked about how a policeman was stripped naked and left for dead in the road while his poor wife in the next village was having a baby. Over and over again, she talked about the massacre – about how the wives had buried their husbands in the barracks wherever they could. She talked about the woman whose husband, father and dog were all murdered in front of her eyes, as she held her eighteen-month-old baby in her arms. She told me about how a boy hid in a wine barrel in the post office when the Nazis came. The officer said to the parents: 'Tell me where your son is or I shall kill you, your husband and your daughter.' But she refused to say a word and the boy watched his entire family being gunned down in front of him, as he watched through a hole in the barrel. Slowly, carefully, I managed to get her to talk about her own abuse and we discussed what had happened to me. She still found this a very difficult topic and I had to tread on eggshells but, to be honest, there was little left to talk about. I knew generally what had happened and had worked through a lot of it. I was aware that there was still work to do, and probably always will be – but that I didn't need to hound her about it. It was enough that she backed me up, that she acknowledged what had happened. It's very easy for people who have been abused to doubt their own memories, to wonder if maybe they made up the whole thing. Mum's testimony rescued me from that torture.

Most visits would depend on the state of her health but, however she felt, she would always come down for Christmas as it was her favourite time of year. Who could blame her? The cottage was idyllic in winter with cosy log fires and a warm embracing atmosphere.

Of course, nothing was truly simple with my mother. She was still feisty and tricksy and each year would insist that this time she *wouldn't* come; that she wanted to spend

Christmas on her own. It became an annual ritual, as predictable as hanging up stockings or decorating the tree. She would insist and insist. We would beg and plead. Then – on Christmas Eve itself – she would rope in one of her friends to drive her down (often a six-hour trip).

The last Christmas she had become more subdued, less tempestuous, and we got on much better. She was funny and warm and much, *much* calmer. It was so much more peaceful than my childhood Christmases, and in some way it laid my bad memories to rest. We all laughed and laughed – she had a wicked sense of humour and clearly loved being with us.

'Why don't you move down, Mum? I'll find you a lovely place nearby.'

'Oh no! What would I do with myself here? It is – what's the word? – *unnerving*. Too quiet, eh?'

'But you'd be close by. We could see more of each other.'

'I don't get it, Michèle. Why do you want to live in the middle of nowhere? It's weird. Why don't you come back to London, eh?'

'I can't live in London,' I said. 'But I want to help you.'

'No, you have your own life. I'm OK. Anyhow, I have Nicholas. He looks after me.'

My poor brother. He had come back home and they had a strange and intense connection. Their relationship was never easy. Nick found it stressful because, while he adored her, he also felt rejected by her. He was struggling with his own demons. Throughout his own nightmare though, he somehow managed to cook and care for my mother, but she appeared to reject everything he did for her. It was the final push that broke his spirit.

I hated it every time my mother went back to London. I felt that the capital was going through a huge energy shift – and not a good one. I wanted her nearer, safer, within my reach. But my mother was my mother – nobody could make her do anything she didn't want to do. So she stayed and left and came back and went again. Each time it was a drama, and how I miss that drama now. None of her friends minded being hauled out to taxi her around – even if it meant giving up their own Christmas Eve. She was just so charismatic and such a character. She never stopped helping people; never stopped gathering up waifs and strays. The phone never stopped ringing, right up until the point where she died. I was horrified that they would ring, begging for one last reading, knowing they were taking her last breath from her.

Above all, she battled her illness as if it were a mythical creature, some monster that required bravery and a stout sword. What she hadn't told me was three years earlier the doctors had told her she had six months to live. She never said a word. When I finally found out, she dismissed it airily.

'I knew I wasn't going to die then. Why all the fuss, eh?'

That was so typical of her – she didn't want to worry me. She was very much the warrior: she felt that her extreme and dramatic life had given her the power to defeat anything.

By sheer luck, I happened to be in London, staying with friends, when the phone rang at 3 a.m. It was Mum saying she didn't feel well. I was dressed in an instant and in a cab racing over to her, phoning the ambulance as I went. When I got there she looked grey and gaunt – not like my mother at all. I have never been so relieved to hear the sound of the ambulance siren.

When we got to Central Middlesex Hospital, it was as if a celebrity were being admitted. The nurses and doctors all knew her, and she still managed to growl to one of them: 'Hello, darling. Did that bastard come back to you like I predicted?'

The nurses fussed around her, and she gave them each little words of wisdom, even though she could barely speak. Her doctor was young and Asian – and, like the nurses he obviously had a soft spot for her. And she for him.

'You are my favourite doctor,' she whispered. 'You are the most handsome one. What can you do for me, doctor?'

He looked at the floor and then gently took her hand.

'Bruna, I am afraid that we are coming to the end. There is nothing left we can do.'

She shrugged. 'When you gotta go, you gotta go.' She smiled at him and patted his hand.

I took him to one side of the dingy corridor, a corridor I was horribly familiar with. It seemed as if I had been here time and time again, and each time standing on the threshold between life and death. It was here I'd been taken when I tried to commit suicide. My mother too had been here when she made her own attempt on her life. A family taking it in turns to try to die, and all in this shabby place with wonderful staff but no soul. Now here I was, desperately hoping that Mum would not die – that I'd have her for just a bit longer.

'Doctor. How long has she got?' I said, hearing my voice crack and feeling an icy energy shift down my body. I knew that this time it was real, this time she could not escape death – her old sparring partner had finally caught up with her.

'The X-rays show she has practically no lung capacity at all,' he said softly. 'I am afraid it could be any time but it is likely to be two weeks maximum.'

Although I feared the worst, I wasn't quite prepared for this. I felt it like a body blow. For all our ups and downs, for all our tempestuous relationship, I loved my mother desperately and deeply. We had resolved so many of our issues since I moved to the country – why did she have to be dying when it was all finally coming right? Despite her protestations, I had always believed that one day I would persuade her to move down to Somerset. Now it was too late.

The doctors said that I could take her home in a day or so. So I went back to her house to get the place cleaned up. I dreaded going through the door – the house had too many ghosts and I felt uncomfortable being there. The place was piled high with nick-nacks and stuff my mother had bought at charity shops. I opened her wardrobe and looked at her old glamorous clothes and handbags, now virtually falling to bits. She would never get rid of anything; she clung to memories like a small child to a teddy bear. But, strangely, I too started to feel a curious comfort in looking through all the things that had shaped my childhood.

Moving back to my old home was surreal. Looking back at that time it feels like an uneasy dream, the kind you have when you're feverish. I had to stay with her all night and I wrapped myself in a duvet and settled down at her feet, snatching odd bits of sleep when I could. She could no longer walk on her own and I would help her to the toilet, each painful step taken with a groan of agony. When she did try to sleep, one eye was always open, peering out from under her mustard-coloured bedspread as if watching out for Death, ready to chase him away should he come calling. If I were Death, I would have been a bit nervous: my mother was never going to go gently into that dark night. I would give her the drops of morphine that lessened her pain and we would watch *Jerry Springer* and endless repeats of *The Golden Girls*. She was eternally amused by them and had a touch of Sophia in her.

But mostly we would just sit for hours holding hands. I lost track of the times she said: 'I do love you, darling. I am very proud of you.'

Blinking away tears, I would reply, 'I love you very much too. I think you're an amazing woman and I'm glad I chose you to be my mother.'

We went through a deep and profound healing. I looked at her hands which were so like mine, with their chipped nails and gold rings. Although she was so weak, her grip remained remarkably strong. We had never sat in this way before: it was like a powerful goodbye. We both knew that this was the time in which we had to say the things we really wanted to say. She started to give me bits of her jewellery, and to talk to me even more about her life. She told me about other horrific things, things she'd never spoken of before: about how she had been raped by six American soldiers just after she had met my father – I was shocked as I had no idea. She talked again about her father abusing her. She talked about her pain and I felt overwhelmed with an unreserved love and compassion for this woman; this woman with the extraordinary energy and life; this woman that was my mother; this woman that had given me her gifts, her power and her bloodline. She had been someone I had always feared getting close to in case she consumed me. I realised I had never really forgiven her for the past, and that I should have known better and practised what I preached. But this time I was ready to hear and understand. I felt total unconditional love and connection with her.

The one thing she wanted above all was one last Christmas with all the family together. Despite being so ill, she was like a child, full of glee and delight. Julien was trying hard to ignore the situation, to pretend it wasn't happening. It was tough on him as he had the closest connection to her; they adored each other. He was fourteen, and his girlfriend had decided to dump him the very day he found out his Nanna was dying: he was unprepared for such intense emotions all at once. Julien and I walked into the garden with the old apple tree and crazy paving; the garden that was so much a part of both our childhoods.

'Nanna loves you very much, but this time she is going to go and we have to send her with as much love as we can. She knows she is going to a better place and has told me she has already seen her relatives there to greet her, including my dad – your grandfather.' I put an arm round his shoulder. 'How do you feel about it?'

'I know she is in pain and that she is ready.' He looked at the ground, brave and uncomfortable, my boy growing into a man through his first taste of death. To lose someone so close at such a vulnerable time himself was incredibly hard.

By the time 11 December came round, I had been at her home for two weeks. My mother had always told me, over the years, that she wanted me to be there when she died. She was terrified that I would not be as I lived so far from her. That day I went shopping and bought all of her favourite foods (salami, olives, stuffed peppers, chicken, Italian bread – many of them things she had not eaten for years). As I was cooking her roast chicken, I said I might nip back to Somerset to pick up my mail and so on.

'The nurse says it's fine for me to go. You're doing well; you're stable.'

'I don't want you to go, Michèle. Don't leave me.'

She started getting terribly upset and I reassured her that I wasn't going to go anywhere.

As I served up the chicken, I couldn't help but remember that she'd always said that she had smelled roast chicken throughout her pregnancy with me. How funny, I thought, a strange echo of life and death and our relationship coming full circle. She ate a little and then complained of feeling unwell and started groaning.

'Michèle, call the ambulance. I have to go to the hospital.'

I didn't quite believe this could be it, as she had been so strong and we had talked so much, and anyway she wanted one last Christmas. The ambulance arrived and I went with her.

When we got there, we had to wait. I couldn't believe it, but my mother managed to be as feisty as ever. 'When you going to flickin' see me? I'm dying here. Get a move on!'

Luckily, one of the nurses knew my mother well and she took her to the front of the queue and got her a bed. As soon as Mum hit the bed she went into cardiac arrest; her body fell back and she was gasping for air. Three doctors rushed to her and started to resuscitate her. Another doctor was yelling that she shouldn't be resuscitated. It was mayhem. I was calling to her in total panic.

'Mum! Mum! Come back. You can't go, it's not Christmas yet.'

She was revived and brought back to life just long enough to look me in the eye and say, 'Let me go, darling.'

I clutched her hand. It didn't seem right. Her hand was still so strong, still filled with life. How could she die? But I knew it was happening and that I had to be strong for her. I gulped and squeezed her hand.

'Don't worry, Mum. Dad will be waiting for you – and Lucy. They will be there. They love you. You are loved, so loved. We all love you. You will be safe.'

Her breathing became shallow. In the struggle to revive her, the oxygen tube had been kicked out of the wall and she was getting no air. We called for the nurse, but she took one look at her and said, 'It's too late. I'm sorry, but she's going.'

I clutched her hand and soothed her, sending her love, praying for her.

Her face changed and became almost like a wild animal's. I waited for her last breath. I expected to see something when she passed over. With all the magic between us, surely there would be something extraordinary? But, at the point of death, it didn't happen. She just looked totally normal and asleep and in a way I felt cheated that I had not seen her leave. I sat with her for ages, holding her hand. She looked at peace, yet I had the strong feeling that her soul had not yet departed. Finally, I left the room to ring Julien and Nick and, when I came back, her spirit had left. Just the empty body remained. She was no longer there.

Julien arrived with three of his friends who had all spent long summer holidays throughout their childhood at my mother's house. Julien walked in, the brave boy-man, and kissed her, as did all his friends. It was one of the most touching sights I have ever seen; those teenage boys filing in, kissing her on the cheek and telling her they loved her. After a while, I gathered them up and we left her. It was such a hard thing to do. We wandered back to her house and the place felt empty, like something phenomenal had shifted. It felt hollow, like an empty church. It felt over. I tried to tune into her, but felt nothing. At the time this really hurt and confused me. I just couldn't understand why I wasn't getting anything from her. But, it was a case of waiting and being patient. She would soon send me a message – and one of great hope.

As I arranged the funeral, I felt totally numb. I couldn't feel anything really. It was like looking at the world through ten feet of water. Every night, when I was alone in bed, I tried to tune in to her energy; I waited for a message. But nothing happened. Then, suddenly, I had an email out of the blue from a friend I had not seen for many years, a Chilean psychic called Andrea. She said that she had had a very vivid dream about an owl and felt it was important. It was – the owl was my mother's symbol. She also recounted a series of events that had occurred the previous day when I had felt very let down by Marie. Andrea immediately said she would come and be around to help me. She told me that my mother was doing fine, but that we needed to do a purification ritual to send her on her way. I accepted this immediately as I knew there was something more for me to do. My mother's body arrived home and I decided that we would have an open casket for twenty-four hours to smudge her body and say prayers.

I wanted to recognise and celebrate both parts of my mother's soul – the Christian and the magical. I also very much wanted to do what I could to help her into the other world. Seeing my mother's body was strange and liberating. It was the first dead body I had ever seen. I knew it was just an empty vessel, a discarded shell: no trace of my mother remained. It didn't even look like her now that her powerful spirit had left. We sat up all night praying for her and burning incense. It felt very powerful and right. I would drift into a hypnotic state and it felt as if I was undergoing an initiation into life, dealing with the death of the person who brought me into the world. There she was in the living room in the exact spot where she had nearly been murdered with an axe all those years ago. The coffin was lying on the dining table right opposite the hatch through which she had escaped. Nick and I talked and told each other that we loved each other and that the past was buried.

I arranged for two black horses and a glass carriage to take my mother to a church in Ealing before the cremation – I knew she would like that.

What pained me more than anything was that hardly anyone came to the funeral. All the people my mother had helped for all those years were nowhere to be seen. It felt very sad. So it was just a small party of us who walked behind the horse-drawn carriage as my mother left the house for the last time. We decided to walk up to the

Hanger Lane gyratory system and up Pitshanger Lane to the church. The Hanger Lane gyratory system was brought to a standstill by a police car as we walked around it and up the hill. It was a powerful and symbolic sight – that busy frenetic road coming to a close even if just for a few short minutes. I helped carry the coffin and, as I walked into the church, I felt a tug of poignancy at the sight of two Christmas trees.

During my speech I felt suddenly grown-up. It was as if something had lifted and changed. As I was talking there was a furious banging on the doors of the church, but when someone went to open it, no one was there. Nick, Julien and I had chosen the music. Nick's choice was 'Pretty Woman' – very apt. Julien's song was 'If Tomorrow Never Comes'. My song was 'The Wind Beneath My Wings' because, in the end, I saw the hero in her: the pain, the suffering and the powerful charisma. I saw how unable she was to deal with her own past. I saw and thanked her for all the gifts she had given me: the ability to be a healer and psychic, the ability to express myself as I am, the ability to be passionate about life and grasp each moment as if it were the last.

A few days later I was back home in Somerset when I felt a tingle down the back of my neck. I looked up and the whole room was filled with a radiant light of pure unconditional love. I was overwhelmed. It was not a separate entity: it was within everything in the room, including me. Everything was shining with love and then I heard my mother's voice quite clearly:

'I am all right, darling. I am so sorry I put you through being with me when I died. It is wonderful here – I should have done it years ago! I will always be here looking out for you, you know.'

With that she was gone. The love and light in the room did not leave immediately, but faded slowly. I knew that nothing would be quite the same again. But I also knew that, from then on, I had a formidable presence protecting me.

27

Daydream Believer

It took me a long time to get over my mother's death. Every time I picked up the phone I still half-expected to hear her gravelly voice, that mad broken English. I missed those tempestuous phone calls and her wild presence. Yet, equally, I felt a strong sense of release. We had talked things through and said what we needed to say. It felt as if a chapter had come to an end, as if we had both somehow fulfilled our karma. We had been through something momentous and had come out the other side. We had released the past and given each other forgiveness. We were OK.

All my life I had been terrified of death, but overnight that changed completely. I now knew, deep in my very being, that there was life after death. Heaven only knows my experiences with the spirit world should have given me enough proof but, in the past, I think I had always intellectualised it. At some deep level I hadn't really grasped it until Mum died and came back to me. I truly feel that ever since that day when I saw the light and heard her voice, my mother has been there protecting me and pushing me towards my goals. In the strangest way she felt closer to me now than she ever did when she was alive. I knew she was looking out for me and I knew without a shadow of a doubt that I was now totally free to create the reality I chose.

It was a big turning point for me. When a parent dies, it does truly feel like an initiation into life. I miss her terribly but she is always around me and the wonderful thing is that only the positive remains.

Death always brings change. It is, of course, the ultimate change, but there were other shifts going on in my life as well. After Mum's death, my brother slipped into a space where I could no longer reach him. I was desperately sad but I simply didn't feel able to help him. Five years later, he is finally on the path to reestablishing his life, step by step, and we have tentative contact. Some bonds are hard to break no matter what.

My relationship with Marie also came to its end. We parted, as we knew we must, sad yet grateful for the wonderful experiences we'd shared.

Julien was happy and settled in his school; both he and I loved the area, so I knew I wouldn't move far. But it was now time for me to start running my own show on my own terms, so I bought a small cottage in the area. It was the first place I had ever owned; the first time I had ever lived by myself (admittedly only during the week – Julien and his friends still came at weekends and holidays). I loved it.

I also knew I needed to take some time out to process my grief, so I took a holiday to Italy. It was the first time I had been there for years and instantly I felt at home again. In fact, I felt Italian in a way I never had before. I had a strong feeling that my luck was changing, and I was right – as when I returned home many things shifted.

I had bumped into Jonathan Ross and his wife, Jane Goldman, a few times over the years. I admired Jane as a very strong woman in her own right – she's a journalist and writer and very much a free spirit. We had not met properly, but when I was asked if I'd be willing to teach her to read the tarot for a TV show, I jumped at the chance. I was sure I would like her straightaway, and I did. We met for the first time in Glastonbury to do some initial shots and then she took my tiny village by storm as she swept in with her crimson hair flying behind her, trotting along with her huge platform shoes. Jane is very emotionally intelligent and unpretentious: it is impossible not to like her.

When I first sat down to teach her the tarot I did my usual technique of chucking her in at the deep end – I asked her to interpret a random card. She got the interpretation spot on, not just that once, but three times in a row. I knew that she was not only a natural card reader, but quite likely a natural psychic to boot. Filming the show felt blessed from start to finish. Ainsley, the producer, was a beautiful and somewhat eccentric lovable spirit who made us all laugh and relax, while Peter, the

director, was also a lovely gentle soul who pulled everything together. Jane became quite a successful reader by
the end of filming, and I believe she still does it now and
quite enjoys it.

It had been eight years since the last series of *Housebusters* and I thought it was done and dusted. But suddenly
there was talk of a new series in the offing. This time round
the show didn't have the wild energy of the earlier series
but it still felt like important work. So many people live
in houses with unquiet spirits and the transformation I was
able to bring to their lives was both exciting and humbling.
I also met the most wonderful people, and felt an instant
connection with many of those I worked with. For instance,
I met Katie, the producer, who has become one of my best
friends. We had many laughs together while making the
show.

One of the other experts on the show was the writer
and holistic home expert, Jane Alexander. We got talking
one evening and, by another wonderful coincidence, it
turned out we were nearly neighbours. We lived in nearby
villages and shared a love for the wild and wonderful South
West. We kept in touch after the show and Jane has worked
extensively on making this book possible. Life seemed to
speed up with coincidences and strange happenings, all
pointing a finger forward on to my path. The media work
was coming in thick and fast.

When a full series of *Housebusters* was commissioned,
I felt it was a gift from my mother. One of the first

programmes I did was for a wonderful family of a mother and two boys. I walked into the house and felt a distinct chill. When I got to one of the boy's bedrooms the feeling intensified. I knew that whoever slept there would feel horribly uncomfortable – there was a looming energy as if someone were watching all the time. It was a dark, disturbed, poltergeist presence, and frankly I couldn't wait to get rid of it as I was seriously concerned about the family. Curiously, I also felt as if I were linked with the family in some way – it felt as if this was something I, and I alone, needed to do. But it took a lot of energy to get rid of it. During filming, the mother and boys were sleeping downstairs when they were woken up by footsteps running upstairs and the lamp shaking. They were terrified, and I could quite see why. Even *I* found the house uncomfortable and I am well used to strange phenomena. I cleared the energy and put crystals in all corners of the house. It took a lot of hard work, but thankfully the problems ceased.

The filming was quite challenging as I was still recovering from the emotional release of my mother. It felt as though, while I had accepted the loss and my work was going on to another level, my own energy still needed to catch up. I was excited about what life was bringing, and also I was cosmically ordering experiences for myself that were coming together at breakneck speed.

Life was good. I was living in my country retreat, walking and connecting with nature, just being. I was finally putting my own demons to bed. I wanted to reflect on what I had learned, so I took some time out from doing individual readings. I developed my writing, which left me with time to be with my son and his friends, to relax a bit. I also wanted to plan my next step. I was aware that there was another phase coming and I wanted it to be right. The trouble with cosmically ordering, though, is that you tend to get what you ask for! I had been single since my mother died as I needed to be on my own to reflect. Lovers are the greatest soul challenge you can have – they make you grow. But sometimes it is important to go it alone and connect deep within you. My tiny home was called Yew Cottage, which was so fitting as the yew tree is the tree of death and rebirth. It was here that I started a deeper inner journey.

But the outside world wasn't going to leave me alone for long. The phone rang, and I was asked if I'd be up for an audition for a new show called *The X Factor*. I loved the title, and felt a hugely positive feeling about the show. I went into the first show brimming with enthusiasm and quite convinced it would be a huge success.

The first person I met was Ben Shepherd, with whom I work on *The Xtra Factor*. Straightaway he said: 'No one ever guesses my star sign. What do you think I am?'

I usually veer away from such questions as the chart is a complex thing, but I looked straight at him and knew immediately there was only one thing he could be.

'Sagittarius,' I said.

His mouth dropped open, and after that we became great working colleagues.

The people on the show were all fantastic to work with and I found it fascinating to get to see the 'real' Simon Cowell. Now, this may be a surprise, but seriously he is one of the happiest people I have ever met! I hate to blow his 'tough man' cover, but really he is a lovely, bright and positive soul. Many people who have achieved great things, and cosmically ordered and succeeded, remain dissatisfied or unhappy. It always surprises and saddens me that many successful people don't allow the joy into their lives; they don't seem able to enjoy their success. But not Simon. He is truly a one-off. Every time I see him he is smiling and giving off a cheerful and delighted energy. It is fantastic to see someone who has manifested such a strong reality and who evidently loves it and revels in it. It's also fantastic to see someone who is so successful, yet also very kind and humble. Yes, humble. That surprises a lot of people, but I can assure you it's true.

However, the biggest magical personality on the show was, without a shadow of a doubt, the wonderful Sharon Osbourne. I always related to Sharon as a sort of kindred spirit. Sharon gives off the most incredible energy. I can only describe her as an avatar of love. She is a true Goddess. Yes, she can have her wrath like any good old Greek Goddess, and can speak directly (like she did to Rebecca Loos), but she is also the most grounded and kindest celebrity I have come across. She takes time to talk to everyone and is always polite to people who go up and talk to her.

I remember once there were some adorable kids who had been doing a magic slot on the show. Sharon walked all the way up several flights of stairs to the dressing room to see the kids, give them a cuddle, and let them take photos. She gave off such a warm loving vibe to those kids that I was quite taken aback. When she was about to leave I felt an overwhelming urge to say something to her, but was unsure if it would be professional. I felt convinced that the run of bad luck she'd been having might have been connected to a statue in her house, a voodoo statue or something that needed to be got rid of.

I decided to take the bull by the horns. 'I hope you don't mind me saying this', I began, 'but I feel there is something in your home which is causing a bit of chaos.'

I described the object and she looked at me with her big green eyes and said, 'Well, I may have something like that in the house.'

I'm not sure if she took me seriously or not, but within a few weeks there was another fire in the property, so most likely she didn't! Either way, whether she believed me or not, she acted and spoke with such kindness and respect. She gave those kids such a treat that they left over the moon – and so did I. I have a lot of respect for Sharon's ability not to let her enormous fame go to her head. She could teach us all a thing or two.

Really, I do my TV performances in order to further my other work. I want to use that energy and any fame I may get so that one day I can (and will!) have that Grief Centre.

I love my media work and it is huge fun, but I'm very aware that it is not real. It is a stepping stone, nothing more. Hopefully one day I will be able to create programmes that are inspiring and have true integrity. Now *that* would be an even better use of the media.

28

Back from the Dead

My mother had left me a small inheritance and I decided I would use some of it to do something I had always dreamed of doing, something that felt very fitting. I would take the Orient Express to Venice. Venice was a place my mother and father loved dearly and they had spent incredibly happy times there. He had proposed to her in Venice – it was their magical city. The Orient Express? Well, as you know, I had vowed that one day I would ride on that renowned train. I had sent out the wish that, some time in the future, I would be on that big beautiful train, trundling slowly over the little bridge at the end of Nursery Road in Brixton. At that time I was a lost young punk, with a mile-high Mohican and a wounded soul. Now I was a grown-up, self-assured woman – an author, a journalist, a successful businesswoman, and a celebrity psychic who hung out in smart hotels and knew wildly famous people.

I thought about all this as I arrived at Victoria Station and was helped up on to the opulent train. This was real rags to riches. This was a real Cinderella story come true. I settled down into my seat and gazed out of the window as we chugged off. London seemed grey and sorry for itself as we slowly passed over the Thames. Then, before long, there I was passing over that bridge, slowly, ever so slowly. I was passing Nursery Road, passing my own past. I looked out and, in my mind's eye, I saw the girl with the lost childhood standing there. She was hunched and turned in on herself, her eyes gazing hungrily at the rich people on the famous train. Her eyes caught mine and I sent her a message from the future. I sent her all my love. I sent her hope. I told her to keep dreaming because it really would all be OK. Love is always rewarded.

It was the stuff of dreams, it really was, and I inhaled every single minute of it. We flew through Switzerland and I couldn't help thinking back to that last train journey through this incredible country – when I was newly pregnant with Julien and in such turmoil. This time, though, I was able to sit back and enjoy the fantastic scenery, my heart soaring at the grandeur of the Alps.

Finally, there I was in Venice. As I first stood on the shore and looked back at Venice in all her glory, I knew this was my spiritual home and that she loved me as I loved her. Venice was alive. It's a mythical city, in itself a powerful dream. It brought my life full circle and made me aware of how far I had come and how much I had come through.

In my mind's eye I saw my mother and father holding hands on the Ponte di Rialto, the Rialto Bridge. I saw the past and the future and knew that I had been here in the past, in many lives before. I knew also that I would return here again, maybe many times. But for that moment, in the present, I was there totally, with my heart full open, giving grateful thanks for my life, that I had been brought through, that I had been granted angels to save me time and time again.

Some people might say, 'Why were you abused? Why did you have such a violent childhood? Was it karma?' I would say this: my soul gave others the opportunity *not* to abuse and to show kindness instead of pain. Some did; some didn't. I gave people the opportunity to make the right choices. Regardless of all the pain I suffered, I feel so strongly that I was protected, right through my life. Without Lucy in the first part of my life, I don't think I would have made it. She showed me it would be all right; she pulled me through the worst of times. She was a divine blessing and I cannot tell you how lucky I was to have her. She kept her promise to stay with me, through the bad times. Lucy was always there when I needed her. When she had to leave, she didn't leave me alone. She simply passed me into the hands of other angels – earth angels – who would turn up at the right moments, to urge me on, to stop me from falling into despair. If you don't believe in angels, just look at my life and tell me who those people were, if not angels?

After Venice, things just got better and better for me. I was finally in a position to make my dreams come true. I moved a little further west, into the most stunning thatched cottage. Really it is the stuff of pure dreams. Imagine the perfect country cottage and there it is – nuzzled into a soft valley with gentle hills protecting it behind. A little waterfall dances into a sacred pool. There are old stone walls and steps leading to hidden places; an English country garden abundant with old-fashioned plants and herbs. The house itself is embracing and nurturing, a very female presence. I have always loved animals and here, with stables and land, I could pursue my dream of rescuing donkeys and ponies. I now have two horses, two tiny ponies and two mad donkeys. A pair of cats stretch out in the sun. Then there's my incorrigible Jack Russell terrier, Ruby, who will always be found staggering around with a huge rock in her mouth. Julien often visits. He left school when he was sixteen – like me, he was a rebel and didn't want to stay on for further education. He moved to Birmingham and now lives with his lovely girlfriend, Julie. Music is his passion and his life – he writes lyrics, performs, and is a very successful MC. We have a great relationship, and I could not ask for a more wonderful son.

My business just got better and better, thanks to the incredible psychics I employ for my psychic phone-line service. I had my feet on the ground for the first time in life, and I was ready again to teach others how to transform their own lives and create their own reality. I continued with some media work, doing television and hosting my own radio show, which is fabulous fun. I've branched out into recording DVDs too, so I can introduce even more people to the tarot and cosmic ordering. I love sharing my knowledge and giving people the nudge they need to create the life they deserve. Reality is a funny old chestnut. I cannot say it enough: we create what we believe. We weave our view of life through our experiences.

One other quite extraordinary experience knocked this truth into me once and for all. Over the years I had never forgotten Michelle, the angel who had saved me when I was hooked on glue, when my life was spiralling out of control as a teenager. I often thought about her and wondered exactly how she had died. In the end it started to bug me. Something wasn't quite right. It felt like a mystery, unsettled, unfinished. I always found it odd that she had never come through to me as a guide or contacted me in spirit.

Her father had been well known, so it suddenly dawned on me that I could use the internet to track down where she was buried. But I couldn't find out anything about it. So I called an Australian private detective and asked him to investigate for me. The very next day the phone rang. It wasn't the detective; it was a very familiar voice. A voice from the grave.

'Hi Michèle? This is Michelle.'

'What?'

'I was only talking about you yesterday. I had to call.'

Michelle was not dead. I was stunned. My jaw dropped and my heart started pounding. It couldn't be. At first I could barely speak. I stumbled over the words. My heart was hammering.

'But your father told me you were dead. He said you'd been in a car accident.'

'What? I don't believe it. Why on earth did he do that?'

She explained that she had lost my details and, try as she might, she couldn't find a way of getting in touch with me. Then time had passed and she had thought I had moved on, as I hadn't been in touch with her. When I calmed down a bit, she told me that the private detective had found her and given her my phone number.

'I couldn't believe it,' she repeated, 'I'd only been talking about you the day before. I was telling someone about this wild girl full of life that I'd met in London. You won't believe this, but I just lost the cat charm you gave me. I was so upset and I kept thinking about you. I was going to try to find you on the web and then, just like magic, the detective called.'

We talked and talked. Our lives were so similar – we were even reading the same book – Jeanette Winterson's *The Power Book*! Over twenty years, and our lives had come full circle. When I put down the phone I had to go and sit down. I was shaking like a leaf. This was monumental and it made me revise a whole chunk of my reality. I had never learned to drive because of my belief that she had died in a car accident and because evil Connie had predicted that I would too. We are not our past. How many years had I been teaching this? I knew it was true, I knew it in the very sinews of my being, but at some level I had never taken it on board 100 per cent. It took something as extreme as this to ram the message home. We are not our past: we are our future. The past moulds us, but should never shape our reality. We are magicians with the power to recreate beliefs and recreate our lives. That is the gift of being human. We all are a unique shard of God come to manifest and evolve the whole. We are one, but have to experience separation to understand the love that is us.

There is nothing, but nothing, we cannot overcome or change. And we all have a one-way ticket home at the end of it. This is a holiday and we can make the most of it, even if it feels like a trip to a resort from hell. Take a wild stab and journey outside the tourist zone – find the magic within your journey on this magnificent Planet Earth!

When we do leave this place ultimately we are going home, home to a beautiful place where we are all one again. No one can miss that journey, no matter how rich or smart. Earth is a centre for our souls' growth. While we are here we are momentarily separated from what we truly are – which is nothing more or less than pure love. Feeling that separation and not knowing that it is only temporary can create terrible problems for people. It can bring them a sense of isolation or fear. If there is one thing I have learned in my life, it is that we are all infinitely loved. All we need to do is to trust and connect to that love.

My life for now is whole. I live in a beautiful place surrounded by hills. My son is happy and last year reached his twenty-first birthday – my baby is all grown up. Also, I have the most amazing partner – a woman with whom I have a strong past-life connection. We recognised each other immediately while sitting under a magnolia tree at a party. Her name is Margi and she seemed so familiar, so wonderful, that I kept experiencing déjà vu. She said she felt exactly the same way. Yes, we had met in past lives, but it felt as if we had known each other from this one too. Then one night, as we lay in each other's arms, it suddenly came to me.

'Did you used to work or live near Neal Street?'

We looked at each other and the penny dropped.

'Oh my God, you're the girl who I told was gorgeous in the Covent Garden General Store.'

'I remember that so clearly. The girl who came up to me, she was you!'

Sometimes Fate can be very kind indeed. Margi is my true soul-mate and her compassion and wisdom have helped me so much through the often excruciatingly painful memories that writing this book has brought to the surface.

Best of all, I have made peace with my past. Every day I try to create a positive reality full of love. Yes, there are challenges, and often I still have to quell my tempestuous Italian temperament, but on the whole life is good. I feel much loved by the gods. Writing this book has shown me just what a charmed life I have led, how loved and protected I have been.

Through all the trouble in my life there were always angels. If you take just one thing from my life, let it be this:

Believe in the power of love; that you too can transform your reality. You are not your past – you are your future. Know that, and you will create something extraordinary.

Appendix

The twinless twin

When I was about halfway through writing this book, I came across the website of an incredible organisation called Twinless Twins Support Group International. As I started scanning through the various articles, I could barely believe what I was reading – they explained so much about why I felt the way I did. What follows are segments from an article on the site.

Leading to the 'Elvis Story' by Peter O. Whitmer, Ph.D

To be born a twinless twin is a potent birthright that spins one's life off in a certain direction, like being born with musical or mathematical genius, or growing quickly to a height of seven feet.

The hallmarks of the twinless twin are clear. Those who have lost a twin at or near birth share reactions that forge the personality in strikingly similar ways. Both the surviving twin and his family show the imprint. The impact and its lifelong psychological repercussions mould these individuals with a common, defining character. In early life, the pressures stemming from this initial loss are felt as identity confusion and an aura of strangeness.

The sensations of alienation and isolation from others crystallize as the person ages. There is a psychic pain that not only endures for life, but also becomes more severe as time passes. To deal with an adult twinless twin is to experience a person suffering the extreme inner torment of unresolved grief.

Fears of injury and death permeate the remaining child's world. Survivors internalize these concerns, which often emerge late in the form of sleep disorders and nightmares.

As youngsters, twin survivors are aware of an uneasy, poorly articulated, yet pervasive emotional sense of 'feeling different' from others in their age group.

When informed they once had a twin, these feelings suddenly make sense and crystallize as part of their identity. With this intellectual awareness, their sense of 'feeling different' is validated, at which point, two opposing forces emerge. The tension created by this inner psychological conflict is driving, compelling, relentless, often more personal than public, and painful in the extreme. The twinless twin wants to prove his uniqueness, to stand as an individual. Yet he is also powerfully pulled towards being re-united with the dead twin.

The over-arching mythical nature of the twinless twin's

predicament is particularly ironic and unresolvable. To win the mother's love, they must grieve for the dead twin. Yet at the same time, to establish self-love and their own security, they must compete with the very person they are compelled to mourn. The compulsion to be unique defines a life-long attempt to prove that they are a separate and whole person. Surviving twins constantly strive to demonstrate their autonomy and completeness. They look to others around them for indications of their success in this. Simultaneously, the opposing force, the tug to be re-united with their lost twin, surfaces, to be powered by survivor guilt. Twinless twins blame themselves for their sibling's death. They reproach themselves for having deprived their mother and father of the special status that is attributed to parents of twins.

Thus begins an emotional pendulum swing. At the mercy of complex and conflicting motivations, the twin strives to assert his uniqueness through behavior designed to demonstrate to others just how special he is. The more successful he becomes in achieving attention and recognition from those around him, the more guilty he feels. Deep down, he is convinced he should be sharing the wealth because he does not deserve to succeed. He believes he should be condemned rather than commended for having reached such levels of achievement. Gradually, this pendulum of emotions swings out of control – farther and farther in each frustratingly contradictory direction.

These two forces – to prove one's individuality, and to

become re-united with the other twin yet always in view of the mother – make it extremely difficult for twinless twins to develop normal relationships with others because they are already intimately involved. Self-imposed alienation is the normal. Yet by definition, the relationship with the dead twin is incomplete and never fully satisfying. Real human closeness is almost impossible, and the sense of pain and isolation becomes intense.

Another characteristic of the twinless twin is an unusually high energy level. The playwright Thornton Wilder wrote his mother about this when he was twenty years old. Saying, 'I suppose that everyone feels that his nature cries out hourly for it knows not what, but I like to believe that mine raises an exceedingly great voice because I am a twin, and by his death an outlet for my affection was closed. It is not affection alone, but energy, and in it I live and because of it I believe I seem to see my life as more vivid, electric, and marvellous than others . . . I am perpetually enthusiastic.' The science fiction writer, Philip K. Dick, was tormented, driven and inspired by his sister's loss for his entire life. He spoke of her powers over him, saying 'She [Jane] fights for my life & for hers, eternally . . . My sister is everything to me. I am damned always to be separated from her/& with her, in an oscillation.'

In the summer of 1956, the performer Liberace first met and discussed with Elvis his feelings due to having lost his twin at birth. He felt this had fuelled his compulsion to perform. Further, he described what he called his need 'to work in a frenzy.' In the process, he gave Presley the first of numerous lessons about how to flaunt his uniqueness, especially through style and dress. Liberace called it 'show-manship.' Both called it success.

Early in Elvis' career, Gladys spoke of her son's source of talent, drive and energy. She pointed to his birth and his twin's, Jesse's, death as the crucible which forged Presley's 'destiny to do great things. He is living for two people,' she proclaimed. 'He has the power of two people.' Elvis himself would refer to his dead twin as his 'original bodyguard.' He sought communion and re-union with the twin, sensing that the dead brother was a spiritual guide who directed him to search for meaning in life. He did this through meditation, numerology, compulsive study of both the Bible and numerous other spiritual tracts and, ultimately, through drug use.

Twinless twins can live a lifetime with most of the people in the world completely unaware of their operative core dynamic. They inhabit, in a sense, the ultimate private world. One speaks with, seeks guidance from, and feels constantly in some form of contact not just with an invisible being – but with a genetic carbon copy of one's self, in fact, who occupies an almost God-like position in this twisted but profoundly spiritual mental relationship. This is not the kind of stuff suitable for open discussion.

Reproduced with kind permission of Twinless Twins Support Group International.

Twinless Twins Support Group International provides support for twins and other multiples who have lost their twin due to death or estrangement at any age. The unique aloneless felt by surviving twins can best be understood by another twinless twin. By providing a safe and compassionate community for twinless twins to experience healing, understanding, and support, we encourage members to reach out to help others cope with the loss of their twin. TTSGI can be contacted via www.twinlesstwins.org.

Getting help

If you are being abused or know anyone who is, please get help. These organisations can help, quite confidentially: NSPCC (National Society for the Prevention of Cruelty to Children): www.nspcc.org.uk.

Childline is a confidential helpline for children – 0800 1111.

NAPAC (National Association for People Abused in Childhood): www.napac.org.uk. Their support line is 0800 085 3330.

Angel Survive: www.angelsurvive.com. This is an on-line community with discussion groups and forums where you can talk with other people who have survived abuse.